Employment law:
an adviser's handbook

THOMAS KIBLING is a practising barrister. He has previously worked as a lawyer in Citizens Advice Bureaux and law centres.

TAMARA LEWIS is a solicitor who works in the employment unit of the Central London Law Centre.

Both authors were founder members of the London Employment Project. They have written and lectured extensively on employment law.

Employment law:
an adviser's handbook

Thomas Kibling

and

Tamara Lewis

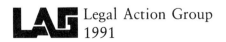 Legal Action Group
1991

This edition published in Great Britain 1991
by Legal Action Group
242 Pentonville Road, London N1 9UN

© Legal Action Group 1991

British Library Cataloguing in Publication Data
Kibling, Thomas
    Employment law: an adviser's handbook.
    1. Great Britain. Employment. Law
    I. Title II. Lewis, Tamara III. Legal Action Group
    344.1041125

ISBN 0-905099-29-X

Phototypeset by Kerrypress Ltd, Luton, Beds
Printed by Biddles Ltd, Guildford, Surrey

Acknowledgements

The development of the Central London Law Centre's employment unit has been greatly assisted by a small group of volunteers, who have shown remarkable commitment over the past seven years. We are particularly indebted to Nicholas O'Brien and Martin Westgate, who have provided such long-standing support and to the rest of our current volunteers, Anne Cutting, Declan O'Dempsey, Anthony Korn and Franco Tizzano. We would also like to thank Robin Allen, John Bowers and Vivien Du Feu for their continuing support for our work.

In relation to this book, we wish to thank Declan O'Dempsey, Anthony Korn and Martin Westgate for checking up on our law and making practical suggestions. Any mistakes of course remain our own. We would also like to thank our editor, Ros O'Brien, for her encouragement and patience in adversity.

The law is stated as at 1 April 1991.

Cover picture courtesy of Vicky White/Photo Co-op

Contents

Table of statutes

Table of statutory instruments and codes

Table of EC Law

Table of cases

Preface

We are constantly asked to recommend a book which covers the wide range of employment problems in a clear and practical form. There is no obvious book to recommend. We have written this book to fill that gap. In particular, we have aimed to provide lay advisers, trade union officials and lawyers with a handbook which is a real support in identifying the relevant law and issues of evidence and which can be used as a self-contained guide while running unfair dismissal and discrimination cases. The book therefore devotes as much space to evidence, precedents and check-lists as to setting out the law.

Employment law is a large subject and inevitably there will be some omissions. We have, however, attempted to cover the major areas of wages, unfair dismissal and unlawful discrimination. Certain areas of employment law are dealt with more thoroughly than others. This is not accidental. We have attempted to give more space to those subjects which cause most frequent problems for advisers of workers. Because of the complexity of the subject and the dangers of over-simplification, the law on race and sex discrimination has been treated in particular detail. The references to issues of disability and discrimination on grounds of sexual preference or AIDS/HIV, are not covered in as much detail as we would have liked.

Tamara Lewis
Thomas Kibling
April 1991

Introduction

The contract of employment

Every worker has a contract of employment, which consists of a number of terms and conditions, some of which are express terms, some implied[1] and some statutory.

Express terms are those agreed between the employer and worker whether in writing or orally. Implied terms are not expressly agreed but are implied into the contract of employment by the courts. Some implied terms are universal (apply to all contracts of employment) and others concern individual contracts. Statutory terms are implied into the contract by Acts of parliament. Employment protection rights (such as the right not to be unfairly dismissed) are examples of such terms.

Express terms

An express term is one which has been the subject of discussion and acceptance by the employer and worker. These terms are usually put in writing but this is not necessary. The main express terms are usually found in the letter of appointment or in the written contract of employment. Sometimes they are found in other documents such as the staff handbook or the rule book. The main express terms are usually:
- the rate of pay, and how often the worker will be paid;
- the hours of work;
- any terms and conditions relating to holidays and holiday pay;
- sick pay;
- notice pay; and
- the disciplinary rules and grievance procedure.

As these are the main terms and conditions of employment, the employer is obliged to supply most workers with written details of these terms.[2]

1

Implied terms

In the absence of express terms, employment contracts need terms to be implied into them in order to make them workable, meaningful and complete. The courts have appreciated that employment contracts involve personal contact between the parties, and it is therefore necessary to have terms implied into them so that they can operate smoothly.

The courts will imply a term only if it is absolutely necessary to do so, or if it is clear that the employer and worker would have agreed to the term if it had been discussed. The courts will not intervene and imply a term if one of the parties has entered into a bad bargain.[3]

The courts may have to invent terms to imply into the employment contract when they are required to make a determination of the terms and conditions which the employer is required to set out in writing.[4] This is necessary where there is no presumption on the evidence as to what the employer and worker would have intended had the matter been discussed. This problem usually arises in respect of the contractual sick pay provisions in an employment contract. The courts have to invent the term if obliged to make this determination and the test is objective – what would be reasonable in the circumstances?[5]

Mutual trust and confidence

This is the most widely applied and influential of all the implied terms. The employer must not, without reasonable and proper cause, conduct him/herself in a manner likely to destroy or seriously damage the relationship of trust and confidence with the worker.[6] This term also applies to the worker. The following are examples of breaches of the implied term:

- physical or verbal harassment;[7]
- failure to support someone who has been the victim of harassment at work;[8]
- moving a senior worker to an inadequate office or location;
- imposing a disciplinary penalty when unwarranted or where the disciplinary procedure is not followed.[9]

Not to act arbitrarily, capriciously or inequitably

An employer treating a worker arbitrarily, capriciously or inequitably without good reason will be in breach of this term. Failing to give a worker a pay increase without good cause when other workers are given an increase can be a breach of this term.[10]

Good faith and fidelity

This term lasts during employment but not after its termination. Any action by a worker which seriously harms the employer's business will be in breach of this term.[11] Likewise, the employer who discloses to a third party information about a worker without good reason or consent will be in breach of this term. Examples are:
- carrying on business in competition with the employer;[12]
- the use of the employer's list of customers including their requirements.[13]

Workers cannot use confidential information for their own personal benefit during their employment.

Not to disclose trade secrets

The worker cannot disclose, either during employment or after, the employer's trade secrets.

To obey reasonable and lawful orders

The worker is obliged to obey reasonable and lawful orders. Lawful means both a requirement of parliament as well as an order given within the ambit of the employment contract. If the worker is asked to perform a function outside the employment contract, this order can be refused.

To employ a competent workforce

The employer owes a duty to employ a competent and safe workforce,[14] safe plant and equipment,[15] to have a safety system at work and to pay attention to workers' complaints in relation to safety matters.[16]

To provide a safe working environment

The employer owes a duty to provide a safe working environment.

Care of employer's equipment

The worker owes the employer a duty of care at work to look after the employer's equipment and machinery. The failure to exercise due care leading to substantial loss to the employer could constitute a disciplinary matter. This will arise if the worker has injured a third party as the claim will usually be against the employer.[17]

All these implied terms are treated as fundamental terms of the employment contract, so the employer's breach will usually entitle the worker to a claim for constructive dismissal.[18] An employer can dismiss workers without notice if they have breached any of these terms.

Statutory terms

Due to unequal bargaining power between workers and employers, successive governments have found it necessary to incorporate into the employment contract certain terms protecting workers during and on termination of employment. The most important statutory terms give the worker the right to receive redundancy pay, to return to work after maternity leave, not to be unfairly dismissed and not to be discriminated against on grounds of race or sex.

Apart from the provisions on unlawful discrimination, a worker qualifies for these rights after a given period of continuous employment. Once the worker has qualified for these rights, they become part of the employment contract and it is not possible for the worker and employer to agree a contract which excludes those rights.

The right to a written statement of main terms and conditions

Most workers on 16 or more hours per week are entitled to receive within 13 weeks[19] of the start of their employment a written statement of the major terms on which they are employed, unless such terms are contained in a written contract.[20] These terms must include:
- the name of the employer and worker;
- the date when employment began, including any period of continuous employment with a previous employer;
- rates of pay or method of calculating pay and frequency of payment;
- hours of work including normal working hours;
- terms relating to holidays and sickness;
- pension arrangements;
- the worker's job title;
- the length of notice required by each party to end the employment;
- if a fixed-term contract, its expiry date;
- the grievance procedure; and
- the disciplinary procedure.[21]

Where there is a change in any of the terms, the employer should notify the worker in writing within one month.[22]

The statement of terms is not itself the contract. It is strong but not conclusive evidence of what the contractual terms are. If no proper statement is supplied within 13 weeks, the worker can apply to the industrial tribunal (IT) at any time up to three months from the termination of employment for the IT to determine what particulars ought to have been given in the statement.[23]

The duty on the IT is to record what has been agreed, not to remake a contract or decide what should have been agreed. It is the contractual relationship alone which is relevant. It is for the IT to make findings of the terms and conditions of the contract as initially made and then consider whether there have been subsequent variations. Where there has been no express nor apparent agreement, it may be possible for the IT to infer a term from the surrounding circumstances or it may be necessary to invent a term. In the case of 'mandatory terms' (identity of the parties, date employment began, rate of pay, hours, job title and the length of notice) the IT must insert a term even if it has to invent it.[24]

Wrongful dismissal

Unlike unfair dismissal which is a statutory right, wrongful dismissal is a contractual right. It arises when an employer terminates the employment contract without giving proper notice or in breach of another contract term, eg the disciplinary procedure.

The general rule is that either party can end the contract by giving the appropriate notice. Where a worker has committed an act of gross misconduct, the employer may end the contract without giving notice. What amounts to gross misconduct depends on the facts of each case but it is an action which completely undermines the employment contract. Although gross misconduct entitles the employer to dismiss without giving notice, whether the dismissal is fair is a separate question under the Employment Protection (Consolidation) Act 1978 (EPCA).

A wrongfully dismissed worker can recover damages for breach of contract. Where the breach of contract is the failure to give proper notice, compensation will usually be loss of earnings for the notice period, subject to mitigation. Where the breach is failure to follow a mandatory disciplinary procedure prior to dismissal, the amount of compensation is hard to predict. In some cases, it may be wages for the length of time it would have taken to go through the compulsory disciplinary procedures. Claims for breach of contract based on failure to follow disciplinary procedures are hard to prove and should be approached with caution. Most contractual disciplinary procedures are guidance rather than mandatory and failure to hold a disciplinary hearing or give a warning prior to dismissal will rarely be a clear breach of contract.

Statutory minimum notice

The EPCA s49 sets out minimum notice periods. An employer must give at least:
- one week's notice to a worker who has been continuously employed for one month or more but less than two years;
- one week's notice for each whole year of continuous employment between two years and 12 years inclusive.

A worker employed for one month or more need give only one week's notice.

CONTRACTS OF EMPLOYMENT: KEY POINTS

- All workers have a contract of employment. Most employment contracts are verbal. They carry the same status as written contracts, the only difference being that they are harder to prove.
- The terms of the employment contract are either express terms (discussed and agreed by the employer and worker) or implied terms (not discussed but forming part of the contract).
- To determine what constitutes the contract of employment, start with the first communications: the job advertisement, the interview, the letter of appointment, the initial written documents etc. Having established the original contractual agreement, then look for any variations which are applicable at the material time.
- Some of the most important terms of the employment contract are put in by Acts of parliament and are referred to as statutory terms. The majority of them are implied into the employment contract to protect workers against unfair treatment. The most important are the rights against unfair dismissal, unlawful discrimination, and victimisation for union membership.

GENERAL GUIDE TO USEFUL EVIDENCE

- All documents, including the letter of appointment, the s1 terms and conditions of employment, staff handbook, and any written procedures.
- The custom and practice at the work place.
- The terms and conditions that other similar workers enjoy.

PART I: WAGES

CHAPTER ONE

Pay and the Wages Act 1986

Introduction

The payment of wages, and the intervals at which payments are made, is a matter of contract between the employer and worker. It is a most fundamental term of the employment contract to pay wages and the failure to do so will entitle the worker to claim constructive dismissal[1] and to recover the wages owing either in the civil courts (county or High Court) or as an unlawful deduction from wages in the IT.[2]

The employer is under a statutory duty to give workers, within 13 weeks of the commencement of employment,[3] a written statement which includes the scale, or the method of calculating wages,[4] and the intervals at which wages will be paid, whether weekly or monthly or by some other period.[5] The employer is obliged to account in writing to the worker for all deductions made from wages at or before each pay day, whether it is for tax, national insurance or for any other reason.[6] This duty is usually discharged by issuing itemised pay statements.

Workers employed in wages council industries,[7] are entitled to receive a minimum rate of pay and an employer who pays less than the legal minimum commits a criminal offence. The worker who has been underpaid is entitled to recover the difference between the legal minimum and the amount which s/he has been paid (the underpayment) for a period not exceeding six years.[8]

The employer's obligation in most work situations is to pay the wages contractually owed. There is no obligation to supply work.[9] The worker's obligation is to be willing and able to perform his/her contractual duties. The failure to do so entitles the employer to deduct a sum equal to the proportion of the time when the worker was not willing and able to work.[10]

Payment in cash and deductions from pay

The legal framework

The legislation

Since 1831 there has been statutory protection for certain workers in respect of their entitlement to be paid 'a current coin of the realm',[11] ie cash for their services.[12] This legislation was introduced to combat the growing practice in the early 19th century of employers paying workers by way of tokens or goods instead of wages. These tokens were valid only in the employer's shop. Employers were not only motivated by profit – they also had religious and paternalistic reasons. Many of these 'tommy' shops, were operated by religious philanthropists who refused to sell alcohol or goods likely to corrupt.

In addition to the right to be paid in cash, the subsequent Truck Acts protected workers in respect of deductions from wages and fines imposed by their employers.[13]

The Truck Acts protected only 'workmen', ie manual workers.[14] A large number of workers who were equally vulnerable were not entitled to the statutory protection.[15]

The Payment of Wages Act 1960 permitted employers to pay wages by credit transfer rather than in cash only with the worker's consent.[16] When this Act was introduced 50 per cent of all workers were paid in cash. Even workers who had consented to credit transfer payments were entitled to retract this consent by giving their employer four weeks' notice.[17]

The Wages Act (WA) 1986 repealed the Truck Acts 1831 to 1940 and the Payment of Wages Act 1960.[18] The WA 1986 abolished a worker's right to be paid in cash, and removed the protection against deductions from wages. Employers since 1 January 1987 are entitled to make deductions from wages as long as they comply with the notification provisions.

Part I of the WA 1986 deals with the employer's right to make deductions from a worker's wage. The WA 1986 limits the size of the deduction that can be made from the wages only of retail workers.[19] However, even the limited protection afforded to retail workers is removed on their final pay day.[20]

The WA 1986 allows employers, if they satisfy the necessary requirements, to make deductions from the pay of workers. There is no control in respect of inequitable deductions, unlike the Truck Acts. The WA 1986 provisions are regulating rather than protective.

Who is covered?

The Truck Acts protected only 'manual workers' whereas the WA 1986 covers most categories of workers and extends the definition of worker beyond the restrictive definition of 'employee' in the unfair dismissal provisions.[21]

The WA 1986 definition of 'worker' covers those who have entered into or work under not only a contract of service (see pp36–37) but also a contract of apprenticeship and any other contract whereby the individual undertakes to do or perform personally any work or services for another party to the contract whose status is not, by virtue of the contract, that of a client or customer of any profession or business undertaking carried on by the individual.[22]

Those working in retail employment are given additional protection in respect of the amount of the deductions that can be made in any given week during their employment on account of cash or stock deficiencies,[23] being no more than 10 per cent of the gross wage due on any given pay day.[24] However, the employer is entitled to recover any total sum over and above the 10 per cent in subsequent weeks as long as the amount is not more than 10 per cent in each week, and on the final pay day, any amount which remains outstanding.[25] Deductions other than for cash or stock shortages are not subject to this ceiling.

This protection was introduced because of the widespread practice of employers in retailing, of deducting cash and stock deficiencies from wages. The worst employers were garage owners who would hold workers responsible for unpaid bills which were occasionally in excess of the wages owing, resulting in the worker owing money to the employer for the privilege of working![26]

Retail employment means employment which involves the sale or supply of goods directly to members of the public or to fellow workers or other individuals, or the collection by the worker of payments in connection with retail transactions.[27] This definition covers workers in shops, banks, building societies, petrol stations, restaurants (waiters and cashiers), homeworkers, those working on the 'lump' in the building trade, and workers involved in the delivery and sale of produce such as those who do milk rounds.

The WA 1986 excludes workers who carry on a business or profession where the other party is a client.[28] This would exclude professionals such as solicitors, doctors, and dentists and also sole traders and taxi drivers. The WA 1986 does not cover crown employment (civil servants),[29] national health service workers,[30] those employed in the armed forces,[31] merchant seamen,[32] and those workers who ordinarily work outside GB.[33]

Payment of wages

A worker who started employment after 1 January 1987 may be paid by credit transfer or by cheque. A worker employed prior to this date who has a contractual right to be paid in cash, continues to enjoy this right. However, if an employer refuses to continue to pay the worker in cash there is very little that the worker can do. A claim for unfair constructive dismissal is unlikely to succeed if the employer argues that the change in paying wages was introduced for sound administrative and/or safety reasons; the reason for any subsequent dismissal would be some other substantial reason justifying the dismissal.

Unauthorised deductions from wages

Definition of 'wages'

For the purpose of the WA 1986, 'wages' are given a wide definition covering 'any sums payable to the worker by his employer in connection with his employment, including any fee, bonus, commission, holiday pay or other emolument referrable to his employment',[34] including guarantee payments,[35] statutory sick pay[36] and maternity pay.[37]

When deductions can be made

The WA 1986 prevents the employer from making any deductions from the wages of workers unless it is:

a) authorised by statute.[38] This enables the employer to deduct from wages the PAYE tax and national insurance payments as required by law;

b) authorised by a 'relevant provision' in the contract.[39] There is no requirement that the term of the contract should be in writing and the term in question can be an implied rather than express term. However, it is necessary for the employer to notify the worker in writing of the existence of the term, and to explain its effect;[40] or

c) the worker has previously agreed in writing to the deduction being made.[41]

If the worker gives prior consent in writing to the deduction being made it will be an authorised deduction. This consent cannot be retrospective. Similarly, the employer cannot receive any payment from the worker unless the payment satisfies one of the three conditions above.[42] This prevents the employer recovering payments by demand rather than deduction.

Even if the above three conditions are absent, the employer is entitled to deduct money:

a) in respect of any overpayment of wages and/or expenses;
b) for a statutory purpose to a public authority (eg taxes owing to the Inland Revenue);
c) as a consequence of strike or industrial action;
d) for any contractual obligation to pay to a third party (eg union dues);
e) in satisfaction of a court or tribunal order requiring the worker to pay the employer.[43]

What amounts to a deduction?

Where the total amount of any wages that are paid by an employer to a worker is less than the total amount of the wages that are properly payable to the worker on that occasion, the amount of the deficiency will be treated as a deduction made by the employer from the worker's wages,[44] even where there is a 100 per cent deduction.[45]

Any unauthorised deduction from any of the different types of 'wages' or a non-payment of them,[46] such as the failure to pay statutory sick pay, maternity pay or accrued holiday pay[47] is recoverable in the IT.

Remedies and time limits

The worker can make a claim to the IT asking for a declaration that the employer has made unauthorised deductions and an order that the employer repay the sums deducted.[48]

This claim must be made within three months of the date of the deduction, or if the worker has made a payment to the employer, the date when the payment was made.[49] If the employer made a series of deductions, the time limit runs from the last deduction.[50] Where there has been a continuous underpayment of wages in breach of the wages council provisions, there is no time limit and the worker can claim back to when the WA 1986 came into force in his/her industry.[51] The IT can extend the time limit if it was not reasonably practicable for the claim to be made within the three-month period.[52] The extension provision adopts the same form of words as used for the unfair dismissal provision[53] and it can only be assumed that the worker will experience the same problems with WA 1986 claims as with unfair dismissal claims.[54] However it might be that ITs will adopt a more flexible approach as with the early unfair dismissal claims when the right was not so well known.

Minimum pay and wages councils

The legal framework

The legislation

Since 1909[55] workers in the 'sweated trades' have had the statutory right to be paid a minimum rate of pay. The trade boards were created in industries where there was no collective bargaining machinery. In 1945 the trade boards were replaced by wages councils.[56] Each wages council was not only directed to set a minimum rate of pay for its industry but also to lay down minimum holiday entitlements. Once the minimum entitlements were decided, the secretary of state for employment would ratify them and thereby give the provisions statutory force.

In 1975[57] wages councils' powers were extended and they were entitled to regulate other conditions of employment. The Wages Councils Act 1979 consolidated the provisions, and vested in the secretary of state the power to create and abolish wages councils.

In order to reduce the scope of the wages councils, and those covered by their provisions, it was necessary for the Conservative government to de-ratify from the International Labour Organisation convention 26 (which requires all member states to have a minimum wage fixing machinery) prior to enacting the WA 1986. It was the first time that one of the 94 member states has denounced any of the ILO conventions which seek to provide minimum protection for workers worldwide.

Part II of the WA 1986 substantially altered the scope of the wages councils and those workers entitled to their protection. Wages councils are now empowered only to set a minimum rate of pay and an overtime rate after 39 or 40 hours in any given week. They can also fix a limit to the amount that will be taken into consideration in respect of the cost of living accommodation.[58] The wages councils no longer have the power to make provisions for holidays or holiday pay.

The Agriculture Wages Act 1948 provides for similar powers to be vested in agricultural wages boards which cover farm workers, and those employed in the agricultural industry. These boards and their powers under the 1948 Act remained unaltered by the WA 1986.

Wages councils are made up of representatives of workers and employers in equal numbers, and not more than five independent members, usually academics. Once a year, after consultation, the wages councils determine the minimum entitlements of those workers covered. Each of the wages councils meets at a different time of the year and introduces its new rates on a specific date, depending on when it meets.

Who is covered?

There are 60 wages councils covering presently about three million workers. The industries covered are varied, the largest being retailing, catering, hairdressing, and clothing manufacturing. The WA 1986 removed from wages council protection workers under the age of 21.[59]

For the purpose of the wages council provisions, the same definition is given for a 'worker' as in WA 1986 Pt I, with the specific addition of homeworkers[60] and those working on piece rates.[61]

The minimum hourly rate of pay applies to all workers covered by a wages council order. Whether a worker is covered depends on the scope of the order and it is necessary to check with the most recent order passed in each industry under the Wages Councils Act 1979, or with the local wages inspectorate office, which is part of the Department of Employment.[62]

Calculating the minimum entitlement

The legal minimum entitlement is based on a weekly calculation.[63] It is necessary first to ascertain the number of hours worked in any given week by the worker. Time worked excludes breaks for lunch or for any other reason during which the worker is not required to work.[64] If the worker is required during a coffee break to serve customers or to be available for some other function (eg a manager supervising) this break will be treated as hours worked.

Having ascertained the hours worked, it is possible to calculate the legal minimum wage entitlement. This is a gross figure (before deductions for tax and national insurance). If the amount of the gross pay paid to the worker is less than the legal minimum, the difference between the two sums can be recovered as a breach of contract or unlawful deduction.

Some workers are paid for production rather than in respect of the time spent at work. These workers are known as 'piece' workers and are found in the clothes manufacturing industry. Homeworkers, who are covered by the wages council provisions are paid in respect of the number of items they produce. In order to work out their entitlement to a minimum wage it is necessary to ascertain the time it would take an ordinary competent worker to do the same work in the factory.[65] Once this has been calculated, it is possible to work out the minimum wage on the basis of the number of items which the worker has produced.

Recovering an underpayment

There are four ways of recovering an underpayment.

Wages inspectorate

The worker can report the employer to the wages inspectorate which is empowered to carry out an investigation and to recover underpayment for up to two years on behalf of the worker in the magistrates' court.[66]

The problem with the wages inspectorate is that it is too understaffed effectively to police the wages council provisions,[67] it is not prepared to use the considerable powers at its disposal, and rarely prosecutes employers who have been found to have acted unlawfully. The inspectorate has recovered on behalf of workers a fraction of the wages owing. To refer a case to the inspectorate will invariably result in delays in recovering the underpayment owed.

The only attraction of using the wages inspectorate is that it will not disclose the identity of the worker to the employer, nor that the worker has reported the employer, and it will investigate whether any other workers are being underpaid at the place of work. It is often able to recover smaller underpayments by coercion short of legal action.

Private prosecution

Recovering underpayment of wages through the civil courts can be a lengthy and costly business. The WA 1986 duplicates the much under-used provisions of the Wages Councils Act 1979 which provided for recovery in the magistrates' courts in the event of a successful prosecution. The magistrates' court can award to the worker the difference between the actual wages paid and the statutory minimum. More importantly, on conviction, the employer can be made to pay in respect of any other worker underpaid, in effect achieving what would be possible only by separate actions in the civil courts.

Although there is a higher burden of proof in criminal than in civil cases, there are certain advantages. The worker has the satisfaction of seeing the employer personally answering charges, the employer is subject to the social stigma of being found guilty of a criminal offence with a higher chance of being reported in the newspapers, and having a personal conviction against his/her name.[68]

Breach of contract

The worker can issue proceedings for the recovery of the underpayment during the last six years in the county or High Court (depending on whether the underpayment is more than £5,000) as a breach of contract claim.[69]

The advantage of a civil claim is that the worker will have to show only on the balance of probabilities that the employer has underpaid. The worker can rely on any failure by the employer to comply with the obligations to keep the necessary records. The claim can go back six years, and interest will be added to the claim at 15 per cent. Legal aid, subject to the means test, will be granted in most cases.

Recovery under the Wages Act

The worker can issue proceedings for a period of three months for unauthorised deductions from pay under WA 1986 Pt I. If the employer has underpaid the worker during the last three months, the worker can make a claim to the IT for the shortfall. In the case of continuous underpayment, there is no time limit other than the coming into force of the WA 1986 (see above p13).[70]

As a matter of tactics, the worker might want to claim three months' shortfall in the IT in the hope that the employer will concede that the deduction was unauthorised. Also, where there is uncertainty as to the claim, an IT's declaration can be used as the basis of a contractual claim in the county or High Court for the full period during which deductions were made. There is no fee for issuing in the IT and no burden of proof. If the employer wishes to settle the IT claim, make sure that the agreement does not exclude the right to sue the employer for the remaining underpayment. It may be that the employer will want to settle the claim for underpayment of wages at this stage, to avoid further litigation.

Employers' obligations in respect of minimum pay – criminal offences

Not to underpay

An employer who fails to pay the legal minimum wage will have committed a criminal offence, and in addition to paying the underpayment to the worker is punishable with a third level fine.[71]

To keep records

Employers are obliged to keep records which contain sufficient information for establising whether they are complying with the wages council provisions.[72] These records must set out the hours worked in each week for the last three years and the amount of deductions for accommodation. Failure to comply with this obligation is a criminal offence punishable with a third level fine.[73]

To supply information

If employers partly or wholly supply false information or allow or cause anyone else to produce such information on their behalf, a criminal offence will have been committed punishable with a fifth level fine.[74]

Holiday pay

There is no statutory right to holidays or holiday pay, not even on bank holidays.[75] The right to holidays is a matter of contract. There is an obligation on the employer to supply the worker, within 13 weeks, with a statement giving details of any terms and conditions relating to holidays, public holidays and holiday pay, including any entitlement to accrued holiday pay on termination of employment.[76]

When there is no express holiday provision, the worker's entitlement might be implied from the custom and practice. There is a presumption that workers are entitled to similar holiday entitlements as their colleagues doing the same job.

On the termination of employment, workers are entitled to receive a payment for any holidays outstanding unless there is an express term excluding accrued holiday pay. Some contracts exclude accrued holiday pay if the dismissal is for gross misconduct. If there is such an express term it will be valid.

If the employer refuses to pay holiday pay, a claim can be made in the IT for an unauthorised deduction from pay[77] or in the civil courts for breach of contract.

Sick pay

Statutory sick pay

Since 1983[78] employers have been obliged to pay statutory sick pay on behalf of the government and to claim this sum back from the national insurance contributions. It is an administrative process which results in many workers not getting sick pay when off work due to illness. Those workers who do not qualify for statutory sick pay claim, if entitled, from the DSS.[79]

The employer is obliged to pay statutory sick pay for a maximum period of 28 weeks.[80] Payment is made after three waiting days' 'qualifying period' for each occasion that the worker is incapable of working due to some specific disease or bodily or mental disablement.[81] Workers do not have to qualify again if two periods of sickness fall within eight weeks.[82]

Statutory sick pay is a flat rate payment, dependent on the worker's normal weekly earnings[83] and is paid at two different rates. Details of the statutory sick pay rates, the entitlement provisions and the remedies available for non-payment can be found in the Child Poverty Action Group handbook on non-means-tested benefits. It is worth noting that the unpaid statutory sick pay is recoverable under WA 1986 Pt I.

Contractual sick pay

The statutory sick pay provisions are a minimum entitlement when away from work on account of sickness. A large number of employers operate contractual sick pay provisions which generally make up the difference between the statutory sick pay figure and normal wages for a fixed period of time in any given year. Usually this right is an express term of the contract. It is possible to imply a term that the worker is entitled to normal pay if it is the custom or practice at the workplace. However there is no longer a presumption that workers are entitled to the normal rate of pay when off sick.[84]

It is a requirement for the employer to provide workers with a written statement of any terms and conditions relating to incapacity for work due to sickness or injury, including any provisions for sick pay.[85]

Itemised pay statements

Employers are obliged to supply workers employed for 16 or more hours per week, at or before each pay day, with an itemised pay statement.[86] If the worker works more than eight hours per week but less than 16, the right to itemised pay statements is acquired after five years' employment. There is no requirement for the worker to request an itemised pay statement. It is an absolute right.[87]

Itemised pay statements must include the gross pay, details of all deductions from the gross pay and the net pay. If the net pay is paid in different ways, the amount and method of payment of each part of the net pay must also be itemised.[88]

If the employer supplies the worker with a written statement of a fixed deduction to be made each pay day (such as the repayment of a season ticket loan), the employer must detail the nature of this deduction only every 12 months.[89]

If the employer fails to give a worker an itemised pay statement, or deductions are made which were not notified, the worker can apply to the IT for a declaration to this effect, and ask the IT to exercise its discretion to make a compensatory award. Whereas the declaration is mandatory, the compensation award is discretionary.

The maximum amount of compensation that can be awarded is calculated by taking the date of application to the IT and determining the amount of the deductions (difference between the gross and net pay) on each of the pay days in the previous 13 weeks.[90]

As ignorance of the law is no defence, employers should be made to pay a compensatory award somewhere near the maximum. If the worker's submission to the IT emphasises the potential for fraud if itemised pay statements are not given, it is likely that the IT will be more willing to make a high award. The EAT, in a decision in 1979, decided that a small award was not appealable as the provisions had come into effect only recently and the employer was a busy professional person in sole practice.[91] After a further decade, and with larger operations, employers should not be allowed to get away with such leniency. It is important to stress to the IT that the failure to supply these statements is often indicative of some unlawful practice by the employer, usually the failure to make the appropriate tax and national insurance returns.

Workers who do not get itemised pay statements, should check with the Inland Revenue and the Department of Social Security to discover whether the employer has been committing fraud by not paying the requisite tax or national insurance, and if so, credited national insurance contributions for the missing payments should be secured.[92]

WAGES: KEY POINTS

- Employers are obliged to pay wages to workers who are willing and able to work even if not required to do so. The only exception is where the contract has an express term allowing the employer to lay off workers when there is no work. Such a term is unusual and could be relied on only for a few weeks.
- Employers are not allowed to make deductions from wages unless there is a statutory requirement to make deductions (tax and national insurance), where it is a term of the employment contract, or where the worker has agreed in writing to the deduction.

- Any deduction made without authority can be recovered by claiming in the IT under the Wages Act 1986 Pt I.
- Certain workers are entitled to be paid minimum rates of pay and overtime pay. These workers are covered by wages council provisions.
- All workers employed for more than 16 hours per week are entitled to receive itemised pay statements at or before each pay day.
- Men and women are entitled to equal pay for equal work. The Equal Pay Act 1970 and EC law apply. Part-timers are generally entitled to pro-rata pay and non-cash benefits.

GENERAL GUIDE TO USEFUL EVIDENCE

- The pay slips, P45, P60 and other tax records.
- Details of what other, similar workers enjoy.
- With wages council workers, the relevant wages council order.

CHAPTER TWO

Equal pay

The legal framework

The legislation

The Equal Pay Act 1970 (EqPA) and, in particular, the concept of equal value introduced by the Equal Pay (Amendment) Regulations 1983 (SI No 1794), are difficult to understand and apply. EC law has been particularly influential in this area, especially Article 119 of the Treaty of Rome (Art 119). This book outlines the key issues so that potential cases may be identified. 'Like work' claims can be relatively straightforward to run in the IT, but complex and lengthy procedures are involved for 'equal value' claims and we only touch on the necessary evidence and procedural issues. An adviser considering running an equal value claim for the first time, should talk to someone who has done it before.

The EqPA and the Sex Discrimination Act (SDA) 1975 cover separate ground. Although the EqPA most often applies to pay, in fact it covers discrimination between men and women in relation to any contractual term. If unsure which statute applies, both should be cited in the application to the IT.

Who is covered?

The EqPA is wider than the EPCA. It protects workers employed under a contract of service or apprenticeship or the self-employed having contracted to execute work personally.[1] Men and women can claim under the EqPA.

The comparable man

Under the EqPA (unlike the SDA) a woman must find an actual man with whom she can compare herself. She cannot simply ask the IT to infer that her terms and conditions are less favourable than those of a man would have been.

The same employment

The male comparator must be employed by the same or an associated employer. An employer is an associated employer where one company owns another or where two companies come under the control of a third person.

The comparator must be employed at the same establishment or at another establishment in GB where common terms and conditions of employment[2] apply generally or to workers of the relevant classes. It would seem that a broad similarity of terms and conditions of employment of the classes to which the worker and her comparator belong will suffice.[3]

Where Art 119 applies,[4] but not under the EqPA, a woman may compare herself with a predecessor, who left before she started.[5] She may also be able to compare herself with a successor.

Comparable jobs

A woman may compare herself with a man in the same employment if:
a) she is doing like work or work of a broadly similar nature;[6] or
b) she is doing work rated equivalent to his in a study which evaluates their work in terms of the demand made on each worker under various headings eg effort, skill and decision.[7] (Such a study is usually known as a job evaluation scheme); or
c) she is doing work of equal value in terms of the demand made on her, eg under such headings as effort, skill and decision.[8]

The following points should be noted:
- A woman can choose which man she wants to compare herself with and may choose more than one.
- Even if there is a man in the same employment doing like work or work rated as equivalent under a JES, a woman may compare herself with a different man who is doing work of equal value.[9] (This prevents equal pay claims being defeated by the presence of one or two low-paid men in predominantly female areas of work.) A woman may not bring an equal value claim comparing herself with a man who is in fact on like work or work rated as equivalent. Her claim against him would have to be on the basis of like work or work rated as equivalent.
- Under Art 119 a woman may compare herself with a man whose work

turns out to be of less value than hers,[10] although she can claim only pay equal to his. This is probably also true under the EqPA.

Job evaluation schemes

A study measuring the relative value of jobs, either solely of the woman and her comparator, or of some or all workers in the same employment, is commonly known as a job evaluation scheme (JES). There are many methods of evaluation, but the principal distinction is between analytic and non-analytic schemes. An analytic JES is one which evaluates jobs according to a breakdown of demands and characteristics. Factors such as responsibility, working conditions, physical and mental requirements are weighted and measured. A non-analytic JES compares jobs on a 'whole-job' basis, eg by ranking and paired comparisons.

There are dangers that a JES may itself be directly or indirectly discriminatory, eg because it over-values traditional male skills and attributes, such as physical strength.

Where there is an existing JES which is both analytic[11] and non-discriminatory,[12] it can serve two functions:
- a woman may claim equal pay and other terms and conditions to those of a man whose work has been rated as equivalent under such a JES;[13]
- where a woman's work has been rated of less value than a man's under such a JES, she will fail in a claim under EqPA s1(2)(c) that her work is of equal value to his.[14]

Sometimes an employer may commission a JES after an equal value claim has been started in an attempt to block the claim. In order to have any effect, the JES must be completed at the latest by the final hearing, and it is in the IT's discretion whether it is willing to stay proceedings if the JES is not ready.[15] A 'completed' JES means one which has been accepted by the employers and workers as a valid study, even though it may not yet have been implemented.[16]

It is uncertain precisely what effect on an equal value claim the completion of a JES after the institution of proceedings will have. Provided the JES relates back to the relevant jobs as at the date the application to the IT was lodged, it is admissible as evidence and, assuming the jobs are differently rated,[17] it may well also block the equal value claim entirely under EqPA s2A.

Equal value claims – the expert's report

In determining equal value claims, the IT must obtain the report of an independent expert.[18] The IT decides at a preliminary hearing whether the case is strong enough to proceed and if so, it appoints an expert to evaluate the jobs on an analytic basis. A case will fail at this preliminary stage if:

a) the woman's work has been valued as less than the male comparator's in a non-discriminatory JES; or

b) there are no reasonable grounds for determining that the work is of equal value.

The IT may also take into account any s1(3)[19] genuine material factor defence put forward at the preliminary hearing.[20]

Independent experts take on average one year to prepare their report, during which time the parties are given opportunities to make representations to the expert. The parties can also cross-examine the expert in the IT once the report is ready. The IT will generally admit the report in evidence unless it can be shown to be unsatisfactory.[21]

Either party may commission their own expert report, although the IT cannot order the worker to co-operate with the employer's expert.[22] The independent expert has no special status,[23] although s/he will usually be more persuasive simply by virtue of being independent. The IT can use its discretion in weighing up all the evidence including the credibility of the different expert evidence and make its own decision as to whether the work is of equal value.

The equality clause

When a claim succeeds, the way the EqPA operates is to insert an equality clause into the contract of the woman. Each contractual term that is less favourable than the equivalent term in the contract of the comparable man is modified to make it equal.

It is irrelevant that, looking at the contracts as a whole, the woman is equally treated. For example, where a woman receives less basic pay, but better holiday and sick pay, she is nevertheless entitled to have her basic pay increased to the male level.[24] Similarly under Art 119, the European Court of Justice (ECJ) has said that the principle of equal pay entails equality in each component of remuneration and does not look at whether the total benefits are the same.[25]

An employer may say that the reason for a woman's lower basic pay is that she has better terms in other respects. This may be a genuine material factor defence under the EqPA, although the employer should be able to show that the lower pay is objectively justifiable and meets a real need of the employer.[26] Where Art 119 applies, it is unlikely that off-setting benefits can amount to a defence.[27]

The defence

The employer has a defence under EqPA s1(3) if it is shown on a balance of probabilities that the variation between the woman's and the man's pay (or other terms) is due to a genuine material factor other than sex. In claims based on like work or work rated as equivalent under a JES, such a factor must be a material difference between the woman's case and the man's. When the scope of the EqPA was broadened to introduce equal value claims, employers were given a wider defence, ie in addition to such a material difference, it can also be any other material factor.

The material difference defence

Originally this defence was limited to personal factors differentiating the woman and her comparator. For example, a man could legitimately receive higher pay because of his longer service or better skills or productivity or because of red-circling. However, the House of Lords decision in *Rainey v Greater Glasgow Health Board*[28] widened the interpretation of the defence to include circumstances other than the personal qualifications or merits of the workers concerned. There is now little practical difference between the defence that can be used on like work and JES cases and that for equal value cases.

The material factor defence

The nature of this defence has been greatly influenced by decisions of the ECJ, although its interpretation by ITs and the Employment Appeal Tribunal (EAT) is inconsistent and needs clarification. The key definition is to be found in the judgment of the ECJ in *Bilka-Kaufhaus GmbH v Weber von Hartz*[29] as applied by the House of Lords in *Rainey*.[30] What the employer must show is that the variation in pay or other terms is objectively justifiable. The variation must be 'reasonably necessary' in order to achieve a legitimate economic, administrative or other objective which corresponds to a 'real need on the part of the undertaking'.[31]

   Unfortunately, many IT and EAT decisions have simply looked at whether the employer can provide an 'innocent' explanation – as opposed to an objective justification – for the variation in pay. In *Davies v*

McCartneys,[32] the EAT said that any genuine reason for the pay difference would be a defence, provided it were not attributable to sex.

A material factor justifying a variation in pay must be 'significant and relevant'.[33] As well as personal differences between the workers concerned, the following are examples of genuine material factors although whether the defence is made out will depend on the specific circumstances in each case:

- market forces and other economic considerations;
- administrative efficiency;
- geographical differences, eg London weighting;
- unsocial hours, rotating shift and night working;
- experience and qualifications;
- different pay structures and bargaining arrangements.

In *Reed Packaging Ltd v Boozer and Another*,[34] the EAT considered the mere existence of separate pay structures governing the woman's contract and the man's contract, neither of which was discriminatory in itself, a sufficient defence. The existence of separate pay structures, often negotiated by different trade unions, is frequently used as a defence to equal value claims. The danger is that while each individual structure may not discriminate between men and women within its remit, there may be lower overall pay within a certain structure precisely because it covers jobs which have always been female dominated. In *Reed Packaging Ltd*, the EAT did not consider the possibility of indirect discrimination as between the two pay structures.

Some equal value cases have confused matters relevant to evaluating the relative worth of each job such as skill, responsibility, effort, with material factors which would justify a pay difference. The EAT in *Davies v McCartneys*[35] suggested that the employer could use as a defence the very matters which were relevant in determining whether a job was of equal value. This approach has been criticised and is open to doubt: once two jobs have been evaluated as equal in terms of these separate demands, an employer ought not to be able to justify a pay difference by saying that s/he personally values one job more highly.

Summary

Despite some of the EAT's decisions, the following test should be argued in any IT with regard to the defence:

- The test is of objective justifiability as defined in *Bilka-Kaufhaus* and *Rainey*. A non-sex-based explanation is not enough. The variation must serve some real need on the part of the undertaking.
- The material factor must be significant and relevant.

- The material factor must be non-sex-based in whole or in part.[36]
- The mere existence of separate pay structures should not be a defence in itself. Further consideration should be given to whether the existence of different structures operates to discriminate indirectly against women.
- Where pay is governed by merit, flexibility, training or seniority, the comments of the ECJ in the *Danfoss*[37] case should be borne in mind.[38]
- A pay differential between full-time and part-time workers must be justified by objective factors unrelated to sex. However, an employer may be able to justify such a practice on the ground that there is a genuine intention to discourage part-time working.[39]
- The burden of proof to show a defence is on the employer, once a worker has shown her work is like work, work rated as equivalent or work of equal value.[40]

Note that the employer may argue a material factor defence both at the preliminary hearing before an independent expert is appointed and again at the final hearing after the expert has reported.

Using EC law

All UK workers can claim under Art 119 in the IT in relation to discrimination in pay. Art 119 requires that 'men and women should receive equal pay for equal work' and is expanded by the Equal Pay Directive (75/117/EEC) which can also be relied on in national courts against any employer.[41]

What does Art 119 mean by 'pay'?

Unlike the EqPA, Art 119 does not apply to all terms and conditions, but only to pay. Art 119 defines pay as 'the ordinary basic or minimum wage or salary and any other consideration, whether in cash or in kind, which the worker receives, directly or indirectly, in respect of his employment from his employer'. This wide definition was confirmed by the ECJ in *Garland v British Rail Engineering*,[42] which added that the consideration may be 'immediate or future, provided that the worker receives it, albeit indirectly, in respect of his employment from his employer'.

Both contractual[43] and statutory redundancy pay[44] fall within Art 119 although it is uncertain whether payment by the redundancy fund when the employer defaults is covered.[45] Some payments made by employers under statutory obligation, eg statutory sick pay,[46] may also be within Art 119. Most significantly, Art 119 covers contributions towards and benefits paid under contractual pension schemes,[47] whether supplementary to[48] or contracted-out from[49] the state pension scheme.

Indirect discrimination

Unlike the EqPA, Art 119 does not require an actual male comparator. Article 1 of the Equal Pay Directive requires 'the elimination of all discrimination on grounds of sex with regard to all aspects and conditions of remuneration'. Hence EC law has developed to prohibit indirect discrimination in pay. The concept is similar to that of indirect discrimination under the Race Relations Act (RRA) 1976 or SDA 1975 s1(1)(b),[50] although without the restrictive wording. In particular, it is not necessary to identify a requirement or condition, and any discriminatory pay practice is covered. For example, the ECJ has suggested that an incremental pay structure using subjective criteria such as 'quality of work' may be discriminatory.

Part-time workers

Many ECJ cases concern lower pay and benefits for part-time workers.[51] There is a general recognition that more women are in part-time work and the issue has been whether employers can justify the differential. In the key case of *Bilka-Kaufhaus GmbH v Weber von Hartz*,[52] a German department store (in line with West German state legislation) excluded part-time workers from its occupational pension scheme. The ECJ said that where a pay practice, applied generally, operated to disadvantage more women than men, it would infringe Art 119 unless it were objectively justifiable.[53]

Working full-time is not a justification in itself for receiving greater hourly pay. Nor would the ECJ in *Rinner-Kühn*[54] accept as justification an argument that part-timers were less integrated into the business than full-timers. However, it may be justification if an employer can show that for economic or administrative reasons it needs to discourage part-time working.

The ECJ's most explicit guidance as to what may be considered justifiable is in *Danfoss* (above). In that case, the employers awarded pay increments on the basis of a number of criteria, ie flexibility, quality of work, vocational training and seniority. It was not apparent to the workers precisely how the level of each person's pay had been arrived at, but the net effect was that women were on the whole paid less than the men. The ECJ said that where a pay system is characterised by a total lack of transparency, that is, where it is impossibe to tell precisely how each worker's pay level was reached, and where there is a statistical imbalance between the pay of male and female workers, the onus is on the employer to justify the difference.

The ECJ then examined each of the criteria. It recognised that proportionally less women were likely to score highly on criteria such as flexibility, vocational training and seniority. Therefore where statistics indicated that women were generally paid less than men on the basis of flexibility or vocational training criteria, the employer must justify the use of each criterion by showing it was 'of importance for the performance of the specific duties entrusted to the worker concerned'. However, an employer need not justify the use of the seniority criterion because that was self-evidently justifiable.

The ECJ's attitude towards seniority is disappointing as it is possible to envisage situations where seniority and experience are not essential. Nevertheless, the ECJ took a radical position in respect of merit payments. It said that if women were, on the whole, paid less on the basis of 'quality of work', this could not be justified because 'it is inconceivable that the work carried out by female workers would be generally of a lower quality'.

Statutory entitlement to certain payments such as redundancy pay and sick pay is often subject to requirements which may have indirectly discriminatory effect. In *Rinner-Kühn*,[55] only workers on more than 10 hours per week qualified for West German statutory sick pay. The ECJ held that this could be indirectly discriminatory under Art 119 unless it could be justified. Similar issues may arise in the UK and the employer may not be able to justify a lower rate of sick pay by saying that the legislation laid down the qualifying requirements. It is likely that the secretary of state would be joined as a respondent to the IT proceedings to put forward the government's justification.[56] The Equal Opportunities Commission (EOC) has started judicial review proceedings for a declaration that the requirement of minimum qualifying hours in order to claim unfair dismissal and redundancy pay is indirectly discriminatory contrary to Art 119, the Equal Pay Directive and the Equal Treatment Directive (76/207/EEC).

Time limits for claiming and remedies

Remedies

If a woman succeeds in her claim, any less favourable term in her contract is modified so that, for example, she is no longer paid less than the male comparator. She may also be awarded pay arrears, or compensation in relation to any non-pay term. Under Art 119, a part-timer suffering indirect discrimination may have her contract modified so that she receives proportionally the same benefits as full-timers.[57]

Under UK law, an IT cannot award compensation for any period more than two years before the application was lodged.[58] However, there is nothing in Art 119 which places a time limit on the period in respect of which compensation may be obtained.

Time limits

According to the EAT in *British Railways Board v Paul*,[59] a worker may bring an equal pay claim at any time during employment or after s/he has left. The EAT may be wrong in its interpreting EqPA s2(4) to mean that no time limit applies. Therefore, where a worker leaves a job, it is safest to claim within six months of departure. It is also unwise to delay starting a claim because of the limitation on how far back damages may be awarded.

There is no time limit for claims made directly under EC law.[60] A worker can probably claim for any contravention of Art 119 taking place after 8 April 1976.[61]

PART II: UNFAIR DISMISSAL AND REDUNDANCY

CHAPTER THREE

Statutory protection

The legal framework

The legislation

The statutory right not to be unfairly dismissed was first introduced by the Industrial Relations Act 1971. The Trade Union and Labour Relations Act 1974[1] repealed the Industrial Relations Act and introduced provisions strengthening the unfair dismissal provisions.

New employment rights were introduced by the Employment Protection Act 1975, which created the Advisory Conciliation and Arbitration Service (ACAS), whose conciliation officers are attached to every unfair dismissal case, with a view to bringing about a settlement.[2] The Employment Protection Act also introduced the right to maternity pay and guarantee payments, it recognised the role of trade unions in redundancy dismissals and it strengthened a worker's right to receive a written statement of the main terms and conditions of employment.

The Employment Protection (Consolidation) Act 1978 (EPCA) consolidated and re-enacted the major legislation on workers' rights relating to their employment contracts and termination of employment. The EPCA consolidated the Redundancy Payments Act 1965, the Contracts of Employment Act 1972 and substantial parts of the Trade Union and Labour Relations Act 1974 and Employment Protection Act 1975.

The statutory framework of unfair dismissal law is now contained almost entirely in the EPCA. Subsequent legislation has made minor adjustments, notably on jurisdictional issues, particularly concerning the required length of continuous employment before bringing a claim.

The Employment Act 1980 reinforced the importance of the Codes of Practice produced by ACAS or the secretary of state.[3] At the same time, the Employment Act 1980 reduced the effectiveness of unfair dismissal protection by removing the burden of proof from the employer to become a neutral burden.[4]

The Employment Act 1982 altered the method of calculating the period of continuous employment.[5] The Sex Discrimination Act (SDA) 1986 introduced an equality clause in respect of normal retirement age, thereby enabling more women to claim unfair dismissal.[6] The Employment Act 1989 increased the qualifying period for a worker's entitlement to written reasons for dismissal from six months to two years.[7] In addition, employers with fewer than 20 workers no longer have to put the disciplinary procedure in writing.[8]

Codes of practice

In deciding whether a dismissal is fair or unfair, the IT is primarily concerned with the fairness of procedures followed by the employer prior to dismissal. This is why, ever since the introduction of unfair dismissal rights, there has been statutory power for the secretary of state or ACAS to produce Codes of Practice. These codes are to give employers practical guidance on how to draw up and effectively operate disciplinary rules and procedures.[9]

There are currently two Codes of Practice relating to unfair dismissal: the Industrial Relations Code of Practice[10] and the ACAS Code on Disciplinary Practice and Procedure.[11]

The ACAS code gives guidance on conduct dismissals although the procedures set out are equally applicable to other types of dismissal. Its essential feature is to require an employer to give fair and appropriate warning to a worker and to give the worker an opportunity to respond to any allegations before decisions are made.[12]

The IT is under a statutory obligation to consider relevant provisions of the Codes[13] in reaching its decision. Significant breach of the provisions of the Codes by an employer should generally result in a finding of unfair dismissal.[14]

Eligible categories

Employees and the self-employed

In order to claim unfair dismissal, a worker must be employed (ie work under a contract of service). A worker who is self-employed (ie working under a contract for services) is not covered. The distinction between these two types of worker can be extremely blurred and difficult to distinguish.[15]

With such a crucial distinction, it is surprising that there is no clear statutory definition of who is employed and who is self-employed. An 'employee' is simply defined as someone who has entered into or works under a contract of employment.[16] A 'contract of employment' means 'a contract of service or apprenticeship, whether express or implied, and (if it is express), whether it is oral or in writing'.[17]

There is no single test which determines whether a worker is employed or self-employed. There have been a large number of reported cases trying to decide an appropriate test. The law at present is that there are four main factors to be considered, some of which are more important than others. This approach is known as the 'economic reality test' and it seeks to adapt to the many different types of employment situation.

The first factor is whether there is a mutual obligation to supply and perform work. This is the most important single factor. If no such obligation exists, the IT will almost invariably say that the worker is not an employee. In *O'Kelly v Trusthouse Forte plc*,[18] butlers who worked in a hotel as 'regular casuals' were not employees, even though they were provided with work on a regular basis, since the hotel was not in fact under an obligation to provide such work. On the other hand, in *Nethermere (St Neots) Ltd v Gardiner and Taverna*[19] a group of homeworkers were employees because, over a period of time, their employer had provided work which they were obliged to accept and perform.

The second main factor is the purpose and intention of the parties. The IT will look at the purpose of the contract and what the parties intended when they formed it. It is the nature of the agreement and the actual performance of the contract which counts, not simply the label attached to the relationship by the parties. Just because a worker is told by an employer that s/he is self-employed does not mean that that is the true legal position. Nor is it conclusive that a worker is paying tax on a self-employed basis, although that will be one of the relevant factors.[20]

The degree of control exercised by the employer is the third factor. Historically this factor alone was the conclusive test. Now it is simply one of several to be considered. If the worker controls when, where and how s/he performs the work, this degree of autonomy would suggest that s/he is self-employed. However, if the employer has the power to tell the worker when, where and how to perform, it would indicate that the worker is an employee.[21]

Finally the method and mode of payment to the worker may be revealing.

Upper age limit

A worker cannot claim unfair dismissal if s/he has reached the normal retirement age at his/her place of work or, if there is no normal retirement age, if s/he has reached 65.[22] Normal retirement age is usually the contractual retirement age unless it can be shown that most or all other employees retire at a different age.[23] If discriminatory retirement ages between men and women apply at the workplace, the normal retirement age for both will be 65.[24]

Working abroad and ship workers

A worker who ordinarily works outside GB is not entitled to claim unfair dismissal.[25] The place of employment will be the place stated in the contract of employment. If there is no written contract or no specific place of work, the appropriate test will be the 'base test', ie where the head office is located or the base from which the worker operates.[26]

A person employed to work on board a ship registered in the UK will be regarded as ordinarily working within GB unless the employment is wholly outside GB or the worker is not ordinarily resident in GB.[27] In determining whether such employment is wholly outside GB, the relevant factor is the extent of the employment which involves working on board the ship, and not where the contract was formed nor where the worker spends his/her paid leave.[28]

Categories excluded from claiming unfair dismissal

- The police,[29] service personnel[30] and certain workers protecting national security[31] cannot claim unfair dismissal.
- A worker employed by a foreign or commonwealth mission in a non-commercial capacity is not entitled to claim unfair dismissal as the employer has immunity in civil claims. The employer can choose to waive the immunity and participate in IT proceedings.[32] Where the mission is a commercial venture, the worker can claim unfair dismissal unless s/he agreed in writing that immunity would apply.[33]
- A share fisherman cannot claim unfair dismissal. This is a worker who has a share in the profits of the fishing vessel on which s/he is employed and who is not paid in any other way.[34]
- A person employed to work on board a ship registered in the UK will be regarded as a person who ordinarily works GB.

Contracting out

A worker employed on a fixed-term contract of one year or more will be unable to claim unfair dismissal if s/he agreed in writing before the expiry of the term to exclude the right to claim unfair dismissal.[35] The exclusion agreement may be either in the contract itself or in a separate document.[36] If the worker is employed on a series of fixed-term contracts, the exclusion agreement will be valid only if the final contract is for one year or more.[37]

The right to claim unfair dismissal will be excluded only if the dismissal consists of the expiry and non-renewal of the fixed term.[38] A worker dismissed during the period of the contract can still claim unfair dismissal.[39]

Illegal contracts of employment

An illegal contract of employment is not enforceable in the courts and a worker will be unable to claim unfair dismissal.[40] An employment contract will be illegal in the following circumstances:

- Where, to the worker's knowledge, the contract of employment involves a fraud on the Inland Revenue, eg the employer is not paying the appropriate tax on the worker's wages. A common indication of a fraud is when wages are wholly or partly in cash. The essential question is whether the worker actually knew that the employer was not paying the appropriate tax, not whether s/he ought to have known. If the worker did not know, the contract is not illegal.[41]
- Where the performance of the employment contract is prohibited by statute, the period of prohibited performance will not count towards the required length of continuous employment for an unfair dismissal claim. A worker on 16 or more hours per week must be continuously employed for two years after the end of the prohibited period in order to qualify.
- Where the performance of the contract is prohibited by common law. A contract for an immoral purpose, eg procuring prostitutes, or for a criminal purpose, eg gun running, will not be recognised by the IT. It is necessary for the main purpose of the employment to be the immoral or criminal purpose rather than it being an incidental part of the employment contract.[42]

Qualifying service

Length of continuous employment

A worker must have been continuously employed for the required period at the effective date of termination (EDT). A worker qualifies who has worked continuously for two years at 16 or more hours per week[43] or for five years at eight or more hours per week but less than 16.[44]

Weeks which count towards continuous service

Continuous employment is measured by 'qualifying' weeks. It is broken by a week that does not qualify and the worker will have to start again in accruing the two years.

A week which counts is one in which the worker either:

a) Actually works 16 or more hours in that week;[45] or

b) works under a contract which normally involves 16 or more hours per week.

If during all or part of a week a worker is away on account of holiday or sickness or other recognised absence, that week will nevertheless count. Equally, if a worker resigns or is dismissed in one week and re-engaged in the subsequent week, each week counts and continuity is not broken, even if the worker works less than 16 hours in each of the successive weeks, provided that the contract normally involves 16 or more hours per week.

Continuity if the worker leaves work and returns

The period of continuous employment must be of unbroken service except in limited circumstances.

Where a worker is absent from work but the contract continues, there is no problem and continuity is preserved. In some circumstances, even though the contract is terminated because the worker leaves, when s/he subsequently returns to the job continuity is preserved and the weeks of absence will count towards the two- or five-year total. Continuity is preserved where the worker is absent from work:

- wholly or partly because of pregnancy or confinement. This is subject to a maximum of 26 weeks except where the absence and return is in accordance with statutory maternity leave;[46]
- on account of a temporary cessation of work[47] - when the employer lays off workers through lack of work;
- because of sickness or injury, subject to a maximum of 26 weeks;[48]
- in such circumstances that, by arrangement or custom, s/he is regarded as continuing in employment for all or any purposes.[49] This can be helpful when, eg an employer agrees that a worker may leave to visit family overseas and return subsequently to the same employment;
- and is reinstated or re-engaged through ACAS conciliation following dismissal.[50]

The presumption of continuity

The period of continuous employment begins the day someone starts work[51] and is presumed to continue[52] until the EDT.[53] The presumption of continuity is very important for workers since it means that it is for the employer to prove there has been a break which is not recognised by the law as preserving continuity.[54]

Identifying the EDT

The EDT is identified in the same way as for time limit purposes[55] save that, for purposes of calculating length of continuous service, it is artificially extended when the employer fails to give notice. In those circumstances, the EDT is when the minimum statutory notice period – not the contractual notice period[56] – would have expired.

Change of ownership of businesses

The Transfer of Undertakings Regulations

The Transfer of Undertakings (Protection of Employment) Regulations 1981[57] protect workers' rights on transfers of the business in which they are employed. Where there is a transfer to which the Regulations apply, the worker's continuity of employment is preserved.[58] The worker must have been employed with the original employer immediately before the transfer except where an earlier dismissal was in connection with the proposed transfer,[59] eg so that the buyer could take over the business free from existing workers.

The Regulations are extremely complicated, but the main points to remember are these:

- The Regulations cover any trade or business which is a commercial venture,[60] ie which has a profit motive. Charitable schools, free advice centres etc are generally excluded.
- There must be a transfer of the undertaking itself, not simply of its assets.
- The transfer may take place by sale or some other disposition,[61] eg lease, franchise, gift. A share takeover is not a transfer since ownership remains in the same legal person, ie the company.
- The Regulations apply to the whole of the UK.
- The worker's contractual rights and obligations also pass to the new employer unless the new employer specifically agrees changes with the worker.

Continuity under the EPCA

Under EPCA Sch 13 para 17, continuity is preserved on transfer of a trade, business or undertaking in GB. The rules are similar to those of the Regulations save that the EPCA does not seem limited to commercial ventures. EPCA s153 defines 'business' as including 'a trade or profession or any activity carried on by a body of persons whether corporate or unincorporate'. Schedule 13 does not preserve the worker's contractual rights.

What is a dismissal?

To bring a claim for unfair dismissal, the worker must have been dismissed in a way recognised by the EPCA. There are various forms of dismissal:
- termination by the employer;
- expiry of a fixed-term contract;
- forced resignation;
- resignation amounting to constructive dismissal; and
- deemed dismissal on returning from maternity leave.

Termination by the employer

The commonest form of dismissal is when the employer terminates the employment with or without notice.[62] Usually there is no doubt that this has taken place, but employers seeking to avoid an unfair dismissal claim often deny that the worker was dismissed.

If there is a dispute as to whether a dismissal has occurred, it is for the worker to show on the balance of probabilities that s/he has been dismissed. If the IT cannot decide this issue on the available evidence, the worker's claim will fail.[63]

Sometimes an employer's words are ambiguous. The IT will look at the purpose and effect of those words in the light of all the surrounding circumstances and, in particular, the conduct of the parties and what happened before and after the disputed dismissal. The IT must then decide how a 'reasonable' worker would have interpreted the employer's words.[64]

If the employer's words clearly indicated a dismissal, they will be taken literally and the IT will not usually consider the parties' intentions.[65] The only exception is where the dismissal – or resignation – took place in 'the heat of the moment', for example as a result of an argument between the employer and worker. If the employer retracts the dismissal very soon afterwards, the IT may consider that s/he was entitled to do so. The period of time in which a party may retract depends on the circumstances but usually it should be within minutes.[66]

Where the worker is immature or below average intelligence and resigns while under emotional stress and in the heat of the moment, the IT will not treat these words as constituting a dismissal if the resignation was never intended.[67]

Expiry of a fixed-term contract

Non-renewal of a fixed-term contract on its expiry is treated as a dismissal.[68] A fixed-term contract is a contract for a specific term and at its commencement, the termination date is ascertainable.[69]

Forced resignation

If the worker resigns as a result of the employer saying that s/he must resign or otherwise be dismissed, this counts as a dismissal. The difficult issue for the IT to decide is whether the resignation was forced.[70] A worker should be wary of resigning in these circumstances, because it may be difficult to prove that s/he was threatened in this way.

Constructive dismissal

If the worker resigns in response to a significant and fundamental breach of the employment contract by the employer, this is a 'constructive dismissal'.[71] Constructive dismissal is usually difficult to prove and a worker should be very careful about resigning if s/he wants to be able to claim unfair dismissal.

Whether there has been a fundamental breach of contract is a contractual matter. The reasonableness of the parties' behaviour is not relevant in establishing whether there was a constructive dismissal, although it will be relevant when considering whether the constructive dismissal was unfair. So, for example, if the employer gives the worker an instruction which is unreasonable but which is allowed by the contract, there is no breach of contract and therefore no constructive dismissal.[72]

Fundamental breach of contract

Not every breach of contract is a 'fundamental breach'[73] which entitles a worker to claim constructive dismissal. Before resigning, a worker needs to consider which term of the contract an employer has broken. A contract may comprise many written and unwritten terms, express and implied. A large number of constructive dismissal claims are based on the employer breaking the following implied terms:
– not to subject the worker to capricious or arbitrary treatment;

- to maintain trust and confidence; and
- to take reasonable care for the health and safety of the worker.

It is difficult to be sure when a breach is sufficiently serious to be a 'fundamental breach' and there are no hard and fast rules. The working relationship will be relevant and, what in one job situation may amount to a fundamental breach, in another will not. The following are examples of what might amount to a fundamental breach: a reduction in pay,[74] a change in the worker's status or job content,[75] changes of work hours[76] or place of work, provided the change was not contemplated by the parties when the employment contract started.[77] The change must not be permitted by the contract.

Sometimes a single breach of contract is enough if it is sufficiently serious. Alternatively the worker can rely on a series of breaches, where each breach in isolation might not constitute a significant and fundamental breach, but taken together they do. This is known as the 'last straw' doctrine.[78]

An anticipatory breach

When an employer breaks a term of a contract with immediate effect this constitutes an actual breach. When the employer merely indicates in advance a firm intention to commit a fundamental breach, this is called an 'anticipatory breach'. A worker who resigns as a result of an anticipatory breach may claim constructive dismissal. However, a worker should be careful not to resign prematurely where the employer has not finally decided to commit the fundamental breach. The employer may still be willing to negotiate. For example, an invitation to use the grievance procedure in response to a proposed step will indicate that the employer has made no final decision. Equally, an employer's statement that 'I expect you to co-operate in the manner asked of you' is only a forceful request, falling short of an actual breach of contract.

When to resign[79]

Once the worker is sure that the employer has committed an actual or anticipatory breach, s/he must resign fairly promptly, since any delay may be taken by the IT as acceptance of the employer's conduct. A worker is often reluctant to resign before s/he has found another job and this can cause problems.

How long a worker can afford to delay depends on the facts of each case. Delay is very risky where the employer's breach has immediate impact on the worker, eg a pay cut, and particularly where the worker has to behave differently to comply with the breach, eg new duties or location. It may be legitimate to object in writing and request a short trial period before resigning.[80] There is less urgency where the breach has no immediate impact, eg a change in retirement age or sick pay entitlement, provided a written protest is made immediately.

When the worker does resign, s/he should make it clear that it is in response to the employer's fundamental breach and not for any other reason.

Deemed dismissal

A woman who is not permitted to return from statutory maternity leave is subject to a deemed dismissal.[81]

Situations where there is no dismissal

Where an unforeseen event occurs which makes future performance of the employment contract impossible or radically different, eg long-term sickness[82] or imprisonment, the contract is frustrated and the worker cannot claim s/he has been unfairly dismissed. This is, however, very rare.

Termination by mutual agreement is usually obvious. However, voluntary redundancy is technically a dismissal,[83] although unlikely to be unfair. Early retirement, unless involuntary, is a mutually agreed termination.

An employer cannot deprive a worker of the right to claim unfair dismissal by agreeing in advance that the contract will automatically terminate on the happening of a certain event, eg the worker's late return from holiday. This would effectively circumvent the IT's jurisdiction and is invalid.[84]

What is an unfair dismissal?

The two stages

EPCA 1978 s57 sets out how an IT should decide whether a dismissal is unfair. There are two basic stages:
a) The employer must show what was the reason, or if more than one, the principal reason for the dismissal.[85] The reason must be one of the five potentially fair reasons set out in s57(1) and (2).
b) The IT then must decide in accordance with s57(3) whether it was fair to dismiss the worker for that reason.

The reason for the dismissal

The potentially fair reasons are the following:
- a reason relating to the worker's capability or qualification for performing work of the kind s/he was employed to do;[86]
- a reason relating to the conduct of the worker;[87]
- the worker is redundant;[88]
- the worker could not continue to work in the position s/he held without contravention of a duty or restriction imposed by or under an enactment;[89]
- for some other substantial reason of a kind such as to justify the dismissal of a worker holding the position which the worker held.[90]

If the employer cannot show the reason for dismissal, the dismissal will be automatically unfair. If there are several reasons, the employer must establish the principal reason. The dismissal will be unfair if the reason shown is insignificant, trivial or unworthy.[91]

The reason for dismissal will be the set of facts known to the employer at the time of dismissal or a genuine belief held on reasonable grounds by the employer which led to the dismissal.[92]

An employer may give one reason for dismissal at the time or immediately afterwards and another one once IT proceedings have started. The IT will be reluctant to accept a change of reason particularly if it will cause prejudice to the worker and the worker will not have had the fullest opportunity to answer the allegations made.[93]

Was it fair to dismiss for that reason?

EPCA 1978 s57(3) sets out the statutory test of fairness:

'the determination of the question whether the dismissal was fair or unfair having regard to the reason shown by the employer, shall depend on whether in the circumstances, (including the size and administrative resources of the employer's undertaking) the employer acted reasonably or unreasonably in treating it as a sufficient reason for dismissing the employee; and that question shall be determined in accordance with equity and the substantial merits of the case.'

The IT must take into account a number of considerations in deciding the fairness of a dismissal under s57(3). The relevant factors vary according to the reason for the dismissal.[94] However, there are also broad considerations which apply to all s57(3) dismissals.

Employer's size and administrative resources
In deciding whether a dismissal is fair, an IT must have in mind the size and administrative resources of the employer. This is particularly relevant when considering the actions taken by an employer prior to dismissal. The larger the employer, the greater the obligation to operate proper disciplinary, grievance and consultative procedures.

Equity and the substantial merits of the case
Equity requires that an employer treats workers consistently ; an arbitrary or capricious dismissal will be inequitable. If, on a different occasion, the employer failed to dismiss another worker for a similar offence, the dismissal may well be inequitable and unreasonable.[95]

Procedural unfairness
In the past, employers successfully argued that although their procedures prior to dismissal were unfair, the same decision would have been reached even if they had consulted and followed proper procedures.[96] This was known as the 'no difference rule'. The House of Lords in *Polkey v AE Dayton Services*[97] held that the 'no difference rule' must no longer be applied.

The Lords stressed the importance of procedures and the obligation on an employer to carry them out fairly in relation to each of the four potentially fair reasons for dismissal. Failure to consult and adopt fair procedures will now in itself render a dismissal unfair except in exceptional circumstances. The employer will be able to justify failure to consult etc only if s/he could reasonably conclude at the time of dismissal and in the light of what s/he knew at that time, that consultation would be 'utterly useless or futile'. An example would be where a worker was caught in the act of theft.

Polkey is probably the most important decision since the introduction of the right not to be unfairly dismissed. Unfortunately some of its beneficial effect has been cut down by ITs on assessment of compensation. Where the unfairness seems more a matter of procedure than substance, the IT can reduce compensation according to the degree of likelihood that the worker would have been dismissed even had fair procedures been followed.[98]

The band of reasonable responses
The real question is not whether the IT would itself have chosen not to dismiss the worker, but whether it was unreasonable of the employer to have made the opposite decision. The IT may think that the dismissal was harsh, but nevertheless within ' the band of reasonable responses' open to

the employer. Within such a band, one employer might reasonably retain the worker whereas another employer might reasonably dismiss him/her. If so, then it is not unfair dismissal, even if the IT would not have dismissed.[99]

This is a very important concept which causes many claims to fail. Section 57(3) gives no scope or support for this idea. It is a judicial creation which benefits only the employer and removes any meaningful role for the IT members, who are appointed for their industrial experience and common sense.

Automatically fair or unfair dismissals

Certain dismissals are not subject to the reasonableness test in s57 because they are automatically either fair or unfair.

Automatically fair dismissals

Lock-out, strike or other industrial action

The IT decides as a matter of fact whether an action amounted to a strike, lock-out or other industrial action. There are statutory and common law guidelines as to the meaning of these terms.

Industrial action includes any action which is intended to pressurise the employer and cause a disruption at work.[100] A strike is a cessation of work by workers acting in combination or a concerted refusal to continue to work for an employer in consequence of a dispute, done as a means of compelling the employer to accept or refuse terms and conditions of employment.[101] A lock-out is the closing of a place of employment or suspension of work or refusal by the employer to continue to employ any number of workers in consequence of a trade dispute.[102]

It is automatically fair to dismiss a worker for taking part in a strike or other industrial action or where the dismissal arises from the employer instituting a lock-out.[103] The employer is able to say that the dismissal was automatically fair unless s/he can establish that:

- the worker was taking part in the industrial action at the time of dismissal and had not already returned to work. The relevant date is the EDT;[104]
- the worker was actually participating in the industrial action and not simply threatening to do so.[105] If the worker was initially on strike but subsequently ceased to intend to participate, s/he will no longer be considered to be taking part;[106]
- the employer has not selectively dismissed or re-engaged workers

involved in the industrial action. If at the time of the industrial action the employer dismisses some of the participants and not others or if, within three months of the worker's EDT, the employer re-engages other participants who were dismissed, the worker can claim unfair dismissal. The purpose of this exception is to prevent an employer using industrial action as a way to dismiss unwanted workers with immunity.[107]

National security

Where a minister of the Crown signs the appropriate certificate stating that a worker was dismissed in order to safeguard national security, the dismisal is automatically fair.[108]

Automatically unfair dismissals

Pregnancy dismissals

A dismissal of a worker due to her pregnancy or for a reason connected with her pregnancy is automatically unfair unless, because of her pregnancy, she is incapable of adequately doing the work for which she was employed or cannot do so without contravention of a duty or restriction imposed by statute.[109] The selection of a woman for redundancy on grounds of her pregnancy is a pregnancy dismissal and automatically unfair.[110]

Dismissal for trade union membership

It is automatically unfair to dismiss a worker for membership or proposed membership of an independent trade union or for refusing to join. It is also automatically unfair to dismiss a worker for taking part or proposing to take part in the activities of an independent trade union at an appropriate time.[111] An appropriate time is outside working hours or, with the employer's consent, within working hours. An independent trade union is one which is not under the control or domination of the employer.[112]

Not declaring spent convictions

The Rehabilitation of Offenders Act 1974 gives certain workers the right not to disclose previous convictions which are 'spent' as a result of the passage of a specified length of time. The length of time depends on the nature of the conviction and the rehabilitation period ranges from six months to 10 years. It is automatically unfair to dismiss a worker for failing to disclose a 'spent' conviction.[113]

Dismissal because of the transfer of an undertaking

It is automatically unfair to dismiss a worker due to the transfer of an undertaking unless the dismissal was for an economic, technical or organisational reason compelling changes in the workforce of either the transferor (the selling employer) or the transferee (the buying employer). If so, the IT will decide the fairness of the dismissal in the usual way.

It is the employer who must prove that the dismissal was for an economic, technical or organisational reason. The IT should interpret this defence narrowly and dismissing workers in order to satisfy the buyer's requirements and obtain a good price is not an 'economic' reason which is acceptable.[114]

Certain redundancy dismissals

Dismissal is automatically unfair where the worker is selected for redundancy:

a) because s/he is a trade union member or proposes to join a trade union or is taking part in trade union activities or proposes to do so.[115] However, if the worker is selected for redundancy because of involvement in industrial action, the dismissal will not be automatically unfair;

b) because s/he refuses to join or remain in a trade union;[116]

c) in breach of a customary arrangement or agreed procedure.[117]

There is no statutory definition of 'customary arrangement or agreed procedure'. A customary arrangement is something which is so well-known, so certain and so clear as to amount to an implied agreed procedure. It includes arrangements which would not amount to a contractual agreement.[118] The employer may depart from a customary arrangement in special circumstances, but there is little guidance on what these are and the IT will look into the facts of each case.[119] An example may be the retention of a worker for compassionate reasons.[120] If the employer wants to depart from a customary arrangement or agreed procedure, s/he has to prove that a special ground exists.

CHAPTER FOUR

Reasons for dismissal

Capability or qualification dismissals

An employer may claim that a dismissal related to the capability or qualifications of the worker for performing work of the kind s/he was employed to do.[1]

The statutory definition of 'capability' is 'capability assessed by reference to skill, aptitude, health or any other physical or mental quality'.[2] 'Qualification' means 'any degree, diploma or other academic, technical or professional qualification relevant to the position which the employee held'.[3]

Skill dismissals

A skill dismissal is one that is due to the worker's inability to perform the job to the standard expected by the employer. It includes situations where that standard is higher than the norm in the industry.[4]

The reasonableness test – s57(3)

It is important to note that the employer need not prove in the IT that the worker actually was incompetent. The employer need show only that s/he genuinely and reasonably believed that the worker was incompetent. The test is as follows:
- Did the employer honestly believe that the worker was incompetent or unsuitable for the job?
- If so, was such belief held on reasonable grounds?
- In forming such a belief, did the employer carry out a proper and adequate investigation? In most cases, this would include giving the worker an opportunity to answer the criticisms.[5]

Other factors are relevant to the fairness of the dismissal. An IT usually expects the employer to have taken steps to remedy the worker's shortcoming before dismissing, eg by offering support and/or supervision, or retraining, setting targets and monitoring progress. The extent of assistance that should have been offered depends on the employer's administrative resources and size of enterprise.

It is rarely fair to dismiss a worker on the basis of one act of incompetence. The exception is where the consequences are so serious that to continue to employ the worker would be too risky and dangerous, eg when a mistake is made by an airline pilot, a coach driver or a scientist operating a nuclear reactor.[6] In this type of situation, dismissal without retraining or being given the chance to improve would be fair.

The IT may also take into account whether the employer had any alternative vacancy which could have been offered to the worker prior to dismissal. An employer will not be expected to create a vacancy or new job for the worker. The failure to offer alternative employment is not an overriding factor in capability dismissals but it is a relevant consideration, particularly where a large employer had appropriate vacancies which were not offered to the worker.

Aptitude and mental quality dismissals

An 'aptitude' dismissal may be because a worker is inflexible at work or is difficult or disruptive or not prepared to adapt.[7] 'Mental quality' would include a worker's lack of drive or having a personality which has a detrimental effect on colleagues' work or on customers.[8]

The reasonableness test – s57(3)

The employer must show that the worker's inflexibility or other mental quality was detrimental to the business. Prior to dismissal, the employer should have given sufficient and adequate warnings detailing the alleged shortcomings and the worker ought to have been provided with a reasonable opportunity to improve. As usual, the employer's size and administrative resources will be relevant in judging the adequacy of the procedures followed.

Sickness, injury and other health dismissals

An employer who dismisses a worker for ill-health or sickness absences may be dismissing on grounds of capability or conduct.[9] It will be a dismissal for conduct if the employer believes that the worker is not ill but is using sickness as an excuse not to work. Since different considerations will be relevant to the fairness of dismissing for conduct, it needs to be established what was the key factor in the employer's mind. This section deals with capability.

There are two distinct forms of absence from work as a result of ill-health:
a) several intermittent absences, not necessarily for the same reason; and
b) a prolonged continuous absence due to a single medical condition.
The proper steps for an employer to take, prior to dismissing a worker, depend on whether the ill-health was intermittent or continuous.

Intermittent absences

Before dismissing, the employer must have made it clear to the worker what level of attendance was expected. If the employer is dissatisfied with the worker's attendance record, s/he should conduct a fair review of the record and give the worker an opportunity to explain the reason for the various absences.[10] Any warning after the review should make it clear that the worker may be dismissed if there is no improvement. If there is no satisfactory improvement following a warning, dismissal will usually be fair.[11]

An employer also ought to take into account the following factors:
- the length of absences and periods of good health;
- the likelihood of future absences;
- the nature of the worker's job and the effect of absences;
- the consistent application of the employer's absenteeism policy;
- any dismissal ought to be handled in a sympathetic, understanding and compassionate manner.[12]

A single period of prolonged absence

The basic question is whether in all the circumstances the employer could be expected to wait any longer and, if so, how much longer.[13]

An IT would expect the employer to have found out the true medical position and to have consulted with the worker before making a decision. A medical report as to the implications and likely length of illness should generally be obtained from the worker's GP or a company doctor or independent consultant. The employer should be willing to consider a report from the worker's own GP or specialist as well as from a company doctor. Whereas the latter may be more familiar with working conditions, the former may be better placed to judge the worker's health.

The employer must get the worker's consent to obtaining a medical report. If a worker refuses to see a company doctor or allow any medical report, s/he increases the risk of being fairly dismissed. The worker is entitled to see the report before it is sent to the employer and to make amendments with the doctor's consent. If the doctor does not consent, the worker has the right to attach a personal statement to the report.[14]

Once the employer has the report, a meeting should be arranged to discuss its contents with the worker. There will be very few circumstances where an employer can justify a failure to discuss the situation with the worker and it would have to be an utterly pointless exercise.[15] In general, the employer must take such steps as are sensible in the circumstances, to discuss the matter and become informed of the true medical position.[16] Consultation will often throw new light on the problem, bringing up facts and circumstances of which the employer was unaware.[17]

The employer's decision ought to be based on the following factors:
- the nature and likely duration of the illness;
- the need for the worker to do the job for which s/he was employed and the difficulty of covering his/her absence. The more skillful and specialist the worker, the more vulnerable s/he is to being fairly dismissed after a relatively short absence;
- the possibility of varying the worker's contractual duties. An employer will not be expected to create an alternative position that did not already exist nor to go to great lengths to accommodate the worker.[18] However, a large employer may be expected to offer any available vacancy which would suit the worker.

There is rarely any useful purpose served by issuing a warning to a worker who is long-term sick. The issue relates to the worker's capability not conduct and the consequence of a warning may be counter-productive.[19]

Sometimes the nature of the illness or injury is such that a worker may never be able to perform his/her contractual duties again or any performance would be radically different from what s/he and the employer envisaged at the outset. If this happens, the contract of employment may be 'frustrated' and just come to an end (see p45 above). Since the employer will not have actually dismissed the worker, the worker cannot claim unfair dismissal.[20] The courts are extremely reluctant to say that an employment contract has ended in this way because of the dire consequences for the worker.

Dismissals due to other physical quality

An 'other physical quality' would include an injury or loss of faculty which affected the worker's ability to perform the job.[21] Although outside the scope of this book, note that an injury sustained at work may give rise to a personal injury claim against the employer including compensation for loss of earnings.

The reasonableness test – s57(3)

The employer will normally be able to justify dismissal if the injury is such that it is impossible or dangerous for the worker to perform his/her job. Before dismissal, the employer should consult the worker concerning the injury and its consequences for future employment. It may be possible for the worker to retrain or use aids to overcome the loss of faculty. An employer should offer any suitable alternative vacancy.

Qualification dismissals

A qualification dismissal is one where a worker loses a qualification or fails to obtain a qualification which was a condition of his/her employment. A common example is disqualification from driving when having a licence is a necessary requirement of the job. This requirement need not be expressly stated in the contract where the job clearly entails driving duties.[22]

An employer may also require a qualification during the worker's employment which the worker does not possess and is unable or unlikely to acquire. An employer's insistence on certain qualifications may be indirect discrimination contrary to the RRA 1976 or SDA 1975.[23]

The reasonableness test – s57(3)

Where a worker loses a qualification which s/he is required to have under his/her contract or which is necessary for the job, it may be fair to dismiss. The employer would not usually be expected to create an alternative job, but s/he should make an effort appropriate to the size and administrative resources of the enterprise and the availability of vacancies.

An employer may require new qualifications because of the introduction of new technology or a different mode of operation. It may be fair to dismiss a worker who fails to acquire the new qualification if the employer can justify the need for it. The employer must also act reasonably in the introduction of the requirement, eg by offering retraining. Failure to give a worker a fair and proper opportunity to satisfy the new requirement will make the dismissal unfair.[24]

CAPABILITY OR QUALIFICATION DISMISSALS: KEY POINTS

• Capability dismissals cover sickness and injury dismissals as well as dismissals relating to the ability to do a job.
• Qualification dismissals relate to relevant qualifications to do the job which may be academic, technical or professional.

- Sickness and injury dismissals fall into two categories, the long-term sickness case and intermittent absence from work. The employer has to satisfy different requirements depending on the category.
- It is a requirement with long-term sickness/injury dismissals for the employer to obtain a medical report (to find out the nature and likely duration of the illness/injury) and to discuss this report with the worker before dismissing.
- With sickness and injury dismissals the employer will be able to dismiss fairly only if s/he can demonstrate that it is necessary for the best interest of the business.
- Only in exceptional cases will a dismissal for a first act of incompetence be fair. The exceptions concern workers who are responsible for the safety of members of the public such as airline pilots or bus drivers.

GENERAL GUIDE TO USEFUL EVIDENCE

- With sickness dismissals, a copy of all the medical reports. If the employer did not rely on a medical report, get a report from the worker's GP for use at the IT hearing.
- Get details of the sickness record of other workers. This might be evidenced by the SSP records. If other workers have had more time off then it is likely to be important and would show inequitable treatment.
- If the dismissal is due to incompetence, get information as to the consequence of the incompetence and also try to discover whether any other workers have committed similar acts and whether they were dismissed.

Conduct dismissals

Unlike with capability and qualification dismissals, there is no statutory definition of conduct dismissals. Perhaps surprisingly, parliament and the courts have made no serious attempt to define exhaustively what forms of misconduct may justify dismissal. Nevertheless, there are a number of activities which are recognised as potential misconduct and are usually listed in the disciplinary procedure if there is a written contract of employment:
- theft or other dishonesty;
- violence and fighting;
- unauthorised absenteeism[25] or lateness;

- disobedience;
- being under the influence of alcohol or drugs;[26]
- threatening or abusive language;
- behaviour undermining the implied term of fidelity and good faith.

Some acts of misconduct amount to 'gross misconduct'. The main relevance of this concept is that an employer dismissing for gross misconduct need not give notice under the contract.[27] Unfair dismissal is a separate issue. It may be fair or unfair to dismiss a worker for gross misconduct. However, as gross misconduct involves more serious forms of misconduct, it is more likely to be fair to dismiss for a single act than for a single act of ordinary misconduct.

Theft and other dishonesty

It is imperative to understand the difference between the criminal law and unfair dismissal law. Many workers feel that the IT is the arena for them to clear their name. Unfortunately the real issue is not whether the worker actually committed the offence but whether, in the circumstances, it was reasonable for the employer to dismiss. An IT may well find that a worker was fairly dismissed for suspected theft, even though by the time of the IT hearing s/he was acquitted. What counts is whether the employer, at the time of dismissal and having carried out reasonable investigations, genuinely and reasonably believed that the worker committed the theft.[28] Equally, it does not automatically justify a dismissal that a worker has been charged with a criminal offence.

A worker may be dismissed for an act of dishonesty whether at work or outside work[29] and against the employer, a fellow worker or the public. Dishonesty dismissals often relate to offences peculiar to the working environment such as borrowing money without authorisation, fraudulent expense claims,[30] unauthorised use of the employer's property[31] and clocking offences.[32]

The reasonableness test – s57(3)

In order to dismiss for dishonesty fairly, the employer must:
- genuinely believe that the worker was dishonest;
- hold that belief on reasonable grounds; and
- have carried out proper and adequate investigations.[33]

If the employer is unable to ascertain which of a group of workers was guilty of the dishonesty, the employer may fairly dismiss all of them solely on reasonable suspicion, provided that:
- after proper investigation, the employer tries and is unable to identify which worker is guilty;

- the employer genuinely believes, on reasonable grounds, that one or more of the group is guilty; and
- any member of the group was capable of having carried out the dishonest act.[34]

It will be inequitable and unfair to dismiss only some members of the group to which the employer has narrowed things down.

It is very important that the employer follows a fair procedure and properly investigates. The degree of appropriate investigation depends on a number of factors including the complexity of the case,[35] the nature of the offence, the size and administrative resources of the employer[36] and whether the worker confessed to the misconduct[37] or was caught red-handed.[38]

The employer's disciplinary procedure should be followed in conducting the investigation, or in its absence, what the IT deems a fair procedure in order to ensure justice. Regard will be had to the ACAS Code of Practice in the absence of a procedure. The disciplinary procedure should state what acts of misconduct are considered by the employer to be gross misconduct, the various stages of the procedure itself, the right to be represented and the right of appeal against any decision reached.[39] Furthermore, it is a requirement of the rules of natural justice that a worker knows the allegations made against him/her, that s/he has an opportunity to answer those allegations fully and that the conduct of the investigation and internal hearings is in good faith.[40]

Since dishonesty is gross misconduct, dismissal for a single act is usually justifed and warnings are not normally appropriate. It is important to emphasise long service and, if relevant, the extent of the dishonesty, on the worker's behalf.

It may not be fair to dismiss a worker for dishonesty taking place outside work, particularly if it does not bear on the work situation. Similarly, in relation to any other criminal acts or convictions occurring off work premises, whether a dismissal is fair will depend on a number of factors such as adverse publicity, implications for the work-place and relevance to the job.[41]

Violence or fighting dismissals

Violence or fighting usually constitutes gross misconduct even if the employer's disciplinary procedure does not explicitly describe it as such.[42] Nevertheless, this does not mean that a dismissal for violence is automatically fair. An employer must carry out an investigation and take into account all relevant matters,[43] eg the nature and circumstances of the violence, whether it was in public view, the proximity to machinery or dangerous objects,[44] the status of the workers, the length of service[45] and the nature of any provocation.

The employer should speak to the parties involved and any witnesses. If the employer cannot ascertain who was responsible for the violence, the employer may dismiss all concerned if it was serious.[46] It will not usually help a worker who participated in fighting to say that another worker initiated it.

An employer should be consistent. Departing from a previous course of action without warning, eg dismissing a worker for an offence for which previous workers have not been dismissed, will usually make the dismissal unfair.[47]

Dismissals for unauthorised absences or lateness

Dismissals for absenteeism may relate to capability and ill-health.[48] Conduct absenteeism is where a worker is absent without authority and it is usually a form of bad time-keeping. A common form of unauthorised absenteeism is where a worker returns late from a holiday.

General absenteeism

An employer is rarely entitled to dismiss for a single occasion of lateness or absenteeism. The usual situation is when a worker is frequently late or absent from work. Some large employers set out in the contract of employment an 'expected level of attendance' below which a worker will be dismissed. However, it is not necessarily fair to dismiss a worker who falls below this level.

The employer should fairly review the worker's attendance record and the reasons for the absences. Appropriate warnings should be given after the worker has had the opportunity to explain. If there is no improvement, the worker's subsequent dismissal is likely to be fair.[49]

As well as fairness in procedures, the IT will take into account:
- the worker's age, length of service and performance;
- the likelihood of an improvement in attendance;
- the effect of absences on the business;[50]
- the known circumstances of the absence, eg temporary domestic problem.[51]

Even if the reason given for the absences is sickness, the employer does not necessarily have to obtain a medical report, particularly if there is no link between the various absences.

Late return from holiday

Where an employer has warned the worker in advance that failure to return from holiday on the due date will be treated as gross misconduct, it will be easier to justify a dismissal. Unless the worker can put forward compelling reasons why s/he should not be dismissed, dismissal will be fair.[52] Usually the employer should wait until the worker comes back to work or invite an explanation by post. However, if there is a significant delay and no obligation under the contract of employment to consult prior to dismissal, the employer may be able to dismiss the worker before his/her return to work, although the IT would expect some efforts by the employer to get an explanation.[53]

Sometimes an employer informs the worker that if s/he returns late from holiday, s/he will be taken to have dismissed him/herself. Legally this is not recognised as a resignation or mutual termination. The worker cannot be deprived of the right to claim unfair dismissal in this way.[54]

Disobedience

This type of dismissal usually arises when a worker refuses to obey an order or instruction of the employer. The instruction may or may not be one with which the worker is required to comply under the contract of employment.

The reasonableness test – s57(3)

The two key considerations are (a) the nature of the employer's instruction and (b) the worker's reason for refusal to comply.

A worker is entitled to refuse any unlawful,[55] unreasonable or dangerous instruction. Although the starting point is whether the worker is obliged to comply with the instruction under the employment contract, this does not necessarily determine whether a refusal is reasonable.[56] It may be unfair to dismiss a worker who refuses to obey a contractual instruction or fair to dismiss a worker who refuses to obey a non-contractual order.

A worker who fails to co-operate with an employer's request to do non-contractual overtime,[57] to adapt to new technology[58] or otherwise go along with a reorganisation[59] will often be found to have acted unreasonably and to be fairly dismissed.

Where a worker is required to comply with a contractual term which has not previously been operated and which will cause inconvenience or hardship, the employer must give reasonable advance notice. If no notice is given, a worker may be entitled to refuse to comply with the instruction in the short term[60] on this ground alone.

The IT must consider also the worker's reason for refusing to obey the instruction and it should weigh up the competing interests and take into consideration the nature of the contractual relationship between the employer and worker generally. There may be good reason for the worker's refusal, eg a pregnant woman refusing to work close to a VDU screen, a risk to the worker's safety in handling money or a risk of civil liability.[61]

Dependency on drugs or alcohol or possession of drugs

Taking or possessing drugs at work, and sometimes out of work, tends to be treated as gross misconduct. Drinking at work may be treated as misconduct depending on the circumstances and what the contract says.

Dependency on drugs or alcohol is now more likely to be treated by an emancipated employer as a medical condition[62] and will not be referred to as an act of misconduct in the disciplinary procedure. The advantage of treating this as a health issue is that the requirements relating to capability dismissals apply. These are more conducive to helping the worker, as medical reports will be obtained and appropriate treatment will be encouraged.

Dependency on alcohol or drugs

The employer must have a genuine and reasonable belief, based on proper and adequate investigation, that the worker is dependent. The worker should be given the chance to answer the allegations and to obtain a medical or specialist report if s/he wishes, particularly if the employer treats it as a sickness issue.

In deciding whether to dismiss, the following factors will be relevant:

- whether the contract of employment or disciplinary procedure treats alcohol/drug dependency as a matter of conduct or capability;
- whether the worker is responsible for the safety of others, eg a coach driver or operator of dangerous machinery. If so, the worker should not be permitted to continue on the job. The employer may dismiss or transfer the worker to safer duties;
- whether the person works in an environment which is potentially dangerous to others or him/herself, eg an electrician. Similar considerations apply;
- whether there is a risk of adverse publicity or harm to customer relations (which would be a dismissal for 'some other substantial reason').

Taking or possessing drugs in or out of work

Most employers are naïve about the different types of drugs and their effect, so summary dismissal is common for using or possessing drugs, particularly when at work. Unfortunately this naïvety extends to many ITs, who take a hard line on any drug-related dismissal. In one case, a worker was arrested for possession of cannabis off the premises during a lunch break. His summary dismissal without investigation or consultation after five years' service was considered fair.[63]

It will usually be fair to dismiss a worker for using or possessing drugs when there is a risk of adverse publicity, harm to customer relations or other harm to the employer's business interests.[64] However, if the possession or use of drugs is outside the work environment, not a matter of public knowledge and could not harm the business, the worker may be able to show that dismissal is unfair.[65]

Drinking at work

This may not be a matter of alcohol dependency at all and it will not necessarily be misconduct to drink at work. This will depend on whether the contract or disciplinary procedure expressly lists drinking as misconduct or, if not, whether the worker and employer clearly contemplated that it would be misconduct. This depends on the nature of the job, factors such as proximity to dangerous equipment and custom and practice.

CONDUCT DISMISSALS: KEY POINTS

- Only with acts of gross misconduct will an employer be able to dismiss for a first offence. Usually acts of gross misconduct will be set out in the disciplinary procedure.
- Whether the dismissal is fair or unfair will depend primarily on the procedure adopted by the employer rather than the nature of the offence itself. Employers will be expected to follow their disciplinary procedure. If there is no disciplinary procedure the IT will take into consideration what type of procedure a reasonable employer would have followed.
- In deciding the issue of fairness, the IT will expect the employer to have had reasonable grounds for suspecting the worker of misconduct, to have carried out reasonable investigations and subsequently come to a reasonable conclusion.
- The IT's function is not to determine whether the worker was guilty of the offence. The IT has to determine whether the employer

acted reasonably in dismissing the worker. If the worker was not guilty then it is unlikely to be a fair dismissal although this is not always the case.

GENERAL GUIDE TO USEFUL EVIDENCE

- It is important to get a copy of the disciplinary procedure and to see whether the employer followed it.
- Get evidence as to whether the disciplinary hearing was fair and properly conducted. Had the decision already been made to dismiss?
- Find out whether any other workers have committed similar acts of misconduct and not been dismissed.

Redundancy dismissals

The right to a redundancy payment was introduced by the Redundancy Payments Act 1965. Not until the general unfair dismissal provisions came into force in 1972[66] was a worker able to challenge the fairness of a redundancy dismissal. In general, redundancy dismissals are now subject to the usual test of fairness in EPCA s57(3). There are however four potentially automatically unfair redundancy dismissal situations, which are dealt with above (see pp49 and 50).

The definition of redundancy

In broad terms, there are three main redundancy situations:
a) closure of the business as a whole;
b) closure of the particular workplace where the worker was employed; and
c) reduction in the size of the workforce.
   The statutory definitions are a little more complex.

Closure of the business

'An employee who is dismissed shall be taken to be dismissed by reason of redundancy if the dismissal is attributable wholly or mainly to the fact that his employer has ceased, or intends to cease, to carry on the business for the purposes of which the employee was employed . . .'.[67]

   The closure may be permanent or temporary,[68] eg closure of a restaurant for refurbishment. The employer's decision to close cannot be challenged unless it is a sham.[69]

Closure of the workplace

A dismissal is deemed to be for redundancy if it is attributable wholly or mainly to the fact that the employer 'has ceased, or intends to cease' to carry on that business in the place where the employee was so employed'.[70]

This situation can arise when a large employer closes down one retail outlet or one branch of a restaurant chain. The facts must be checked against these definitions; there is no redundancy situation unless the wording is satisfied.[71]

The first matter to be established is where the worker is employed under the contract, ie where the worker can be required to work. The contract may expressly state that the worker is employed to work for the employer generally in any of its premises, or there may be a clear mobility clause which allows the employer to require the worker to move to another location or within a geographical area. If so, there will not be a redundancy situation just because the worker's actual workplace closes, if s/he is required to work elsewhere.

If there is no express mobility clause, the IT may nevertheless imply one by custom and practice, if the worker has moved around for the employer in the past.[72] The IT will also take into account what was said when the worker was appointed and whether the worker was paid expenses when working away from the normal workplace in the past.[73]

Even if the worker has not moved around in the past, an IT may imply a term that s/he can be required to work at another location in close proximity,[74] where the additional travel required will not cause hardship or undue inconvenience.[75]

Subject to the above exceptions, if there is no express contractual term, written or oral, as to workplace, the IT will usually find that s/he was employed to work at the location where s/he has in practice always worked. When that location closes, s/he is redundant.

Reduction of the workforce

It is a dismissal for redundancy where it is 'attributable wholly or mainly to the fact that the requirements of that business for employees to carry out work of a particular kind, or . . . to carry out work of a particular kind in the place where he was so employed, have ceased or diminished or are expected to cease or diminish'.[76]

This is where the employer reduces the workforce due to a downturn in business[77] or as the result of a rationalisation.[78] The particular worker's job either disappears or is absorbed by other workers.

Note that the test is not whether the employer needs fewer workers but whether s/he needs fewer workers to do the particular kind of work. The first question is what work the worker can be required to do under the employment contract, as opposed to what work s/he is actually doing. If the employer's requirement for workers to do the contractual work has ceased or diminished, the worker will be redundant.[79] This is so even where a worker is still needed but his/her job is radically redefined.[80]

Difficulties arise when the employer reorganises the method of production so that the worker is doing the same job but in a different way. The commonest situation is the introduction of new shift patterns although the actual work remains the same. A worker dismissed in the light of such reorganisation is not redundant[81] and an employer will have to justify the dismissal as being for some other substantial reason.[82]

Finally, an employer may offer a redundant worker another worker's job. The other worker is then treated as dismissed for redundancy.[83] This process is known as 'bumping' and usually occurs in recognition of long service.

Redundancy payments

A worker dismissed on the ground of redundancy is usually entitled to redundancy pay.[84] If the dismissal is also unfair, the worker will be awarded additional compensation for unfair dismissal.[85]

Suitable alternative employment

If the worker unreasonably refuses an offer of suitable alternative employment, s/he will lose his/her entitlement to redundancy pay.[86]

What constitutes a valid offer

The offer of alternative employment must be made before the old job ends and the new job must start immediately or within four weeks of the end of the previous employment. The offer need not be in writing, but it will be for the employer to prove that a suitable offer was made.[87] If the worker says s/he is not interested in receiving any alternative offer and the employer therefore does not make one, the worker will not be taken to have unreasonably refused a suitable offer and is entitled to a redundancy payment.

The offer must set out the main terms of the new job in enough detail to show how it differs from the old one[88] and the starting date should be clear.

The trial period

The worker can try out the new job, where it differs from the old one, for a trial period of up to four weeks.[89] The trial period starts on the date the worker begins the new job and ends four weeks later, by which time the worker must have decided whether to accept the new job permanently. If the worker works beyond the four-week period, s/he will lose the right to claim redundancy pay. It is a strict time limit and can be extended only for the purpose of retraining the worker; such agreement must be in writing and specify a new date when the trial period will end.[90]

Unreasonable refusal of a suitable offer

The employer must prove both that the offer was suitable and that the worker's refusal was unreasonable. There is very little case-law guidance as to what a worker may refuse and it depends on the particular situation. 'Suitability' tends to mean objective job-related factors such as pay, status, hours and location. The reasonableness of a refusal depends more on the worker's individual circumstances, eg domestic factors and health. A very common form of alternative offer is of the same job but in a different location. Whether this is a suitable offer which the worker cannot reasonably refuse depends on a combination of factors such as extra travelling time and expense, childcare responsibilities, health, and status of the job (the higher the status, the more an IT would expect a worker to travel).

Unfair redundancy

A dismissal for redundancy may be unfair because:
a) there was no genuine redundancy situation;
b) the employer failed to consult;
c) the worker was unfairly selected; or
d) the employer failed to offer alternative employment.

No genuine redundancy situation

If the employer maintains but cannot prove that the dismissal was wholly or mainly attributable to a redundancy situation,[91] s/he will have failed to show the reason or principal reason for dismissal and the dismissal will be unfair. Employers frequently argue in the alternative, ie that the dismissal was either for redundancy or for some other substantial reason. An employer would need to show which was the principal reason for dismissal[92] and justify it. An IT is more likely to be cynical as to the true reason for dismissal where an employer appears uncertain by arguing in the alternative.

Failure to consult

The importance of consultation in redundancy dismissals has been recognised since the introduction of the unfair dismissal legislation. Where redundancy dismissals become necessary, the Industrial Relations Code of Practice[93] requires the employer to give as much warning as practicable and consult with workers or their representatives in order to:

- consider the introduction of schemes for voluntary redundancy, retirement or transfer;
- decide which workers should be selected for redundancy and the mode of discharge;
- help workers find other work and give time off for this purpose; and
- ensure that no announcement is made before the worker has been informed.[94]

The obligation to consult applies equally with unionised and non-unionised workers.[95] When making redundant unionised workers, the employer also has a statutory obligation to consult with the trade union at the earliest opportunity and to comply with the minimum notice periods ranging from 30–90 days according to the number of workers being made redundant.[96]

The requirement to consult takes many forms. At one end of the spectrum it involves detailed discussions and meetings; at the other end it will entail discussions with individual workers who are likely to be made redundant. Consultation means jointly examining and discussing problems of concern to both management and workers. It involves seeking mutually acceptable solutions through a genuine exchange of views and information.[97]

Following fair procedures is extremely important and an employer will be able to justify failure to consult only if it would have been utterly useless to do so.[98] Given the various functions of consultation, this will rarely be the case.

Unfair selection

If the worker is selected contrary to a customary arrangement or agreed procedure, the dismissal is automatically unfair.[99] If there is no such agreement or procedure, the employer must show that the selection criteria adopted were objective and that they were fairly applied.

The employer should usually take account of all matters which can be objectively assessed, eg length of service (which is usually the most important single criterion),[100] productivity (if it can be objectively assessed), age, time-keeping, the worker's adaptability and the employer's future needs. The application of certain criteria such as pregnancy or part-time working may be directly or indirectly discriminatory.[101]

The lengths to which the IT expects an employer to go in drawing up and applying criteria will depend on the employer's size and administrative resources.[102] Usually the IT expects the medium or large employer to have adopted a clinical approach, awarding each potentially redundant worker with points against each criterion and dismissing those who score least.[103] This selection process will in most cases fall within the band of reasonable responses and be fair. However, even small employers must show that they used an objective selection method.

Failure to offer alternative employment

The employer must offer any available alternative employment which the worker is able to perform. The employer's duty is not limited to offering similar positions or positions in the same workplace. In certain situations, the employer is expected to have carefully considered 'bumping' another worker and offering the job to the redundant worker.[104]

When offering alternative employment, the employer must give sufficient detail of the vacancy and allow a trial period. Failure to do so is likely to make the dismissal unfair.[105] It is up to the worker whether to accept the alternative employment which might even involve demotion or a reduction in pay.[106] However, workers who unreasonably refuse a suitable alternative offer will lose their entitlement to redundancy pay.

One of the main purposes of consultation is to consider other employment, eg transfer to another workplace, as an alternative to dismissal.[107] The IT will consider what vacancies exist throughout the employer's operation and with any associated employer.[108] The IT will look at vacancies existing during the consultation period (regardless of whether there was actual consultation) and during the worker's notice period as well as at the time of dismissal itself.

REDUNDANCY DISMISSALS: KEY POINTS

• Even where there is a genuine redundancy situation the worker may have been unfairly dismissed.
• A worker who is dismissed on the ground of redundancy where there is no redundancy situation will have been unfairly dismissed.
• A redundancy dismissal is also unfair if there has been inadequate consultation by the employer, unfair selection for dismissal or where there has been a failure to offer available alternative employment.
• The most important requirement is for the employer to consult adequately with the worker before dismissal. The only exception to

this requirement is where such consultation would be utterly pointless or futile.
- The most important factor when it comes to the selection of workers for redundancy is the length of service. Larger employers will be expected to have more sophisticated selection criteria than small enterprises and they should be objective rather than subjective.
- The employer is expected to offer any alternative available employment which the worker is capable of doing. It is for the worker to decide whether to accept the offer, and not for the employer to make this decision.

GENERAL GUIDE TO USEFUL EVIDENCE

- Get copies of all minutes, notes and memoranda of meetings at which the redundancy dismissal was discussed.
- Get a list of all workers who could have been selected for redundancy and discover when they started their employment, and why they have been kept on.
- Find out all vacancies available shortly before and after the dismissal (including the whole of the notice period) to see whether the worker could have done any of them.
- Find out from those workers who are still employed, what happened, to the worker's job after the dismissal. Was the worker simply replaced? If so find out who the new worker is, and get a copy of the job advert, and the letter of appointment.

Statutory restriction dismissals

There are very few cases where the empoyer relies on a statutory restriction as the reason for dismissal. The most common example is the loss of a necessary qualification for a job, eg a van driver losing his/her driving licence. If the employer wrongly believes a statutory restriction applies, this will not be a potentially fair reason for dismissal, even if the employer was acting in good faith. The dismissal will then be justifiable only if it falls within one of the other potentially fair reasons for dismissal – usually for 'some other substantial reason'.

The employer must show that the statutory restriction affected the work that the person was employed to perform and that no alternative employment was available. The larger the employer, the greater the duty to try to find an alternative to dismissal.[109]

Consultation as to the consequences of the ban and possible alternatives is very important.[110] Where a restriction does not prevent the worker from doing his/her job but makes it difficult, eg a salesperson losing a driving licence, the employer should consult as to what assistance may be possible. Even where continued employment of the worker would be unlawful, eg where a GP has been struck off the medical register, the employer should still consult as to the likelihood of the decision being reversed.

Dismissals for some other substantial reason (SOSR)

A dismissal which is not for one of the four potentially fair reasons may still be fair if it is for 'some other substantial reason of a kind such as to justify dismissal'.[111] The most common SOSR dismissals are for reorganisation, in order to protect the employer's business interests or as a consequence of the transfer of a business. However, a substantial reason is one which is not trivial or unworthy but one which would justify the dismissal.[112]

Dismissals due to reorganisation

It is sometimes hard to differentiate between a reorganisation and a redundancy situation. Employers usually try to claim that the dismissal is because of reorganisation, in order to avoid making a redundancy payment and also because an employer's obligations to a worker in relation to a reorganisation dismissal are substantially less than for a redundancy.

A worker may be dismissed because s/he cannot or will not accept a change in terms and conditions resulting from the reorganisation. If an employer cannot establish that the reorganisation – and the worker's refusal or inability to fit in with it – was a substantial reason such as could justify dismissal, the dismissal is automatically unfair.[113] In practice, it is fairly easy for the employer to meet this initial requirement.

An employer is entitled to reorganise the workforce and terms and conditions of employment so as to improve efficiency and to dismiss a worker who does not co-operate with the changes.[114] It is sufficient for the employer to show that the reorganisation is for sound business reasons requiring a change in the worker's terms and conditions.[115] The reorganisation need not be essential.

It is very hard for a worker at the IT to challenge the employer's reasons as not being sound and good. The employer needs only to demonstrate the benefits to the business of the reorganisation, perceived at the time of dismissal. If the employer cannot demonstrate the benefits and the importance attached to them at the time of dismissal, the dismissal will be unfair as the employer will not have established a 'substantial' reason for dismissal.[116]

The reasonableness test – s57(3)

Although the IT should consider a number of factors as to whether it was fair to dismiss, it primarily looks at the situation from the employer's point of view, ie whether a reasonable employer would make those changes to the worker's terms of employment.[117] The IT considers the competing advantages and disadvantages to the employer and the worker, but the main emphasis in reorganisation dismissals is on the employer's interests which are paramount.

Consultation now plays an important part in all types of dismissal including reorganisation, after the *Polkey* decision.[118]

Dismissals to protect employers' business interests

There is an implied term of fidelity and good faith in every employment contract which lasts as long as the worker is employed. Some workers also agree to express terms which restrict their future employment in the same industry for a given period. These terms are known as restrictive covenants.

A worker dismissed for breaking the implied term of good faith and fidelity will be dismissed for SOSR and perhaps also misconduct. In addition, there may be a substantial reason potentially justifying dismissal if:

- a worker refuses to sign a restrictive covenant and the employer is genuinely seeking to protect the business interests;[119] or
- there is a genuine risk arising from a worker's relationship with a competitor.[120]

Other situations where a dismissal might be deemed to be for SOSR are where the interests of the business might suffer as a result of friction at work between two colleagues or a worker is incompatible and does not fit in, or adverse publicity on any matter, eg relating to a worker taking drugs[121] or having a criminal conviction.[122]

The reasonableness test – s57(3)

Where dismissal is for refusing to sign a restrictive covenant, the IT will take into account the necessity of applying it, whether the industry usually requires employers to take this precaution and whether the worker's job was of sufficient importance. The IT will also consider the manner and method of the introduction of the clause and whether it was consistently introduced among other workers.

Where dismissal is due to a personal relationship with a competitor, the IT should take into account the nature of the relationship and its bearing on the work situation. The manner of the worker's dismissal and the degree of notice or warning of impending dismissal are also relevant.[123]

Before an employer dismisses a worker for incompatibility, s/he should do all that is reasonable to try to remedy the problem, which might involve transfering the worker.[124]

Dismissals on transfer of an undertaking

A dismissal of a worker on or after the transfer of an undertaking for an economic, technical or organisational reason entailing changes in the workforce of either the buyer (transferor) or seller (transferee) is treated as a substantial reason of a kind that can justify dismissal.[125]

Dismissals at the time of a transfer usually arise out of the desire of the buyer or seller or both to reduce the workforce so as to make the business a more valuable asset. Any reduction in the workforce means a reduction in potential liability for wrongful dismissal, unfair dismissal and redundancy claims. An 'economic' reason is interpreted narrowly and does not include dismissing workers in order to effect a sale.[126]

The reasonableness test – s57(3)

There is no presumption that the dismissal is fair just because it was for an economic, technical or organisational reason,[127] but if it is not, it is automatically unfair on transfer. The employer would be expected to justify the decision on the basis of sound, good business reasons.

'SOME OTHER SUBSTANTIAL REASON' DISMISSALS: KEY POINTS

- The most common type of 'some other substantial reason' for dismissal is where the dismissal arises out of a reorganisation at the workplace.
- It is necessary for the dismissal to be for a substantial reason. The courts treat the interests of the employer as being more important than those of the worker. The dismissal of a worker who may prejudice the interests of the employer will generally be treated as substantial, and usually justifiable.

- Dismissals due to incompatibility with other workers will be for some other substantial reason.

GENERAL GUIDE TO USEFUL EVIDENCE

- Any evidence to show that it was not prejudicial to the employer to continue to employ the worker will be valuable.
- Find out if any other workers in a similar situation were dismissed.

Returning after maternity leave

A woman who leaves work in order to have a baby may be entitled to return by virtue of:
a) her statutory rights under the EPCA;
b) a contractual agreement with her employer;
c) a composite right, combining both.

The law is very complex in this area[128] and the worker has to ensure that she takes the correct steps before she leaves work. She may also be able to claim that any refusal to allow maternity leave or permit her return is unlawful sex discrimination.[129] This may be easier to prove under EC law than under the SDA. Nevertheless, women in non-state employment may find that the SDA assists where they have not acquired the necessary two years' service or if they fail to take the proper procedural steps under the EPCA.

The statutory right to return

A woman has a statutory right to return after maternity leave provided that she acquires that right in the first place and properly exercises the right when returning. The smallest mistake in following the necessary steps and time limits under the EPCA will almost certainly deprive the woman of her rights.

Acquiring the statutory right

A woman must be employed until immediately before the start of the eleventh week before the expected week of confinement (EWC).[130] She need not actually be at work, eg she may be on holiday or on sick leave. As at that date, she must have been continuously employed for at least two years.[131] The EWC is the week, starting with Sunday, in which it is expected that the birth will take place.

The woman may work beyond the eleventh week before the EWC if

she wishes.[132] At least 21 days before her absence begins, she must write to her employer stating the following:[133]
- that she will be absent from work wholly or partly because of pregnancy or confinement as from [the date she is leaving];
- that she intends to return to work after her confinement; and
- the date of the EWC.

If a woman is unable to notify her employer within 21 days before her departure, she should do so as soon as is reasonably practicable afterwards.[134] If she is uncertain whether she will want to return, she should nevertheless notify the employer of her firm intention, so as to preserve her rights.

If the employer requests, the woman must produce a certificate from a registered medical practitioner or midwife stating the EWC.[135]

No sooner than seven weeks after the baby is born, the employer may request written confirmation that the worker intends to return. The woman must supply written confirmation within 14 days or as soon as reasonably practicable thereafter.[136] There are certain requirements which the employer must meet in making this request, but it is safest for the woman to reply however the request is made.

Exercising the right of return

A woman may return at any time up to 29 weeks after the date of birth. There are very limited extensions of time. The notification requirements are very strict.

The woman must give written notice to her employer, at least 21 days in advance, of her intention to return on a specified date.[137] This date becomes the notified date of return (NDR). The woman must specify a date. It is not enough to suggest that the employer contacts her to discuss a convenient date.[138]

The NDR must fall before the end of 29 weeks starting with the week in which the birth actually occurred.[139] A week is a week ending with a Saturday unless the worker's pay is calculated weekly on the basis of a week ending with any other day.[140]

Once a woman has notified a date of return, even if it is well within the 29-week period, she can postpone the date only once for up to four weeks.[141] She should therefore be careful not to notify a date too early if she is unsure about her fitness. The postponement may be on grounds only of her unfitness to work and must be supported by a medical certificate stating that 'by reasons of disease or bodily or mental disablement she will be incapable of work' on the NDR.[142]

The certificate must be submitted to her employer before the original

NDR. If the woman has not yet given a NDR, the certificate must be supplied before the end of the 29-week period.

If the woman is still unfit after the end of the postponement, she should return to work, if only for one day, and then go on sick leave. Otherwise she will lose her right to return altogether.

A woman may also postpone her return if there is an interruption of work, eg industrial action.

An *employer* may postpone the worker's return for up to four weeks for any specified reason provided these are notified to her before the NDR.

Each of the three forms of postponement may follow on from the other.

The job returned to

The woman is entitled to return to the job she was originally employed to do, on terms and conditions no less favourable than those which would have applied to her had she not been absent for maternity.[143]

Refusal to allow return

If a woman is not allowed to return to her old job on equally favourable terms and conditions, she is treated as continuously employed until the NDR (or properly postponed NDR) and dismissed on that date.[144] The reason the employer does not allow her to return will be taken as the reason for dismissal.[145]

This kind of dismissal is called a 'deemed dismissal'. It occurs regardless of whether the woman's contract continued through her maternity leave. A 'deemed dismissal' occurs only where the worker has a statutory right to return and gives proper notification.

The usual rules as to the reason for and fairness of the dismissal apply. The test under EPCA s57(3) is whether it would have been reasonable to dismiss the woman for the particular reason, had she not been absent from work.[146]

Where the reason for the deemed dismissal is redundancy, the dismissal is automatically unfair if the employer fails to offer a suitable, available, alternative vacancy.[147] The woman is thus in a better position than an ordinarily redundant worker.

Exceptions to the right to return

Where an employer (and any associated employer) has no more than five employees immediately before the woman's maternity absence begins, there is no deemed dismissal for not letting her return to her old job, provided that it is not reasonably practicable for the employer:
- to let her return to her original job; or

- to offer her alternative work which is suitable and appropriate for her to do in the circumstances and is on terms not substantially less favourable than the original job.[148]

Where it is not reasonably practicable, for a reason other than redundancy, for the employer to let the worker return to her old job, there will be no deemed dismissal if the employer offers her alternative work which is suitable and appropriate for her to do in the circumstances and is on terms not substantially less favourable than the original job.[149]

A contractual right to return

A woman who does not qualify for the statutory right to return, eg because she does not have the requisite length of service or she fails to give the proper notification prior to her maternity absence, may nevertheless have a contractual right to return. This right may come from a written contract or derive from a separate verbal agreement with the employer prior to her going on leave.

Provided that the woman's contract continues to run throughout her maternity absence, the employer's refusal to let her return will be an ordinary dismissal under EPCA s55 on that date.

Whether the contract does continue through a woman's maternity leave depends on the circumstances. Unless there was an express agreement in advance that the contract would continue, the IT will look at all relevant factors, such as whether the worker was contacted in her absence for advice or information and whether she received any pay, eg sick pay. If she resigned or was dismissed as she went on maternity leave, her contract will have terminated then.

A composite right

Sometimes a woman may have a contractual right to return as well as acquiring a statutory right. If so, she needs to be very careful about following the correct procedures. The contractual right cannot be operated separately from the statutory right. What happens is that any aspect of the statutory right may be modified by an express contractual term which is more favourable. Where the contract is silent, the statutory procedure applies.

For example, a composite right may lead to a woman being entitled to return up to one year after the birth. However, unless there is express agreement otherwise, the woman must still give 21 days' notice of her NDR. If she fails to give the correct notification, she loses her right to return altogether, even if her contract continued throughout her leave.[150]

This is because there is no deemed dismissal, as she has not complied with the notice requirements of a statutory or composite right, and there is no ordinary dismissal since her contractual right cannot stand independently.[151]

Dismissal during maternity leave

If a woman's contract continues after she goes on maternity leave, any dismissal during her leave is treated as an ordinary dismissal as at the date that it occurs.

If the woman has acquired statutory maternity rights, she has a choice. She may wait and claim a deemed dismissal if she is not permitted to return in due course (see p75 above). Alternatively, if her contract runs throughout her maternity leave, she may claim an ordinary dismissal as at the date it occurs and also try to exercise her right to return subsequently. If she is then allowed to return, she must repay any unfair dismissal compensation if her employer requests.[152]

CHAPTER FIVE

Evidence in unfair dismissal cases

What kind of evidence is helpful?

Burden of proof

If dismissal is disputed, the burden is on the worker to prove that it occurred.

Once dismissal is proved, the employer must show the reason (or principal reason) for the dismissal and that it was one of the potentially fair reasons set out in the EPCA.

Proving a disputed dismissal

If the worker seeks advice very shortly after dismissal, unless s/he already has a dismissal letter, a request should immediately be written asking for confirmation of the dismissal and written reasons for it.[1]

If there is a dispute as to whether the worker was actually dismissed, supporting documents and witnesses will be needed. As early as possible, a signed statement plus name and address of any witness to the dismissal should be obtained.

Any documentary proof that the employer had decided to dismiss before s/he did so will be helpful, eg copy job advertisements which had already appeared for the worker's job.

If advising on a potential constructive dismissal claim where the worker must show a fundamental breach of contract, all contractual documents must be obtained. These may comprise a letter of appointment, statement of main terms and conditions, notices of variation of contract[2] and staff handbook.

Conduct and capability dismissals

It should be ascertained whether the worker has received any written or verbal warnings in the past, particularly concerning the matter for which s/he was dismissed. Copies of the written warnings should be obtained. With verbal warnings, it is necessary to check when they were given, by whom and roughly what was said.

The relevant provisions of the contract of employment or staff handbook must be examined, in particular the notice provisions, the required disciplinary procedure and, if relevant, what offences are listed as disciplinary matters. Ascertain whether the contractual procedures were in fact followed.

The worker should be asked what disciplinary hearings took place, who was present, whether s/he was advised s/he could bring a representative, how much warning s/he got of the hearing and whether s/he knew what it would be about in advance. All these are matters of procedural fairness. In particular, it should be asked at what point in the meeting s/he was told that s/he was dismissed. If the employer said something at the start of the hearing to indicate that the decision to dismiss had already been taken, this would be unfair. Who took notes at the hearing and whether the worker has any should be ascertained. An effort should be made to get the worker's best recollection of the detail of the meeting and, in particular, what each person said.

In general, what the employer knew or ought to have known, had s/he properly investigated or consulted, at the time of dismissal is what is important.

If relevant (eg with fighting, alcohol or lateness dismissals) how the employer treated similar offences or problems in the past should be established.

With sickness, injury or qualification dismissals, what other jobs the employer had available at the relevant time should be noted.

Absenteeism and lateness

Discovery of the attendance record of similar workers should be sought to see whether the employer was acting consistently in deciding to dismiss. The names of the other workers will be needed so that their statutory sick pay or attendance records can be obtained from the employer to make this comparison. However, it will be for the employer to show the reason for the differential treatment.

To what extent the worker was made aware of the employer's dissatisfaction with his/her attendance should be ascertained and whether it was made clear that dismissal would follow a failure to improve. If there was only a verbal warning, given to a group of workers, it should be clarified from another of those workers what was said and whether it was clear that dismissal might ensue.

Whether the employer properly reviewed the worker's attendance record prior to giving any warning or dismissing should be checked. This should have involved consulting the worker as to the reasons for the absences or lateness. In general, it should be considered whether the employer approached the dismissal of the worker with sympathy, understanding and compassion.

Prolonged sickness absence

If the employer obtained a medical opinion on the worker's state of health (no medical opinion could have been obtained without the worker's consent), a copy of any medical report should be obtained. Was the worker consulted in respect of the employer's medical report? If so, copies of notes taken of the meeting and a statement from the worker as to what was said should be obtained. The worker should be asked whether s/he was offered the opportunity of getting his/her own medical report.

The importance of the worker's job and whether the employer could be expected to hold it open any longer should be considered. What arrangements were made during the worker's absence? What other short-term solutions were possible? How soon after the dismissal was the vacancy filled?

Injury

It should be clarified whether the injury was such as to make the performance of the job impossible. Could the worker, through retraining or the use of aids, have continued to do the job?[3] Was there any form of consultation with the worker as to the medical prognosis and what s/he could do?

If the worker seeks advice while still employed, the employer may have a beneficial sickness retirement scheme in certain circumstances. It may also be worth considering whether the worker should take advice in respect of a personal injury claim if the injury occurred at work.

Qualifications

It should be established whether the qualification was a term of the contract or otherwise a genuine requirement of the job. If not, the employer will find it hard to justify dismissal. If the employer has changed the requirement, why was the change necessary? Are there any other workers doing the same job who do not have the qualifications and are new workers expected to be qualified? Also, whether other jobs were available which the worker was qualified to do at the time of dismissal should be ascertained.

Finally, whether the requirement had a discriminatory effect on the worker should be considered (see pp93 ff below).

Redundancy dismissals

If relevant, the selection criteria adopted by the employer should be established. Were there other workers in similar jobs who were not made redundant, particularly any who had shorter service?

To check whether it was a genuine redundancy, it should be established whether a new employee has simply replaced the worker in the same job. It is important to obtain all internal and external advertisements and vacancy lists relating to suitable vacancies at the time of dismissal and for a short period before and after. These are relevant both as to the genuineness of the redundancy (advertisements for the same job) and as to the availability of alternative jobs which should have been offered. The worker should be asked what other jobs s/he could and would have done for the employer and whether s/he was consulted about vacancies or doing any other work.

PART III: DISCRIMINATION

CHAPTER SIX

Discrimination on grounds of race and sex

The legal framework

The principal statute prohibiting race discrimination in employment is the Race Relations Act (RRA) 1976. The legislation prohibiting discrimination on grounds of sex or marital status is more complex and contained in several Acts of parliament. Similar provisions to those in the RRA are contained in the Sex Discrimination Act (SDA) 1975 as amended by the SDA 1986. However, sex discrimination in pay and other contractual terms is dealt with separately[1] under the Equal Pay Act 1970 (EqPA), amended by the Equal Pay (Amendment) Regulations 1983 (SI No 1794).

A 'Code of Practice for the elimination of racial discrimination and the promotion of equal opportunity in employment' came into effect on 1 April 1984. The Code of Practice was made by the Commission for Racial Equality (CRE) under RRA 1976 s47. The Equal Opportunities Commission issued a similar 'Code of Practice for the elimination of discrimination on the grounds of sex and marriage and the promotion of equality of opportunity in employment' under SDA 1975 s56A, which was brought into effect on 30 April 1985.

The Codes of Practice lay down guidelines for good employment practice, but they are not legally actionable in themselves.[2] However, the Codes are admissible in evidence at a hearing and the IT can 'take into account' any relevant provision in reaching its decision. In 1988 the Court of Appeal endorsed the importance of the Race Relations Code of Practice.[3]

EC legislation

In some circumstances EC legislation applies to discrimination on grounds of sex and marital or family status. The material legislation is:

a) Article 119 of the Treaty of Rome (Art 119), which lays down the principle of equal pay for equal work;
b) Directive 75/117/EEC ('the Equal Pay Directive'), which expands the principle set out in Art 119; and
c) Directive 76/207/EEC ('the Equal Treatment Directive') which provides for equal treatment between men and women in their access to employment, training, promotion, working conditions and dismissal.

The advantage of EC legislation is that its ambit is often wider than the UK legislation. Wherever possible, UK legislation enacted to implement an EC directive should be interpreted to effect the purpose of the directive.[4] Where there is a conflict between UK and EC law, the latter can be applied to individual cases in the IT only in the following limited circumstances:

The Equal Treatment Directive

Individuals in ITs and other national courts can use the Equal Treatment Directive against any employer which is a state authority.[5] A 'state employer' includes health authorities,[6] the police[7] and probably nationalised industries.[8] The best definition of 'state employer' is in *Foster v British Gas*,[9] where the European Court of Justice (ECJ) said that the directive can be used by individuals employed by any body made responsible by the state for providing a public service under the control of the state and which has special powers for that purpose.

Article 119/the Equal Pay Directive

In almost all cases, a worker can claim directly under Art 119 against private as well as state employers.[10] In so far as the Equal Pay Directive merely interprets Art 119, it can also be used directly against a non-state employer, but it cannot be used insofar as it establishes rights additional to those contained in Art 119.

Where a question arises as to the interpretation or applicability of EC law, any UK court or tribunal can ask the ECJ to give a preliminary ruling. UK courts can choose to interpret EC law themselves, but where there is no further route of appeal, ie in the House of Lords, the ECJ must be referred to.

Who is covered?

The RRA 1976 and SDA 1975 are wider than the EPCA. They protect job applicants, employees, contract workers and those working on a contract personally to execute any work,[11] in relation to employment at an establishment in GB.[12] Employment agencies must not discriminate in their provision of services.[13]

Since the Employment Act 1989, any person providing or making arrangements for the provision of training facilities is covered.[14] This protects trainees on work experience and work placement programmes. The prohibition on discrimination by training bodies now mirrors the range of discriminatory acts forbidden to employers save that discrimination in the arrangements made for determining who should be offered training is still excluded.[15]

With limited exceptions, employers are liable for the discriminatory acts of their employees or agents, regardless of whether they knew or approved those acts.[16] This is a particularly important issue in claims of sexual harassment.[17] There are statutory provisions as to where employers' liability lies in the case of the police.[18]

Sex Discrimination Acts 1975 and 1986

The SDAs prohibit discrimination against women, men or married persons. It is not prohibited to discriminate against an unmarried person although this may be unlawful under the Equal Treatment Directive Art 2(1).

Race Relations Act 1976

The RRA 1976 prohibits discrimination on 'racial grounds' or against members of any 'racial group'. Section 3 defines 'racial' in these contexts as 'by reference to colour, race, nationality or ethnic or national origins'. For the purposes of the RRA, a particular racial group may comprise two or more distinct racial groups.[19] For example, a person of Cypriot nationality could claim s/he has suffered discrimination not only as a Cypriot, but as a non-British national or as someone not of EC nationality.[20]

A British national from Northern Ireland who is discriminated against on grounds of being 'Irish' is covered by the RRA.[21] English-speaking Welsh people are not a distinct racial group as against Welsh-speaking Welsh people.[22]

Ethnic groups

There are seven essential characteristics which a group must have to fall within the meaning of 'ethnic group' under the RRA 1976.[23] In summary, these are:
- a long shared history;
- its own cultural tradition;
- a common language;

- literature;
- religion;
- a common geographical origin; and
- being a minority or oppressed group within a larger community.

It does not matter if the size of a particular ethnic group has diminished due to intermarriage or lapsed observance, provided there remains a discernible minority.[24]

Jews, Sikhs and probably Rastafarians[25] are covered by the RRA 1976, but Muslims are not.[26] 'Gypsies' in the narrow sense of 'a wandering race (by themselves called "Romany") of Hindu origin' are an 'ethnic group' although a prohibiton against 'travellers' may refer to all those of a nomadic way of life and amount only to indirect discrimination[27] against those of Romany origin.[28]

Discrimination on the ground of religion

The RRA 1976 does not prohibit religious discrimination as such, but where there is discrimination on the ground of religion, the RRA 1976 may be helpful in two ways:

a) Where an employer attacks a religious practice associated solely with a particular ethnic group, this may be indirect race discrimination. Example: a rule against wearing turbans may indirectly discriminate against Sikhs, or a requirement that a manager work Saturdays may indirectly discriminate against Jews.[29]

b) Where an employer openly discriminates against a worker because of his/her religion, but that religion is prevalent among that worker's racial group. Example: an employer refuses to employ a worker of Pakistani nationality or national origin because of his/her muslim religion. This religious discrimination would particularly disadvantage Pakistani workers, and so could amount to indirect racial discrimination.[30] Example: an employer insists that a Pakistani female worker wears a short dress as uniform. Since most Pakistani women are of the muslim religion which has certain dress requirements, the employer's requirement may be indirect racial discrimination against the Pakistani racial group.

In these last examples, if the worker concerned were an Indian person of the muslim religion, s/he probably could not claim indirect racial discrimination, since Indian citizens are not predominantly muslim.

Employment outside GB

The RRA 1976 and SDA 1975 do not apply to those employed wholly or mainly outside England, Wales or Scotland. People working on a ship or airline registered in the UK and operated by a person based in GB are deemed to work in GB unless they work wholly outside GB.[31]

It is not unlawful race discrimination for an employer specifically to train in GB a non-GB resident, in skills which are to be exercised outside GB.[32]

Private households

The RRA 1976 does not apply to direct or indirect discrimination in employment in private households, although victimisation is covered.[33] Thus, if a worker in a private household complains about discrimination and is dismissed as a result, this is unlawful victimisation.

Workers in private households are usually domestic servants or private chauffeurs. Sometimes it is difficult to know whether the worker is employed for the purposes of a private household or not. For example, it will depend on all the facts whether a chauffeur, employed to drive a company chairperson to and from work as well as the chair and his/her spouse on leisure trips, may be employed by the company rather than in the chair's private household.[34]

The armed services

The SDA 1975 does not cover employment in the armed forces and auxiliary services. The RRA 1976 does not cover recruitment into the armed forces but otherwise applies, although members of the armed forces have access only to an internal procedure, not to industrial tribunals.

Police and prison officers

Discrimination in height requirements as between male and female prison officers is allowed by SDA 1975 s18, as are requirements for height, uniform or equipment within the police force (s17).

Ministers of religion

The SDA 1975 does not apply to employment for the purposes of an organised religion (s19).

Prohibited actions

Unlike the law on unfair dismissal, the law on discrimination covers all aspects of employment, including recruitment, promotion and dismissal. RRA 1976 s4 and SDA 1975 s6 prohibit discrimination in the arrangements made for determining who should be offered employment, in the terms on which employment is offered, in refusing to offer employment, in access to opportunities for promotion, transfer, training or any other benefits, facilities or services. Finally, RRA 1976 s4(2)(c) and SDA 1975 s6(2)(b) prohibit discrimination 'by dismissing him/her, or subjecting him/her to any other detriment'.

The law is not clear as to what amounts to 'subjecting' the worker to 'any other detriment'. Basically it means putting the worker at a disadvantage,[35] but a worker cannot bring a case in respect of discrimination on a trivial matter. The worker must show that 'by reason of the act or acts complained of a reasonable worker would or might take the view that he had thereby been disadvantaged in the circumstances in which he had thereafter to work'.[36]

The statutes do not expressly prohibit racial or sexual harassment and abuse, but this behaviour is covered if the worker is subjected to a 'detriment'.

The meaning of discrimination

There are three kinds of unlawful discrimination – direct discrimination, indirect discrimination and victimisation. Each of these has a precise legal meaning, which is set out in the sections below. In summary, the meaning of each form of discrimination is as follows:

a) Direct discrimination is where one worker is treated differently from another because of his/her race, sex or marital status. If different requirements are imposed on workers according to their race or sex, this is direct discrimination. Example: if an employer required all male workers to be over six foot and all female workers to be over five foot, a male job applicant of five foot five inches would suffer direct discrimination.

There is no defence, although there are some exceptions for genuine occupational qualifications and for positive action (see below).

b) Indirect discrimination is where a requirement or condition is applied equally to all workers, but workers of a certain race or sex are less able to meet the requirement. Example: an employer requires all workers to be over six feet tall. Women would be disproportionately less able to meet this requirement. A female job applicant below six feet would suffer indirect discrimination.

Requirements which can be objectively justified are not unlawful indirect discrimination.

c) Victimisation is when a worker is treated differently because s/he has previously complained of discrimination, given evidence for another worker in a discrimination case or done any other 'protected act'.

Example: an employer sacks a worker because s/he complained of race discrimination.

The only defence for the employer is if the worker made a false allegation and did not act in good faith.

Direct discrimination

This is the most obvious form of discrimination. It entails differential treatment on grounds of race, sex or marital status.

The formal definition is in RRA 1976 s1(1)(a) and SDA 1975 ss1(1)(a), 2 and 3(1)(a). RRA 1976 s1(1)(a) states:

'A person discriminates against another if on racial grounds he treats that other less favourably than he treats or would treat other persons.'

The SDA 1975 s1(1)(a) is similar except that it prohibits discrimination against a woman 'on the ground of her sex'. Discrimination against men is also prohibited[37] and s3 prohibits less favourable treatment of a married person 'on the grounds of his or her marital status' compared with an unmarried person of the same sex. It is not unlawful to discriminate against someone on the ground of their unmarried status.

Segregating a person on racial grounds is regarded as less favourable treatment under RRA 1976 s1(2).

Direct discrimination is best thought of in terms of comparative treatment. Comparisons between workers of different racial groups or of different sex or marital status must be made where the relevant circumstances are the same or not materially different[38] so that the comparison is significant. A worker will usually have a stronger case if s/he can point to an actual person of different race or sex who was treated more favourably in similar circumstances. However, it is not essential to find an actual comparator if it can be shown that the employer 'would have treated' someone of different race or sex more favourably.

A possible example of direct discrimination is where an employer does not appoint a woman with appropriate qualifications and experience for a job. If the woman was not appointed because she was a woman, then direct discrimination has occurred. This is so regardless of whether an actual man with similar qualifications and experience has applied and been appointed, although the woman would find it harder to prove her case if there was no actual comparable man.[39]

In certain cases it is hard to make a direct comparison with someone of the opposite sex, eg unfavourable treatment of pregnant women[40] or cases concerning dress. Where women are not allowed to wear trousers, the IT will probably make comparison with men required to meet equivalent standards of smartness.[41]

Where there is more than one ground for an employer's action, it is sufficient if race or sex was 'an important factor'.[42]

The employer's state of mind

Employers often tell the IT that they are not personally prejudiced and insist that they acted with the best of intentions in everything they did.

This is irrelevant.[43] What counts is what the employer does, not what s/he thinks. If an employer in fact treats a black worker worse than s/he would treat a white worker, this is direct discrimination in any of the following situations:
- the employer intended to treat the black worker worse out of personal racial prejudice or malice;
- the employer intended to treat the black worker worse, but out of a non-malicious or even benevolent motive;
- the employer in fact treated the black worker worse but without realising it, ie unconscious discrimination.

Examples of direct discrimination where the employer was not personally prejudiced are: where a headteacher refused to appoint a teacher because the pupils wished to be taught English by someone of English national origin;[44] or where a Pakistani worker was not re-employed because the employer feared industrial unrest among fellow Pakistani workers resulting from an earlier incident between him and a white foreman.[45]

Examples of discrimination outside the employment field are where a council offered free swimming to persons over state retirement age (ie women from 60 and men from 65) in order to alleviate financial hardship of pensioners;[46] where a council inherited a situation whereby there were more grammar school places for boys than for girls and therefore had to set higher entrance requirements for girls.[47]

Recent cases have suggested that the 'but for' test should be applied to direct discrimination.[48] The question is whether the worker – but for her race or sex – would have been treated differently. The advantage of this test is that it focuses on actions not intentions and the IT need not try to assess the employer's state of mind.

Unconscious discrimination is hard to prove and there are few reported cases which deal with it. Nevertheless, it is a concept which the law recognises. The Court of Appeal has talked about the possibility of 'a conscious or unconscious racial attitude which involves stereotyped assumptions about members of that [racial] group'.[49]

Defences to direct discrimination

An employer cannot claim that for some reason s/he was justified in directly discriminating. Only indirect discrimination can be justified. Direct discrimination is absolutely unjustifiable, although in certain special circumstances it is permitted, eg where authenticity is required for an acting role or to preserve privacy and decency between the sexes. These limited exceptions – which are basically common sense – together with positive action provisions are set out below in chapter 7.

DIRECT DISCRIMINATION: KEY POINTS

- Look for different treatment of the worker and of someone not of the worker's race, sex or marital status. If possible, find another worker for comparison, but a hypothetical comparison will suffice.
- The employer's prejudices, motives and intentions are irrelevant.
- If direct discrimination has occurred, it cannot be justified. However there are exceptions for positive action or if the genuine occupational qualification defence applies.

GENERAL GUIDE TO USEFUL EVIDENCE

- Evidence discrediting the employer's likely explanation of events.
- Indications of prejudice on the part of the relevant managers. (Although this is not legally necessary, it can strengthen the case.)
- Directly comparable examples within the workplace where workers of the same race or sex as the worker have been treated less favourably than those of a different race or sex.
- Statistics as to the position and treatment of workers, of the complainant's race or sex, generally within the workforce.

Indirect discrimination

This is a more difficult concept for practitioners and tribunals alike. The definition of prohibited discrimination was extended in the RRA 1976 to include indirect discrimination, as it was recognised that the law against direct discrimination did not go far enough to eliminate institutionalised disadvantage in the workplace. The great difficulty of indirect discrimination is that it is not always easy to detect and advisers need to be particularly alert.

Indirect discrimination occurs where there is apparently equal treatment of all groups, but the effect of certain requirements or conditions imposed by employers has an adverse impact disproportionally on one group or other. For example, a requirement that all job applicants speak fluent English, while applied equally to everyone, would disproportionally debar persons born outside the UK from employment.

It is important to stress to ITs that the prohibition on indirect discrimination does not reduce standards or entail any kind of reverse discrimination. This is a common misconception. If a discriminatory requirement or condition can be justified, then it is not unlawful. The law simply prohibits unjustifiable requirements or conditions which have a discriminatory effect.

The definition

The definition of indirect discrimination is recognised to be tortuous. It is set out in RRA 1976 s1(1)(b) and SDA 1975 ss1(1)(b) and 3(1)(b). The former reads as follows:

'A person discriminates against another . . . if – (b) he applies to that other a requirement or condition which he applies or would apply equally to persons not of the same racial group as that other but—
(i) which is such that the proportion of persons of the same racial group as that other who can comply with it is considerably smaller than the proportion of persons not of that racial group who can comply with it; and
(ii) which he cannot show to be justifiable irrespective of the colour, race, nationality or ethnic or national origins of the person to whom it is applied; and
(iii)which is to the detriment of that other because he cannot comply with it.

Put more simply, the following steps are necessary to identify indirect discrimination:
–   there must be a requirement or condition which is applied to workers generally, regardless of their race or sex;
–   the particular worker bringing a case must be unable to comply with the condition or requirement;
–   proportionally fewer people of the worker's race or sex than those not of the worker's race or sex must be able to comply with the condition or requirement; and
–   the requirement or condition must be unjustifiable.

There is a wealth of case-law on the meaning of each part of the s1(1)(b) definition.

Identifying the requirement or condition

Not everything which an employer does is covered by s1(1)(b). The CRE in its *Proposals for Change*[50] has suggested that the wording be extended to cover any 'practice, policy or situation' involving an employee or job ·

applicant. As things stand, however, it is only discriminatory requirements or conditions which are unlawful. A 'requirement or condition' bears its natural meaning and should not be narrowly construed.[51]

It is not always easy to identify which is the relevant requirement or condition imposed by the employer. Formulating the requirement wrongly can make the difference between winning and losing a case.[52]

Common requirements or conditions which may be discriminatory under the RRA are those requiring certain dress,[53] languages, qualifications, duration or area of residence. Those under the SDA could relate to mobility, height, shift-working.

If an employer does not apply a condition absolutely but operates only a preference, this will not be covered by the definition of indirect discrimination.[54] This is a big loophole in the law.[55] It means that an employer can work to discriminatory preferences with impunity.

For example, an employer might advertise a job stating 'English A-level preferred'. An applicant without English A-level may still be considered but will be at a disadvantage compared with a person who has the qualification. Nevertheless, the RRA will not apply.

In another example,[56] an employer used twelve informal criteria for short-listing for the post of local government solicitor. Failure to meet any of the criteria did not bar candidates, but lowered their score for the purpose of short-listing. One criterion was Tower Hamlets' experience. Mr Meer, who was of Indian origin, did not have such experience and indeed no Indian solicitors would have been able to fulfil such a condition. Nevertheless, because it was merely preferable and not essential that candidates could satisfy the criterion, the case failed.

Unfortunately it is common to find the 'person specifications' issued by large employers containing lists of 'essential' and 'preferable' requirements.[57] This is not thought to be good equal opportunities practice.

EC law, where it applies, is not confined to mandatory requirements and conditions. Under Art 119, an indirectly discriminatory 'pay practice' is unlawful.[58] There are no ECJ decisions as yet on indirect discrimination under the Equal Treatment Directive, but the position is likely to be the same.

Ability to meet the requirement

The relevant time at which a person's ability to comply with a requirement or condition must be measured, is the same both for testing the particular worker's ability to comply and for measuring generally whether others of the same and different racial or sexual groups can comply.[59] It is the date on which the worker suffered a detriment because s/he could not comply with the requirement and when the requirement or condition had to be fulfilled.[60]

For example, a woman of Asian origin who qualified as a teacher in Kenya could not comply with a requirement for a clerical post of having English O-level. It was irrelevant that she had the ability to gain an O-level and could in the past or in the future have obtained one. At the time that the requirement was applied, she could not meet it.[61]

In another case,[62] part-timers were selected first for redundancy. At the time of the redundancy dismissals, Mrs Clarke was a part-time worker. It was irrelevant that she could have changed to full-time working several years ago once her children had grown-up, since she had not in fact done so and at the time of the selection, she was still a part-timer.

The test is whether someone can in practice comply with the condition or requirement at the relevant time, not whether they could in theory.[63] For example, a Sikh could in theory comply with a requirement that he wear no turban. He need only take it off. However, in practice, he could not comply. The test is whether someone 'can consistently with the customs and cultural conditions of the racial group' comply.[64]

A civil service requirement that candidates for the post of executive officer must be under 29[65] does not in theory bar any more women than men. However, in practice, many women take career breaks to raise children, so that this requirement was held to discriminate indirectly against women.[66] The court said that it was relevant to consider 'the current usual behaviour of women in this respect, as observed in practice, putting on one side behaviour and responses which are unusual or extreme'.[67]

Comparing proportions who can and cannot comply with the requirement

A worker must show that within a 'pool' chosen for comparison, a considerably smaller proportion of those of the worker's own race or sex than those not of the worker's race or sex can comply with the requirement.

The question is within what section of the community does the proportionate comparison fall to be made?[68] For example, is the ability to comply measured among the total female and male population or only those in a particular town or a specific workplace or with appropriate qualifications?[69] The appropriate 'pool' will depend on the facts of each case and which section of the public is likely to be affected by the requirement. In choosing the pool, people must be compared in the same – or not materially different – relevant circumstances.[70]

Clearly the statistical outcome will vary according to the pool chosen. The IT's selection of the appropriate pool is a matter for its discretion.[71] However, the pool must not be such that it incorporates the act of discrimination. For example, in one case[72] only those who had been resident in the EC were eligible for lower college fees. It would have been misleading to choose as a pool, people who had actually applied to the college, because many would have been deterred from applying.

In another case,[73] lone parents who had never married were not eligible for grants. Ms Shaffter complained that this indirectly discriminated against women. The statistics showed that whereas 80 per cent of all lone parents were female, 20 per cent of the male lone parents and 20 per cent of female lone parents had never married. The court said that the appropriate pool for comparison was among all students with dependent children claiming grants and not among all lone parents who had never married. The latter pool was a 'trap' and would disguise the discrimination.

Indirect discrimination is concerned with whether a requirement or condition adversely affects one particular sex or racial group more than others. The law compares the proportions (fractions or percentages) of people who can comply with the requirement, not absolute numbers. This makes a difference.[74]

For example, a Spanish worker may claim indirect discrimination because s/he cannot meet a potential employer's requirement for fluent English. The appropriate comparison is not the total number of Spaniards who can speak fluent English as against the total number of non-Spaniards who can speak fluent English. The proper comparison is the proportion of all Spanish people who can speak fluent English as against the proportion of all non-Spanish people who can do so. The calculation could be done as follows:

A = The total number of Spaniards within the chosen pool.
B = The number of Spaniards within the pool who can speak fluent English.
C = The total number of non-Spaniards in the pool.
D = The number of non-Spaniards in the pool who can speak fluent English.
Then B is divided by A and D is divided by C to get the fractions to be compared. Percentages can be calculated by multiplying each fraction by 100.

Taking a sex discrimination example: a university advertises a full-time lectureship. A woman with childcare responsibilities is not employed because she can work only part-time. An appropriate pool may be among all those already holding GB university lectureship posts or qualified to do so. The proper comparison is B÷A compared with D÷C where:

A = The total number of women who are or are qualified to be lecturers in GB universities.

B = The number of those women who can work full-time.

C = The total number of men who are or are qualified to be lecturers in GB universities.

D = The number of those men who can work full-time.

What amounts to a 'considerably smaller' proportion? The percentages should be looked at in terms of each other; it does not matter if the practice under attack has no relevance to the vast bulk of humanity.[75] Thus a difference of one per cent or two per cent with very small percentages would be no less significant than a difference between between 30 per cent and 60 per cent.

It does not defeat the claim if no one of the particular sex or racial group can comply.[76]

Is the requirement or condition justifiable?

The concept of justifiability is central to the law on indirect discrimination. In practice there are numerous, often hidden, requirements and conditions with discriminatory effect in every workplace. The possibility of bringing a successful case often turns on whether the requirement or condition is justifiable.

Justifiability is very much a question of fact. It is difficult to gain guidance from past cases since tribunals have applied different tests for what is justifiable. At one time, an employer needed to produce only what 'right-thinking people' would consider were 'sound and tolerable reasons' for applying a requirement.[77] Now it is not so easy. What an IT would consider justifiable requires 'an objective balance between the discriminatory effect of the condition and the reasonable needs of the party who applies the condition.'[78] An employer must show that:

- the requirement was objectively justifiable regardless of race or sex;
- the requirement served a real business need of the employer;[79] and
- the need was reasonable and objectively justifiable on economic or other grounds, eg administrative efficiency; it is not sufficient that the particular employer personally considers it justifiable.[80]

The greater the discriminatory effect of the requirement, the greater the objective need an employer must show s/he has.[81]

Examples of factors which may justify a discriminatory requirement are hygiene, safety, consistency of care, consistency of management, important economic and administrative considerations. Each case will depend on its precise facts and the principle of balance. Note that the

Employment Act 1989 exempted turban-wearing Sikhs from any statutory requirements to wear safety helmets on construction sites and declared that any requirement imposed by an employer to that effect would not be justifiable indirect discrimination.[82] Note also that the special treatment of lone parents participating in employment training is now permissible.[83]

Although the burden of proof in discrimination cases is generally on the worker, once a worker has proved that there is a prima facie discriminatory requirement, it is for the employer to show that it is justifiable.[84] This crucial distinction is often forgotten by ITs who expect workers to show why the requirement is not justifiable and to suggest alternative ways for employers to achieve needs. For example, a majority of the EAT has said that the employer is:

'under no obligation to prove that there was no other possible way of achieving his object, however expensive and administratively complicated. If an alternative or alternative criteria are thought to be reasonable, then that method will no doubt be put forward by the applicant'.[85]

Obviously it is helpful if workers can show how employers could meet their needs by taking action with less discriminatory effect, but workers should not be required to provide such evidence.

INDIRECT DISCRIMINATION: KEY POINTS

- Find the requirement or condition which the worker cannot meet. It must be one that is applied to everyone.
- The requirement or condition must be such that people of the worker's race or sex are generally less able to meet it than other people.
- Consider whether the employer is likely to be able objectively to justify applying the requirement or condition.

GENERAL GUIDE TO USEFUL EVIDENCE

- Statistics or other evidence showing that proportionally fewer people of the worker's race or sex could meet the requirement.
- Evidence showing that the worker cannot in practice meet the requirement.

Victimisation

It is unlawful to victimise a worker because s/he has made a complaint of discrimination or done any other 'protected act' under the RRA 1976 or SDA 1975. This protection is particularly important for workers who risk dismissal by bringing up controversial issues, but do not have the requisite length of service to qualify for a claim of unfair dismissal. Unfortunately, it is very hard to prove that victimisation has taken place. A worker must show three things:[86]

- s/he has done a 'protected act', ie an act within RRA 1976 s2(a)-(d) or SDA 1975 s4(a)-(d);
- s/he has been treated less favourably by the employer because s/he did the protected act. The comparison is with the way another worker who had not done the protected act would have been treated;[87] and
- the less favourable treatment is precisely because the worker's conduct was under or by reference to the RRA 1976, SDA 1975 or EqPA.

It is unlawful under RRA 1976 s2 to treat someone less favourably because they have done any 'protected act', ie if they have brought proceedings under the RRA 1976 or have given evidence or information in proceedings (brought by themselves or anyone else) under the RRA 1976, or intend to do any of those things.[88] More generally, it is unlawful to treat someone less favourably because they have done – or intend to do – anything under or by reference to the RRA 1976 or because they have alleged – or intend to allege – that anyone has committed an act which would in fact amount to a contravention of the RRA 1976.[89] Section 4 of SDA 1975 grants similar protection in relation to the SDA 1975 and the EqPA.

The precise scope of doing anything 'under or by reference to' the statutes is uncertain. A Leeds IT thought that the activities of three local authority race trainers in pursuance of the authority's obligations under RRA 1976 s71 were protected acts under s2(c) and their dismissal when the authority changed hands was unlawful victimisation.[90]

Since a worker first has to prove that s/he has done a 'protected act', which s/he feels has led to victimisation, it is advisable that any complaint of discrimination or statement of intention to bring proceedings or give evidence should be put in writing at the time. If appropriate, such written statement should be accompanied by a reminder to the employers of the right not to be victimised under the appropriate sections.

As a matter of evidence, it is difficult to prove that the reason the employer has treated the worker unfavourably is precisely because the worker has done a protected act. It is particularly hard to prove that what caused the employer's reaction was that aspect of the worker's act which related to the RRA 1976, SDA 1976 or EqPA.

For example, Ms Cornelius claimed she was victimised in that she was refused a transfer and grievance hearing while her proceedings for sex discrimination were pending. Her victimisation claim failed because the court accepted that her employer would have acted in the same way, whatever the nature of the proceedings. The court believed that the employer's concern was as to the risk of acting in a way which might embarrass the handling of existing legal proceedings, regardless of whether those proceedings were under the SDA 1975 or quite a different matter.[91]

In another case,[92] Mr Aziz was a taxi driver and member of TST, a company promoting the interests of taxi drivers in Coventry. He made secret tape recordings of other TST members, as he felt he was being discriminated against. He later decided to make a race discrimination claim against TST. When the recordings were disclosed during the case, he was expelled from TST. Mr Aziz claimed that he was victimised by being expelled. He claimed that the protected act was making the tape recordings with a view possibly to bringing a race discrimination case. He lost his case because the IT found that the reason for his expulsion was the fact that the recordings were underhand and a breach of trust. The IT accepted that TST would still have expelled Mr Aziz even if the purpose of the recordings was nothing to do with the race relations legislation.

As is apparent from these examples, the difficulties in proving motive or causation severely limit the effectiveness of the victimisation provisions in practice.

An employer has a defence to a victimisation claim in relation to a worker's allegation under the RRA 1976, SDA 1975 or EqPA, where such allegation was false and not made in good faith.[93]

CHAPTER SEVEN

Permitted race and sex discrimination

Genuine occupational qualifications

Under RRA 1976 s5 and SDA 1975 s7, discrimination is permitted in certain circumstances[1] where being of a particular racial group or gender is a genuine occupational qualification (GOQ) of the job. The GOQ defence may apply to discrimination in refusing to offer someone employment or in the arrangements made for determining who should be offered employment or in access to opportunities for promotion or transfer or to training for employment.

The GOQ defence is *not* available in the following circumstances:
- under the SDA 1975, where discrimination is against married persons;
- where discrimination occurs in the terms of employment offered or afforded to workers, or in access to benefits, facilities or services (other than promotion, transfer or training), or in dismissing someone or subjecting them to any other detriment;
- to the filling of a vacancy at a time when the employer already has workers of the particular race/sex who are capable of carrying out the duties in question, whom it would be reasonable to employ on those duties and who could carry out those duties without undue inconvenience to the employer.[2] For example, in *Etam plc v Rowan*,[3] a shop selling womens' clothes refused to employ a male shop assistant because the job was likely to involve contact with women in a state of undress.[4] The GOQ defence failed because the part of a sales assistant's job which involved contact with women in changing rooms could have been carried out by other (female) shop assistants without causing undue inconvenience to the employer.

For a full list of GOQs, it is important to read the wording of the sections. In summary, they are as follows:

Under the RRA 1976:
- for reasons of authenticity as an actor, entertainer, artist's or photographer's model;

- for reasons of authenticity, working in a place where food or drink is served to the public in a particular setting; or
- to provide personal services promoting the welfare of persons of the same racial group.

Under the SDA 1975:

- for reasons of authenticity as an actor or entertainer or for reasons of physiology (excluding physical strength or stamina);
- to preserve decency or privacy because of likely physical contact or contact with persons in a state of undress or using sanitary facilities or, where work is in a private home, because of close physical or social contact with someone living in the home;
- because it is necessary to live on work premises and there are no separate sleeping and sanitary facilities and it is not reasonable to expect the employer to supply these;
- where the work is in a single-sex establishment or part of an establishment for persons requiring special care, supervision or attention, eg a hospital or prison;
- where the job is one of two to be held by a married couple; or
- to provide personal services promoting the welfare or education or similar services to persons of the same sex.

An employer can invoke the GOQ defence even where only some of the duties of the job are covered by the section,[5] although of course it is then more likely that the duties can be covered by other workers.

Positive action

The Codes of Practice encourage positive action.

Personal services

The RRA 1976 s5(2)(d) says that being of a particular racial group is a GOQ where:

'the holder of the job provides persons of that racial group with personal services promoting their welfare, and those services can most effectively be provided by a person of that racial group.'

SDA 1975 s7(2)(e) is similar in relation to gender except that it refers to personal services promoting 'welfare or education or similar personal services'.

To gain the protection of the sub-sections:

- The job must involve wholly or partly the provision of 'personal services'. The post-holder must be directly involved in the provision of

the services,[6] ie in face to face contact with the recipient. Purely administrative and managerial positions such as assistant head of a local authority housing benefit department[7] are not covered.
- Those services must be such that they are most effectively provided by a person of the same sex or racial group. It is not necessary to show that the services can be provided only by a person of the same sex or racial group.[8] It is recognised that 'where language or a knowledge and understanding of cultural and religious background are important, then those services may be most effectively provided by a person of a particular racial group'.[9]
- The EAT has said that the provider of services must be of a particular racial group which is the same group as that of the recipients and not simply black.[10] However, Balcombe LJ in the Court of Appeal suggested obiter that in some circumstances, eg a health visitor, personal services may be most effectively provided to persons of 'a racial group defined by colour', eg black people, by a person of the same colour, regardless of which ethnic group each person came from.[11]
- There must be no other workers already employed who could, without undue inconvenience, provide those services.[12]

Encouraging applications/offering training

Under RRA 1976 s38 and SDA 1975 s48, an employer can:
- encourage people of only a particular sex or racial group to apply for jobs; and
- offer training only to people of a particular sex or racial group;
provided that in the previous 12 months the number of women or people of that racial group doing the work in question was comparatively small, either generally or in the employing organisation in particular.

Note that, although it is permissible exclusively to encourage job applicants who are women or of a particular racial group, it is not permissible to discriminate at the point of taking someone on. Employers can therefore place advertisements expressly encouraging applications from women and particular racial groups or ask job centres to tell such people that applications from them are particularly welcome, but it should be made clear that selection will be on merit, regardless of race or sex.

Special needs

It is not unlawful under RRA 1976 s35 to afford someone of a particular racial group access to facilities or services to meet their special needs in regard to their education, training or welfare.

Discriminatory advertisements

Under RRA 1976 s29 and SDA 1975 s38 it is unlawful to publish or have published an advertisement which indicates or might reasonably be understood as indicating an intention to discriminate, unless a GOQ or other exceptions apply.[13] Proceedings in respect of unlawful advertisements are brought by the Commission for Racial Equality or Equal Opportunities Commission not by individuals.[14] However, a discriminatory advertisement may be evidence supporting an individual's claim of unlawful discrimination if a person goes on to apply for the job and is unsuccessful.

Statutory authority

Section 41 of RRA 1976 excludes from the ambit of the RRA any discriminatory act done in pursuance of a statute or statutory instrument. It is now established that 'in pursuance of' is confined to acts done in necessary performance of an express obligation contained in a statute or statutory instrument and does not include anything done merely in the exercise of a power or discretion conferred by statute.[15] For example, the secretary of state was not protected by s41 when exercising his discretion under the Education (Teachers) Regulations 1982 to decide whether to grant qualified teacher status to an overseas teacher on the basis of his own non-statutory criteria.

The sex discrimination exemption is quite different and SDA 1975 s51 has been significantly amended by Employment Act 1989 s3. Discriminatory acts which are 'necessary' to comply with a requirement of any statute passed before the SDA 1975 are permitted, provided that the purpose of the provision was to protect women as regards pregnancy, maternity or any other risks specifically affecting women.[16] The Employment Act 1989 Sch 1 sets out specific health and safety legislation which is also excluded.

Pregnancy or childbirth

Section s2(2) of SDA 1975 permits (but does not require) special treatment afforded to women in connection with pregnancy or childbirth.

Private households

Acts of direct or indirect discrimination within a private household are not covered by the RRA 1976 although victimisation is still prohibited.[17]

CHAPTER EIGHT

Special situations

Pregnancy dismissals

Under EPCA s60, it is automatically unfair to dismiss a woman because she is pregnant or for a reason connected with her pregnancy (see p49 above). Women who do not qualify to claim unfair dismissal may be able to claim under the SDA 1975. Where possible, women may choose to claim under both statutes, since a successful sex discrimination claim would lead to additional compensation for injury to feelings.

Originally, the provisions of the SDA 1975 were applied rather literally so that discrimination against pregnant women was permitted. It was said that no comparison could be made for the purposes of s1(1)(a) because men could not be pregnant.[1] Similarly, under s1(1)(b), a requirement of not being pregnant could not be applied to men and women alike.

The EAT in *Hayes v Malleable Working Men's Club and Institute* and *Maughan v North East London Magistrates' Courts Committee*[2] interpreted the law more sensibly, noting:

'It will usually be the consequences of pregnancy, rather than the condition itself, which provides the grounds for dismissal; the general effect upon the employee's performance at work or the need to take time off for her confinement and for periods of rest before and afterwards.'

The EAT went on to suggest that a pregnant woman employee could properly be compared with a sick male employee for the purposes of the SDA 1975.

Several difficulties face a worker following this decision. First, she has to prove that the reason for her dismissal was in some way connected with her pregnancy. This is frequently denied by employers. Then she must identify which of the consequences of her pregnancy has caused the dismissal. For example, is it her occasional absences, her anticipated absence for having the baby, her desire to return after maternity leave, any reduced work performance? Finally, she must prove that her employer 107 would have treated more favourably a man requiring leave, eg for an operation, study or travel or performing less well due to temporary sickness. This last stage carries all the usual evidential difficulties of discrimination cases, where the burden of proof lies on the worker.

The cases tend to concern dismissal. However, action short of dismissal may also be sex discrimination, eg refusing maternity leave.[3]

The law is still unsatisfactory. Many pregnant women do not consider their condition is analogous to sickness. Moreover, *Hayes* deals only with the situation where a woman is dismissed because of the consequences of pregnancy. It is uncertain what approach would be taken if dismissal were solely due to the fact of pregnancy. As pregnancy is a condition exclusively connected with women, then any discrimination on the ground of pregnancy ought to be automatically considered discrimination on the ground of sex. This argument was recently aired before the EAT but rejected.[4] However, the law may change on this, following developments in EC law (see below).[5]

A claim of indirect discrimination may be worth trying. For example, there may be a requirement that a worker 'be available for work without interruption'. This is likely to have disparate impact on women and the issue will be justifiability.

Note that men cannot claim sex discrimination if an employer chooses to give special treatment to women in connection with pregnancy or childbirth.[6]

Women employed by state employers (see p86 above), are in a much better position than private sector employees, since they can claim under the Equal Treatment Directive. This makes it unlawful discrimination to treat a woman less favourably on grounds of pregnancy.[7] It is not necessary to make any artificial comparison with a man; thus a woman who is dismissed due to her pregnancy or the need for maternity leave suffers unlawful discrimination regardless of the way a man in comparable circumstances would have been treated. Equally, a woman who is not recruited because she is pregnant is discriminated against even though the person who gets the job is also a woman, who is not pregnant. Since pregnancy relates only to women, then it is automatically sex discrimination contrary to the directive.

It is likely that British courts will now interpret the SDAs consistently with this approach, so that there is no difference in women's rights between public and private employees.[8]

PREGNANCY DISMISSALS: KEY POINTS

• Dismissals for pregnancy or a connected reason of a worker employed for over two years are automatically unfair.
• Under the SDA 1975, consider what aspect of the pregnancy has led to the dismissal, eg the need for time off intermittently or the anticipated future period of longer absence. The relevant comparison is with how the employer would treat a man requiring similar time off.
• Indirect discrimination may also apply.
• EC law may be useful with a public employer since it treats pregnancy discrimination automatically as sex discrimination.

GENERAL GUIDE TO USEFUL EVIDENCE

• Evidence proving that the dismissal was for pregnancy or a related reason as opposed to the reason put forward by the employer.
• Evidence or statistics showing how a man would have been treated in comparable circumstances, eg if he required time off for an operation.

Part-time working and job-shares

Part-timers and job-sharers may have some protection under the SDA 1975. Two broad issues arise here: whether women can claim a right to work part-time and whether part-timers are entitled to enjoy the same terms and conditions as full-timers.

The basic principle behind these issues is that more women than men work part time and wish to work part time, by reason of childcare responsibilities. Thus, any less favourable treatment of part-timers or any prohibition on part-time working is likely to have adverse impact on women. Similar arguments can be made in respect of married persons as against unmarried persons. In most cases, the real issue concerns justifiability.

Is there a right to work part time?

There is no absolute right to work part-time or to job-share. However, a number of cases have accepted that women are adversely affected when only full-time work is available and this can be unlawful as indirect sex discrimination. Even if an IT declares that insistence on full-time working in a particular case is discriminatory, an employer cannot be compelled to employ someone part time and the only remedies are for compensation for sex discrimination, victimisation or unfair dismissal.

The main case establishing that refusal to let women work part-time may be unlawful indirect discrimination was *The Home Office v Holmes*[9] in 1984. The EAT in 1989 under the presidency of Mr Justice Wood revealed itself to be extremely hostile to the principle of women's rights in this area. In *Clymo v Wandsworth LBC*,[10] the EAT interpreted every stage of the law of indirect discrimination restrictively. This is a precedent to be wary of, although in several respects its interpretation of the law may be considered wrong. Fortunately, the Northern Ireland Court of Appeal in *Briggs v North Eastern Education and Library Board*[11] effectively overruled *Clymo* in many respects. Although the decision is not strictly binding outside Northern Ireland, it is of strong persuasive value and should be quoted in the IT.

The stages of proving indirect discrimination are dealt with above.[12] Where a woman claims that an employer's insistence on full-time working is indirect discrimination, the following special considerations apply.

Is full-time working a requirement or condition?

It is now fairly well-established that an employer who insists on full-time work is imposing a requirement or condition within the meaning of the SDA 1975.[13]

In *Holmes*, a full-time executive officer asked to work part-time after returning from maternity leave. All workers on her grade were employed on rigid full-time contracts. The Home Office argued that full-time service was not a condition of the job, but was the job itself, ie a full-time job was one kind of job and a part-time job was another. The EAT disagreed. It said that the words 'requirement or condition' could include any obligation of service, including the obligation to work full-time.

The EAT in *Clymo* (above) thought that in some situations, full-time working was not a separate requirement, but was part and parcel of the job itself. The EAT seemed to think that status was the determining factor, saying that for a managing director, full-time working would be part of the nature of the appointment, whereas with a cleaner, it would simply be a requirement.[14] However, the Northern Ireland Court of Appeal[15] has rejected this approach, saying that a requirement applies even where the nature of the job entails full-time attendance.

Is the requirement to work full-time a detriment?

Is the full-time working requirement to the worker's detriment because she cannot comply with it? In *Holmes*, the IT considered that the applicant could not comply with the requirement and that was to her detriment. It said that attempting to fulfil parental responsibilities and work full time entailed excessive demands on Ms Holmes' time and energy.

In *Clymo*, the IT was less sympathetic. Ms Clymo, a senior branch librarian, wished to job-share with her husband after returning from maternity leave. The IT thought that Ms Clymo could comply with the full-time requirement since the council had offered child-minding and she and her husband were earning enough to pay for it; she was merely exercising a personal preference to care for her child. The EAT agreed with this view,[16] revealing its attitude by stating: 'in every employment ladder from the lowliest to the highest, there will come a stage at which a woman who has family responsibilities must make a choice'. This seemingly contradicted the EAT's earlier comment that Ms Clymo 'should not be coerced into a position of complying with a situation wholly alien to her womanhood or motherhood'. However, it does seem that the IT and EAT were influenced by Ms Clymo's relatively high status and income and the council's offer of childcare.

In view of the restrictive approach in *Clymo*, a woman bringing IT proceedings should be careful not to demonstrate in the meantime that she can in fact work full time. On the other hand, she will not want to resign if there is a chance that the IT can help her. Sometimes an employer may agree that she works part time pending the result. If not, she will have to show the IT that her childcare arrangements could only be sustained in the short term and were causing great stress, expense or inconvenience. Ms Clymo tried to avoid this trap by using up her days off to work part time in practice. Ms Holmes took six months' sick leave.

Is the requirement justifiable?

This depends on the facts of the particular case. In *Holmes*, the Home Office tried to justify the requirement by arguing that the bulk of industry, national and local government service was still organised on a full-time basis. The EAT was unimpressed with that argument and found the requirement unjustified.

In another case,[17] a health visitor was permitted to work part time after maternity leave, provided her hours were spread over five days. The worker objected that this involved her in greater expenses for the same wage. Nevertheless, the EAT found the requirement justified because

patients needed regular personal contact and visitors should be available
five days a week for consultation with doctors or social workers.

Treatment of existing part-timers

The application of the redundancy selection criterion of part-timers first
may well be unlawful sex discrimination.[18] Most difficulties facing part-
time workers, however, concern less favourable terms and conditions,
particularly indirect discrimination in 'pay' in its broadest sense. Because
Art 119 is binding on all employers, EC law has been very helpful in
securing equality of pay, pension contributions, sick pay etc.[19]

Indirect discrimination commonly affecting women with children

A requirement that an employee work shifts or flexible hours may
indirectly discriminate against a woman because of childcare
commitments. Similarly, an employer's attempt to alter a woman's hours
(whether or not permitted to do so by her contract) even in a minor way,
may be indirect discrimination if, for example, it interferes with her
arrangements for collecting her children from school. Again, the main
issue is likely to be whether the change is justifiable. Similar
considerations apply with mobility requirements.

Any assumption made by an employer that women will be less mobile
or flexible is directly discriminatory. Interview questions concerning
mobility or flexibility, if asked only of female candidates, are likely to
lead to poorer interview performance and constitute direct discrimination
in the arrangements made for determining who should be offered
employment.[20]

PART-TIME WORKING: KEY POINTS

- Refusal to permit a woman to work part time may be unlawful
  indirect discrimination against her as a woman or as a married
  person.
- The main issue on part-time working will usually be whether the
  employer can justify insisting on full-time working.
- It may also be indirect sex discrimination to treat part-time workers
  less well than full-timers. Where part-timers are given less equal
  terms and conditions including pay rates, EC law usually applies as
  this may contravene Art 119 and the Equal Pay Directive.

GENERAL GUIDE TO USEFUL EVIDENCE

When an employer will not permit part-time working —
- Evidence generally and within the appropriate pool showing that women more often work part time and are less able to work full time than men.
- Evidence showing that the particular worker cannot in practice work full time.

Sexual or racial harassment or abuse

Meaning of harassment

There is no express prohibition in the RRA 1976 or SDA 1975 against harassment or abuse. If a worker wants to bring a claim solely about harassment, the treatment complained of must fall within the range of prohibited behaviour under RRA 1976 ss1 and 4 or SDA 1975 ss1 and 6. The worker must prove:

- less favourable treatment on grounds of race or sex, ie direct discrimination (RRA 1976 s1, SDA 1975 s1);
- that the less favourable treatment took the form of a prohibited act under RRA 1976 s4 or SDA 1975 s6. Most commonly, the worker will claim s/he has been 'subjected to a detriment'.

It is confusing to think in terms of proving 'sexual harassment' which has certain non-legal meanings which are not relevant for proving unlawful sex discrimination. Two important cases have emphasised that the test is simply whether direct discrimination occurred. In *Strathclyde RC v Porcelli*,[21] the court said that the primary question was not whether there was sexual harassment, a phrase not found in the SDA 1975, but simply whether the worker was less favourably treated on the ground of her sex than a man would have been.

In *Bracebridge Engineering v Darby*,[22] a worker was sexually assaulted by two supervisors. The employer argued that a single incident could not be described as 'sexual harassment'. However, the EAT said 'whether or not harassment is a continuing course of conduct, there was here an act which was an act of discrimination against a woman because she was a woman'.

What happens if the employer claims that the way the woman was treated was not based on her sex but, for example, on the fact that she was disliked? In *Porcelli* (above), the worker was subjected to a campaign of sexual harassment by two male colleagues. The court said it was irrelevant that an equally disliked male colleague would have been treated just as unpleasantly. It was not necessary to show that the treatment of Mrs Porcelli had any sex-related motive or objective:

'This particular part of the campaign was plainly adopted against Mrs Porcelli because she was a woman. It was a particular kind of weapon, based upon the sex of the victim, which would not have been used against an equally disliked man.'[23]

Similarly, if a chosen insult is expressly racial, an employer cannot evade the RRA 1976 by saying that s/he would have been equally insulting to other workers.

'Any other detriment'

The act or acts of discrimination concerned must fall within the areas of behaviour covered by the RRA 1976 and SDA 1975.[24] There is no difficulty where, for example, refusal to accept sexual advances leads to lack of promotion, dismissal or other discriminatory acts prohibited under SDA 1975 s6. Where harassment does not lead to such easily identifiable consequences, the question arises as to whether it is unlawful. In order to bring such a claim under the RRA 1976 or SDA 1975, a worker would have to show that the harassment or abuse, in itself, amounted to 'any other detriment'.[25]

Several cases have dealt with what amounts to an unlawful 'detriment'. For example, can a single racist insult amount to unlawful race discrimination, or the display of a pin-up calendar amount to unlawful sex discrimination? The *Jeremiah*[26] case said detriment simply meant 'putting at a disadvantage'. Subsequent cases have been more explicit.

In *Porcelli*,[27] the employer conceded that if the worker had suffered discrimination, then she had been 'subjected to a detriment' under SDA 1975 s6(2)(b). A single incident of harassment can amount to a detriment 'provided it is sufficiently serious'.[28] A one-off racist 'joke' or remark is unlikely to be enough, but the surrounding circumstances will be relevant.

It is not necessary to show that by reason of the harassment, the worker has suffered some contractual disadvantage, but rather that the worker has suffered a disadvantage in her working circumstances. In *De Souza v The Automobile Association*,[29] a secretary claimed racial discrimination after she overheard a manager tell a senior clerk to give some typing 'to the wog'. The Court of Appeal said:

'Racially to insult a coloured employee is not enough by itself, even if that insult caused him or her distress; before the employee can be said to have been subjected to some "other detriment" the court or tribunal must find that by reason of the act or acts complained of a reasonable worker would or might take the view that he had thereby been disadvantaged in the circumstances in which he had thereafter to work.'

It is therefore necessary to show (a) subjectively that the particular worker was disadvantaged in his/her working circumstances and (b) objectively that a reasonable worker of the same sex or race would have been disadvantaged. Ultimately it is a question of fact whether, objectively and subjectively, an unlawful detriment has occurred. The nature of the workplace, the worker's age, status and vulnerability are all likely to be relevant.

Unfortunately it would seem that a woman's sexual attitudes are also relevant. The EAT has said that evidence as to a worker's mode of dress at work[30] and evidence showing that a woman talked freely about sexual matters to fellow workers[31] can be relevant both as to whether she suffered a detriment and as to compensation for injury to feelings. Somewhat inconsistently, the EAT also acknowledged that 'a person may be quite happy to accept the remarks of A or B in a sexual context, and wholly upset by similar remarks made by C'.[32]

On the facts of *De Souza*, the court felt that the woman was not 'treated' less favourably, because it was not intended that she overhear the remark. For the same reason, she was not subjected to a detriment under RRA 1976 s4(2)(c). There was no evidence to show that both the woman and 'the reasonable coloured secretary in like situation would or might be disadvantaged in the circumstances and conditions in which they were working'. Perhaps the court was persuaded by the employer's argument that the RRA 1976 was 'not intended to prevent the mere holding or indeed expression of racial opinions'.

Employers' liability

Under RRA 1976 s32 and SDA 1975 s41, the employing organisation is legally responsible for any discriminatory action by one worker against another, provided that the action is carried out in the course of employment. The employer is responsible even if the perpetrator is not of managerial status.[33]

How can a discriminatory act be perpetrated 'in the course of' employment? In most cases, the employing organisation will not have actually instructed or authorised a worker racially or sexually to harass another worker. An employer is responsible for an authorised act which is carried out in an unauthorised way, but not for an entirely unauthorised act.[34]

The distinction is difficult to apply in practice and is a question of fact. A postman writing racist comments on envelopes to be delivered has been considered to be acting outside the course of his employment.[35] In *Bracebridge*,[36] however, where the assault was perpetrated by two supervisers as the worker was washing her hands preparatory to going home, the act was considered to be in the course of employment, because the two men were exercising a disciplinary and supervisory function.

The employer's defence

The employer is responsible regardless of whether s/he knew or approved of the unlawful act, unless s/he 'took such steps as were reasonably practicable' to prevent unlawful acts of discrimination.[37]

In *Balgobin and Francis v LB Tower Hamlets*,[38] two women were subjected to sexual harassment by a cook who worked with them in a hostel. An inconclusive enquiry was held by the employer, once the women complained, after which the cook returned to work with the women. A majority of the EAT accepted the employer's defence under SDA 1975 s41(3), that the employer was running the hostel with adequate supervision and had 'made known' its policy of equal opportunities.

It is to be hoped that this view will not be adopted in other cases since the employer did very little to earn the s41(3) protection. It had given no guidance to hotel staff on the operation of the equal opportunities policy which did not mention specifically that sexual harassment was unlawful.[39]

The EAT also said that requiring the women to continue to work with the cook after the enquiry did not constitute less favourable treatment, even though it was a hostile working environment. The harassment itself had ceased and the women were required to continue working with the cook because they were employees, not because they were women.

Constructive dismissal

If an employer commits a repudiatory or fundamental breach of contract, a worker may resign and claim constructive dismissal.[40] What amounts to a repudiatory breach is a question of fact, but in the key case of *Western Excavating (ECC) v Sharp*,[41] Lawton LJ said that:

'Persistent and unwanted amorous advances by an employer to a female member of his staff would clearly be such conduct.'

In *Bracebridge Engineering v Darby*,[42] the employer's failure to treat seriously and fully investigate the worker's allegations of assault clearly amounted to a repudiatory breach of the implied term of trust and confidence and the obligation not to undermine the confidence of female staff.

An employer's failure to investigate an allegation of discrimination may itself be an act of discrimination, but only if the refusal was on grounds of race or sex.[43] In addition, if the employer refuses to investigate simply because the allegation made was one of discrimination, this may amount to unlawful victimisation.

Common law claims

Where the harassment involves physical contact, particularly if there is a severe assault, the worker may have a claim for damages at common law either in civil assault against the perpetrator or negligence against the employer. The advantage of such claims is that they are heard in the civil courts where legal aid may be available and there is no ceiling on compensation. However, any concurrent claim under the SDA 1975 or RRA 1976 must be brought separately in the IT.

HARASSMENT: KEY POINTS

- Sexual or racial harassment or abuse is not prohibited as such under the RRA 1976 or SDA 1975. The worker must prove that the harassment amounts to direct discrimination in the usual way.
- The discrimination must amount to a disadvantage in the person's working conditions.
- The harasser's motive is irrelevant. What is relevant is the form that the harasser's action takes, eg unwanted sexual advances or racial abuse.
- The employer is normally legally responsible for harassment carried out by a manager or other worker.
- The harassment – or the employer's failure to deal with a complaint about it – may also constitute fundamental breach of contract entitling the worker to resign and claim constructive dismissal.

GENERAL GUIDE TO USEFUL EVIDENCE

- Evidence proving that the harassment occurred, eg as to visits to a GP.
- Evidence of any efforts to inform management and the response.
- Evidence as to any substantial preventative measures taken by the employer, eg equal opportunities training of its staff.

Retirement: age, redundancy pay, pensions

The SDA 1986 amended the SDA 1975 and the EqPA in respect of retirement provisions. It is unlawful discrimination to make men and women retire at different ages[44] or to reduce a worker's status or refuse promotion, training or transfer because of a worker's proximity to a discriminatory retirement age. The SDA 1986 did not prohibit all forms of discrimination in connection with retirement and pensions, so in many cases the only protection will be under EC law if the discrimination amounts to unlawful discrimination in 'pay' within the meaning of Art 119.[45]

The SDA 1986 did not make it unlawful for redundancy payments to cease being payable at 60 years for women and 65 years for men. However, it is unlawful, as a result of EC law, for an employer to discriminate in either contractual[46] or statutory[47] redundancy pay. It is uncertain whether payments made by the redundancy fund on the employer's default are covered.[48] Furthermore the Employment Act 1989 amends EPCA s82(1) in respect of dismissals after 15 January 1990 to give women as well as men a redundancy entitlement up until 65 years or any earlier non-discriminatory normal retirement age.

As a result of different state pension ages, occupational pension schemes still tend to discriminate. This is not prohibited by existing UK legislation, although Art 119 will usually apply. The Social Security Act 1989, effective from 1 January 1993[49] states that occupational pension schemes must not discriminate on the ground of sex, although there are a number of exceptions.[50]

Payments made by an employer towards the state pension scheme do not fall within Art 119 as these relate to a social security scheme. However, benefits paid under a contractual occupational pension scheme, supplementary to the state scheme, constitute 'pay' under Art 119.[51] Benefits paid under a private pension scheme, contracted out of the state scheme, are also covered by Art 119 and there must be no discrimination in entitlements first accruing after 17 May 1990 – or earlier, if legal proceedings were already under way by that date.[52]

The law on pension payments and benefits is complex and undergoing rapid change. Developments need to be closely watched.

RETIREMENT: KEY POINTS

- It is unlawful sex discrimination to apply different retirement ages to men and women.

- Men and women are entitled to redundancy payments if made redundant before the age of 65.
- Men and women can claim unfair dismissal if dismissed before the age of 65 unless there is an earlier normal retirement age applicable equally to men and women.
- Men and women are entitled to equality in their occupational pension schemes.[53]

GENERAL GUIDE TO USEFUL EVIDENCE

When a woman is retired before 65 —
- Obtain documents relating to the contractual retirement age of male and female workers,[54] eg the worker's original contract, standard contracts of male and female workers and any subsequent memoranda purporting to amend the contractual retirement age.
- Evidence/statistics as to the age at which men and women in the workplace, particularly those with similar jobs to the worker, have retired in the past.

Discrimination against gay men and lesbians

Discrimination against gay workers is not in itself unlawful although the law on unfair dismissal and the RRA 1976 and SDA 1975 may sometimes afford some protection.

Unfair dismissal

There are very few reported cases above IT level concerning unfair dismissal on the ground of homosexuality. Those there are indicate a lack of understanding and – often – hostility towards gay workers. It is to be hoped that despite the AIDS hysteria which has become associated with gay men in particular, prevailing attitudes towards homosexuality will become more enlightened and in turn improve judicial attitudes. However, as with cases of unlawful discrimination on grounds of race or sex, the prime difficulty is in proving that dismissal was connected with a worker's homosexuality.

In one case,[55] the EAT upheld an IT's decision that it was fair to dismiss a woman for refusing to remove a 'Lesbians Ignite' badge at work. A similar test as to issues of dress generally was applied. It was fair to dismiss because a reasonable employer 'on mature reflection' could reasonably have decided that the badge would be offensive to customers and fellow workers. It was not necessary to wait and see whether the business was disrupted or damaged.

In another case,[56] an IT found it fair to dismiss a maintenance man from a children's camp because he was homosexual. The EAT agreed that dismissal was within the band of reasonable responses even though expert evidence had been called to the effect that homosexual men were no more likely to interfere with children than heterosexual men. The point was that there was a considerable body of popular opinion which took the contrary view, which was shared by the employer, who was entitled to dismiss regardless of whether that view had a proven foundation. The Court of Session refused to overturn the decision on the facts found and noted that the reason for dismissal was not solely for being homosexual. Presumably the Court had in mind the employer's concern about the risk to children and anxiety of parents.

Much of the existing case-law concerns dismissal of gay men for holding criminal convictions for sexual offences. Since most such offences have no heterosexual equivalent, this is a process which itself discriminates. For example, any sexual contact between two men in a place regarded by the law as public or where one is under 21 may be 'gross indecency'. Many men plead guilty in the hope of minimising publicity so as not to risk losing their jobs, when their chances of acquittal by a jury may be high. Consequently, it is important to understand the context in which such convictions occur and not to take them at face value.[57]

In one case,[58] an IT found it fair to dismiss a drama teacher of boys aged 16–19 following two convictions for gross indecency with men in public lavatories. The EAT would not accept it as self-evident that someone who behaved as the teacher did would not be a risk to teenage boys in his charge; although there was a respectable body of opinion supporting that view. It was a highly controversial subject and an employer could not be said to have acted unfairly by concluding that there was some risk in continuing to employ the teacher.

Gay men wishing to work with children have particular difficulties because organisations which work with children often have access to information about potential employees from the police and other sources. Also, certain professionals, those working with young people under 18 and employees in the courts, police or prison service, are not protected by the Rehabilitation of Offenders Act 1974 and can be dismissed for failing to reveal a 'spent' conviction.

Sex discrimination

In some cases, it may be possible to invoke the protection of the SDA 1975, which of course covers detriments other than dismissal. Under SDA 1975 s5(3), any comparison must be made in the same – or not materially different – relevant circumstances. Therefore, if a lesbian would be treated differently from a gay man, for example because of different stereotyped ideas about each group, sex discrimination may be proved.

Workers with HIV or AIDS

As with discrimination against gay men and lesbians, there is no specific legislation prohibiting discrimination against workers with AIDS or who are HIV positive. As far as possible, the ordinary unfair dismissal and race and sex discrimination provisions should be used. AIDS and HIV-related discrimination is not a difficulty which affects only gay workers.

Unfair dismissal

HIV infection is not itself usually sufficient reason to justify dismissal.[59] Where the worker becomes ill, the usual rules as to dismissals for ill health apply, including adequate consultation with doctors and the worker (see pp52–54 above). Because of the variable state of health of AIDS/HIV sufferers, proper consultation is particularly important.

In the rare event that a worker with AIDS/HIV constitutes a health risk to others, dismissal for 'some other substantial reason' may be fair, although an employer should discuss with the worker the possibility of transfer to alternative employment.

Where no health risk exists, but another worker refuses to work with someone having AIDS, dismissal may be fair but only as a last resort.[60] An IT would probably expect the employer to have made reasonable attempts at conciliation and supplied information on the transmission of AIDS in order to allay fears. If these steps fail, an employer should consider transferring one or other worker or possibly disciplining the employee refusing to work.

Where an employer dismisses someone with AIDS/HIV because of the threat of industrial action, such pressure is disregarded by the IT in determining the fairness of the dismissal.[61] If the dismissal is because of customer pressure, the employer should consult and try to allay fears. If that fails and there is nowhere else to employ the worker, dismissal will probably be fair.

HIV testing

It is probably a fundamental breach of contract (and therefore constructive dismissal) to require a worker to undergo an HIV test, even if there is a contractual right to do so, unless there is reasonable ground for suspecting that the worker is infected and that there may be a risk to the health and safety of others.[62] However, in the latter case, it is probably fair to dismiss a worker who refuses to have the test, provided that the employer has explained why the test is necessary and warned that a refusal will lead to dismissal.

It is a breach of the implied duty of trust and confidence for an employer to disclose that a worker has AIDS/HIV without the worker's consent. In rare cases, disclosure may be permitted where it is only to persons who have a real need to know and in the public interest, for example where health risks are concerned.

Discrimination

Because of the popular misconception that only gay men are likely to have AIDS/HIV, male workers may be discriminated against solely because they are homosexual (see above p121). Therefore if men are treated adversely on the basis of assumptions about who is likely to have AIDS/HIV, this is probably contrary to the SDA 1975. Similarly, if an employer refuses to recruit job applicants from central African countries or requires only such applicants to undergo HIV tests, (because AIDS is apparently more widespread in some of those countries), this is unlawful under the RRA 1976.

The difficulty is that any comparison for discrimination purposes must be in the same relevant circumstances. If the relevant circumstance is the worker's sexual orientation, then a gay man may successfully claim sex discrimination if a lesbian would not have been treated in the same way. However, if the relevant circumstance is membership of a high-risk group, the SDA 1975 may not help, as an employer might have treated a woman who was an intra-venous drug-user in the same way as s/he would have treated a gay man.

Any requirement imposed by an employer that, for example, a potential employee must not come from a high-risk group, may adversely affect men or people from certain countries and the issue will be one of justifiability.

Disability

There is no equivalent to the RRA or SDA to protect workers with disabilities. Under the 1944 and 1958 Disabled Persons (Employment) Acts, employers have limited obligations to employ a percentage of registered disabled, but there is no specific prohibition on discrimination. In practice, relatively few employers are meeting the required quota.[63] Under the Companies Act 1985, directors of a company employing on average 250 workers per week must include in their annual report a policy statement about the employment of disabled persons,[64] although such a company is under no obligation to have any specific policy beyond meeting the quota. There is a MSC *Code of Good Practice on the Employment of Disabled People*, which is not legally binding although it is backed by the TUC and the CBI.

The ordinary law of unfair dismissal applies, although a person's disability is likely to be taken into account by an IT in considering whether a dismissal is fair.

Obligations to take on registered disabled

Employers with 20 or more employees must employ registered disabled workers as 3 per cent of their workforce. The disabled worker must be employed for at least 30 hours per week, although someone working between 10 and 30 hours counts as half a worker.

It is purely voluntary for disabled persons to apply for registration on the Department of Employment's register. Applications are considered by Disablement Resettlement Officers (DROs). A person with any form of disability is eligible, but certain prescribed conditions of 'employability' must be met. Once registered, a person obtains a 'green card'. A person can be disqualified from holding a green card if s/he is in prison, a full-time in-patient or of 'habitual bad character'.[65]

Government departments and the NHS are not covered by the Disabled Persons (Employment) Act 1944, although they have voluntarily undertaken to be bound by the quota scheme. It is a criminal offence to:
- offer work to a person who is not registered disabled if the quota has not been fulfilled;
- dismiss a registered disabled worker without reasonable cause if the employer would then be below the quota; and
- fail to keep records to show whether the quota has been complied with.

Employers can apply on a 12-month basis for an exemption on the ground that the quota is too large having regard to the circumstances of employment. They can also apply for a permit to count disabled workers who are not registered.

In addition, the secretary of state can designate specific classes of employment as particularly suitable for disabled workers. So far, passenger electric lift attendants and car park attendants have been designated. Any employer of any size who gives designated employment to a person who is not registered disabled commits a criminal offence, unless the employer has obtained an exemption permit.

Obligations to provide access and facilities for disabled workers

Obligations to provide access and facilities for disabled workers are very limited. Under the Chronically Sick and Disabled Persons Act 1970,[66] factory, office and shop employers are obliged to provide access to and within premises, car parking and sanitary facilities for disabled workers, but only insofar as it is practicable and reasonable to do so.

Assistance for employers taking positive steps

The MSC Code (see above p123) has information on sources of advice, finance and services, available to employers wishing to take on disabled workers. Many of the services are provided by the Disablement Advisory Service and the DROs. One of the main functions of the latter is to put employers in touch with suitably qualified job-seekers. There are also job introduction and sheltered placement schemes. Grants can be obtained for adaptations to premises and there is financial assistance towards costs of travel to work. Special tools and equipment are available on loan.

Unfair dismissal

Under EPCA s57(3), an IT must consider whether a dismissal is fair having regard to all the circumstances. The EAT has said[67] 'If an employer knowingly takes a disabled person into his employ, he must have regard to that fact and any decision to dismiss must take fairly into account both the disability itself and the basis on which the person has been employed.' For example, in a multiple redundancy situation where selection is based on standards of work performance, an employer should specifically consider a disabled worker's individual situation.[68]

Different considerations apply where a worker becomes disabled during employment. An employer should consider what steps can be taken to enable the worker to continue in his/her existing post or any suitable alternative position. (The Disablement Advisory Service gives free help in assessing a disabled worker's capabilities and, as mentioned above, various sources of financial and other assistance are available to the willing employer.)

Whether it is fair to dismiss a worker for failure to disclose a disability at the recruitment stage depends on all the circumstances. The nature of the work and risks to the safety of the worker or others are relevant, and also whether the worker had been specifically asked about health and whether s/he deliberately misled the employer.[69]

In all dismissals concerning disabled workers, fair procedures are particularly important and similar considerations apply as with sickness dismissals (see above pp52–54).

CHAPTER NINE

Evidence in race or sex discrimination cases

The burden of proof

The standard of proof in direct and indirect discrimination cases is the normal civil standard, namely whether, on the balance of probabilities, (ie 'more likely than not'), discrimination occurred. The IT should be reminded of this at the hearing.

The 'legal' burden of proof is on the worker, who has to prove overall that discrimination happened. However, there may come a stage during the hearing when the worker has provided strong initial evidence suggesting discrimination which, if uncontradicted by the employer, will probably lead to the IT deciding that the worker's case is proved. This stage is sometimes described as when the 'evidential' – although not the 'legal' – burden of proof moves from the worker to the employer.

If and when this stage is reached, the employer's explanation becomes crucial. If the employer cannot satisfy the IT that there is an 'innocent' explanation for whatever happened, the IT should decide that there was unlawful discrimination.[1]

Thus, the following stages need to be established to prove race or sex discrimination, with the burden of proof on the worker in the first two stages:

a) Is there different or less favourable treatment (ie discrimination) of the worker than his/her comparator?

b) If so, are the circumstances consistent with the different treatment (ie discrimination) being on the ground of race or sex? (It may be sufficient simply to show the worker is of a different race or sex from the comparator.[2])

c) If stages (a) and (b) are shown (ie there is a prima facie case), the evidential burden shifts and the employer must provide an adequate explanation. If this is not done, the IT should infer unlawful race or sex discrimination.

It is often hard to know whether stages (a) and (b) have been fulfilled. For example, is it sufficient to show that a man was appointed to a post whereas a female applicant was not? Or is it necessary to show that the woman was equally or better qualified?[3] In some circumstances, statistical evidence demonstrating less favourable treatment of the racial group to which the worker belongs may suffice.[4] Even greater problems arise where there is no actual comparator. For example, a woman fails to obtain a post, but no one else has applied. How can stages (a) and (b) be answered hypothetically without determining the entire issue?

Because of these difficulties, it is often best simply to refer the IT to all pieces of evidence from which an inference of unlawful discrimination may be drawn,[5] laying particular emphasis on any inadequacies in the employer's explanation.

Even where the worker does not seem to have made out a prima facie case, the IT will usually want to hear the employer's evidence and explanation and the worker should have the opportunity of questioning the employer's witnesses.[6]

In indirect discrimination cases, the burden of proof is on the worker to show that there is a requirement or condition with discriminatory impact and which is to his or her detriment because s/he cannot comply with it. However, if the employer seeks to claim that a discriminatory requirement is justifiable, it is for the employer to prove it. Since the test of justifiability balances a requirement's discriminatory effect with the employer's needs,[7] it is unclear precisely what the employer must prove.

It seems that the employer does not need to show that s/he considered the discriminatory effect of the requirement, as it is for the IT to carry out the balancing exercise.[8] The EAT has said that the employer need only show that s/he took a 'broad and rational view'.[9]

If indirect discrimination is proved, the burden is on the employer to show it was not intentional, so that damages should not be awarded.[10]

Helpful kinds of evidence

Direct discrimination

In *Khanna*,[11] the EAT said that as direct evidence of discrimination is rarely available, the necessary evidence will 'normally consist of inferences to be drawn from the primary facts'. In other words, the IT must look for clues and draw conclusions. The concept of the IT making 'inferences' is central to running a discrimination case.

Since such an indirect approach is necessary, a wide range of evidence may seem relevant. Choosing which evidence to use in a case is important. A good case can become discredited by taking weak points. Excessive and inconclusive evidence clouds the real issues and lengthens the hearing, increasing the risk of a costs award if the claim fails (see below).

Other acts of discrimination

Every act of discrimination within the three months prior to lodging an application to the IT may form the basis of a claim. However, acts of discrimination falling outside the time limit may be mentioned in the application purely as evidence in support of the discriminatory acts founding the claim.[12] It should be made clear which acts form the basis of the claim. Earlier alleged acts of discrimination will usually be helpful only if they took place relatively recently and relate to the same managers.

Acts of discrimination or evidence of discriminatory attitudes occurring after the acts founding the claim are also admissible as supporting evidence of a tendency to discriminate.[13]

The employer's explanation

The employer's likely explanation for what has happened must be anticipated as it will have to be discredited. If, for example, a worker has clearly committed a dismissable offence or is obviously the least qualified and experienced for an appointment or promotion, then it will be extremely difficult to prove unlawful discrimination, even if it could be shown that the employer was generally prejudiced against workers of the same sex or racial group. The issue is less favourable treatment and if, for example, a man would similarly have been dismissed for the same offence, it is irrelevant that the employer was pleased to have the opportunity to dismiss a woman.

Where the alleged act of discrimination is dismissal, ITs often suspect that the case is an attempt to claim unfair dismissal for a worker without the necessary qualifying service. It must therefore be remembered that the IT is not interested in whether or not the dismissal was fair, but whether it was on the ground of race or sex. Nevertheless, in some cases it can be argued that the dismissal was so patently unfair as to be irrational unless explained by hidden grounds.

Discrimination cases are more than usually dependent on the quality of the employer's evidence at the hearing, which makes their outcome hard to predict. Much will depend on how well the employer's explanation stands up to cross-examination. Any contradiction between different witnesses for the employer or between the explanation given at the hearing and that in any contemporaneous document or in the defence or questionnaire reply may well lead the IT to infer race or sex discrimination. However, it will not usually be enough simply to discredit the employer's version of events; some other indication of unlawful discrimination may be required.

Comparative treatment

The central concept in direct discrimination is that of actual or hypothetical comparative treatment. If a worker of a different sex or racial group can be identified who, in similar circumstances, was treated more favourably, then the case will be much stronger. Other variables should also be checked because these could provide an explanation for the different treatment. They include:

- relevant experience
- relevant qualifications
- age
- marital or family status
- whether an internal or external candidate for a post
- trade union membership.

Where someone fails to gain a post after interview, despite having equal or better qualifications and experience than the person appointed, it is common for the employer to say that the successful candidate interviewed better. This is extremely difficult to contradict. All notes made by the interview panel in relation to each candidate during or after the interviews should be obtained. Also, while the interview is still fresh in his/her mind, the worker should note down the questions and answers as near verbatim as possible.

It may be relevant to know how the employer generally treats male and female workers or workers from different racial groups, in circumstances other than those of the alleged discriminatory act. It may be that an employer generally speaks more politely to white workers than to black workers, or that black workers are penalised for arriving late to work whereas white workers are not. In *West Midlands Passenger Transport Executive v Singh*,[14] the Court of Appeal said that evidence of discriminatory treatment against a group may be more indicative of unlawful discrimination than previous treatment of the particular worker, which may be due to personal factors other than discrimination. Sometimes it is appropriate, as in *Singh*, to request statistics showing comparative treatment of groups of workers.

Statistics

The *Singh* case established the potential importance of statistical evidence in cases of direct discrimination. The Court of Appeal said:

'Direct discrimination involves that an individual is not treated on his merits but receives unfavourable treatment because he is a member of a group. Statistical evidence may establish a discernible pattern in the treatment of a particular group.'[15]

Mr Singh claimed racial discrimination in his failure to gain promotion to the post of senior inspector. The Court said that if statistics revealed a regular failure of members of a certain group to gain promotion to certain jobs and an under-representation in such jobs, it may give rise to an inference of discrimination against members of the group.

If statistical evidence is not available because, for example, an employer has not monitored the workforce and applications for employment and promotion, the IT could be invited to draw an adverse inference from this fact. Unfortunately, although monitoring is recommended by the Race Relations Code of Practice and encouraged by the higher courts,[16] most ITs will not draw an inference from failure to monitor. Nevertheless, with a large employer and particularly a public authority, it may be worth citing at the hearing the numerous public bodies who do now monitor,[17] so that it is clear that the particular employer is acting unusually.

Failure to follow the Codes of Practice

The Codes of Practice are admissible in evidence and, under RRA 1976 s47(10) and SDA 1975 s56A(10), an IT can take into account relevant provisions of the codes in determining any question in the proceedings.

The codes make recommendations on good practice in recruitment and promotion procedures. In cases concerning discrimination in these areas, the employer's procedures should be examined to see whether the guidelines of the Codes have been followed. The Court of Appeal has expressly referred to the importance of paragraph 1.13 of the Race Relations Code of Practice.[18] Questions in the questionnaire (see p163) and requests for discovery (see p168) should be aimed at establishing what procedures were adopted and these will be a matter for cross-examination at the hearing.

The Commission for Racial Equality's Code of Practice encourages record-keeping by employers and paragraphs 1.22 and 1.23 recommend that in any disciplinary matter, the employer should consider the possible effect on a worker's behaviour of racial abuse or other racial provocation. Furthermore, any complaint of racial discrimination by a worker should not be treated lightly. The IT's attention should be drawn to those provisions, where the worker has complained of discrimination at some stage during his/her employment, including the final disciplinary hearing, and has been ignored.

Racist remarks/overt indications of prejudice

Although prejudice need not be present to prove discrimination, it strengthens the case if it is demonstrably present. Difficulties often arise because it is only the worker's word and s/he can be accused of making up such remarks while giving evidence. It is therefore important that any crucial remarks are mentioned in the IT1 form from the start.

Another difficulty is that certain words, 'jokes' or actions may not be taken as indicative of a racist or sexist attitude by the IT. Even if they are, a tribunal will not automatically conclude that prejudiced attitudes lead to discriminatory treatment.[19] In an appointment or promotion case, an employer's comment that someone 'who would fit in' was wanted should be regarded as a danger signal.[20] In certain cases, racist comments may themselves constitute one of the acts of discrimination basing the claim (see p113 above).

Previous complaints of discrimination

Recorded previous complaints of unlawful discrimination against relevant managers should constitute useful evidence, particularly if the employer has failed to investigate such allegations (see p130).

There are many and obvious reasons why a worker may not complain of discriminaton while still employed. Nevertheless, a worker who alleges that discrimination has been occurring for some time is likely to be heavily cross-examined as to why s/he did not complain at the time, and should be prepared to answer this question at the hearing.

Where a worker, during employment, seeks advice in respect of discrimination, proceedings will usually be regarded as a last resort. However, s/he should be advised of the risks of not registering the allegation in writing, should some issue of discrimination ultimately end up in the IT. According to the circumstances, the worker could make a formal complaint under the grievance procedure or write a low-key letter just putting the matter on record. If appropriate, the employer's attention could be expressly drawn to the prohibition on victimisation under RRA 1976 s2 or SDA 1975 s4.

Failure to respond to the questionnaire

Under RRA 1976 s65(2)(b) and SDA 1975 s74(2)(b), if the employer 'deliberately and without reasonable excuse' fails to answer the questionnaire within a reasonable time or answers in a way that is 'evasive or equivocal',[21] the IT may draw an inference that the employer committed an unlawful act of discrimination. So far, ITs have been slow to draw such inferences, although the EAT has encouraged the use of the questionnaire procedure.[22] It should be borne in mind when drafting the questionnaire, that it should not be so onerous that an employer has a 'reasonable excuse' for not answering (see p163).

Indirect discrimination

Proportions who can comply

The necessary comparison under RRA 1976 s1(1)(b)(i) and SDA 1975 s1(1)(b)(i) will almost invariably require statistical evidence. The IT can take account of its own knowledge and experience in determining whether a requirement or condition has disparate impact[23] and it is often undesirable to present elaborate statistical evidence.

It is well-established that determining the correct pool for comparison of the proportions of people of different sexes or racial groups who can comply with a requirement is a question of fact for the IT.

It may choose a pool not anticipated by the worker and catch him/her unprepared. It may be possible to avoid this difficulty by agreeing a pool with the employer prior to the hearing, by holding a preliminary hearing on the point or even adjourning the main hearing once the pool is decided if the necessary statistics are not available. However, it is wise to prepare statistics on all the potential pools.

Clearly some pools will be more helpful than others and less helpful pools which the IT might choose should therefore be anticipated with, if possible, explanations as to why they are misleading or irrelevant, for example because they incorporate discrimination.

Justifiablity

Although the onus is on the employer to justify a condition or requirement, it seems that s/he is not required to produce evidence of its discriminatory effect, or at least no detailed statistical evidence.[24] The worker should, therefore, be prepared to supply such evidence. The type of evidence will be similar to that used to show the lesser proportion of women etc who could comply with the requirement at the relevant date.

Furthermore, the employer is under no obligation to prove that there is no other possible way of achieving his/her objective. If the worker thinks that there are reasonable alternative requirements with less discriminatory effect, s/he must put forward the suggestion and supporting evidence.[25]

PART IV: REMEDIES

CHAPTER TEN

Unfair dismissal remedies

An IT, having found that a worker has been unfairly dismissed, must first consider making an order for reinstatement, and if reinstatement is not practicable, an order for re-engagement. If neither of the re-employment orders is practicable or desired by the worker, the IT will make an award of compensation.

It was envisaged when ITs were first introduced that the re-employment orders would be the primary remedy. It is however rare after the conclusion of an IT hearing for the parties to want to work with each other again, making re-employment orders rare.[1] It is not unusual when workers win, that the IT has decided either that the employer has lied or that s/he has treated the worker in a callous and/or arbitrary fashion. Such a public finding is hardly conducive to the re-commencement of the employment relationship.

Reinstatement

Reinstatement is where the IT orders that the worker returns to his/her old job, whereas re-engagement is where the worker returns to a similar job either with the employer or an associated employer.

The IT is under a statutory duty to ask the worker after the hearing whether s/he wants to be reinstated even if no mention of it was made on the IT1 form (the application to the tribunal). As will be noted from the sample IT1 forms, both reinstatement and compensation should be requested as an employer might be able to avoid an order for reinstatement if the worker does not put the employer on notice of this desire (see below).

When making a reinstatement order the IT decides the date when the worker will return to work, the amount of the missing wages and benefit that the employer must pay for the period between dismissal and reinstatement, including restoring any rights that the worker would have acquired during the period of absence.[2] The terms of employment cannot be less favourable then those previously enjoyed.[3]

Whether it is practicable involves the consideration of a number of issues. The factors which the IT must consider are: the worker's wish to be reinstated, whether it is practicable for the employer to comply with the order (the job may no longer exist), and whether the worker caused or contributed to some extent to the dismissal.[4] The IT must not take into consideration the fact that the employer has employed a permanent replacement unless the worker has delayed in putting the employer on notice that s/he wanted to be reinstated, or if it was not practicable for the employer to have the work carried out on a temporary basis.[5]

The IT must consider each case on its own merits, and decide whether such an order is capable of being put into effect with success.[6] Factors that should be taken into account include whether the reinstatement of the worker is going to cause problems with the other workers, the size of the employer,[7] and the workability of such an order.[8] ITs are encouraged to adopt a common sense approach and to avoid treating it as a techincal exercise.

Finally, the IT must consider whether the worker has to some extent caused or contributed to his/her dismissal and, if s/he has, whether it is just to make an order for reinstatement.[9] It might be that, although the dismissal was unfair, subsequent information implicated the worker or demonstrated that there had been a degree of contributory fault.[10] The IT in the circumstances can refuse to make an order for reinstatement although it may make a re-engagement order instead if it would be just to do so.

Re-engagement

Re-engagement is where the worker returns to a similiar job either with the employer, a successor or an associated employer on such terms as the IT may decide,[11] being comparable or suitable employment.[12]

The IT must, in making a re-engagement order, state the identity of the employer, the nature of the employment (including any rights or privileges which must be restored), the rate of pay, and the amount of the arrears of pay and loss of other benefits for the period when the worker was not employed by the employer.

In deciding whether to make an order for re-engagement, the IT must again take into consideration the worker's wishes, the practicability of such an order, contributory fault, whether it is just to make an order and, if so, on what terms.[13] The statutory provisions entitle the worker to put forward his/her own views as to the terms of the order and the investigation by the IT is thereby made more flexible and conciliatory than with reinstatement.

Compensation

Compensation consists of two elements, the basic award and the compensatory award. If the employer fails to comply with a reinstatement or re-engagement order, the IT can make an 'additional' award. If the dismissal relates to trade union membership a 'special' award is made.

The basic award and redundancy payment

The basic award was introduced to compensate workers for the loss of job security following dismissal.[14] It has been described as the 'paid-up insurance policy' against redundancy. The basic award is calculated broadly in the same way as a redundancy payment. The only difference between them is that the redundancy payment does not recognise any service below the age of 18, and in the final year before retirement the redundancy payment is reduced by 1/12th for each completed month.

The basic award is calculated by reference to the period ending with the effective date of termination (see p41 above) during which the worker has been continuously employed and allows for one and a half weeks' pay for each year of employment in which the worker was not below the age of 41, one week's pay for each year of employment when the worker was not below the age of 22, and half a week's pay for each year of employment below the age of 22. A maximum of 20 years' employment will be counted. A table allows easy assessment of the number of weeks of entitlement.

A week's pay is subject to a maximum figure which increases each year. The figure is presently £198.[15] If there are fixed working hours, a week's pay is the amount payable by the employer under the contract of employment. If the worker's pay varies with the amount of work done ('piece rate') the amount of a week's pay is calculated by reference to the average hourly rate of pay over the last 12 weeks of employment, and where there are no normal hours, a week's pay will be the average weekly pay over the last 12 weeks of employment. The basic award may be reduced if the worker:
- behaved before the dismissal or before the notice was given in such a way that it would be just and equitable to do so;[16]

- received a redundancy payment whether paid under statute or otherwise;[17]
- received an ex gratia payment which is expressly or impliedly referrable to the basic award;[18]
- unreasonably refused an offer of reinstatement, in which case the IT will reduce the basic award by such amount as it considers just and equitable;[19] or
- is 64, in which case the basic award is reduced by 1/12th for each completed month of employment during that year. Workers who are 65 or more are not entitled to a basic award.[20]

A worker dismissed for trade union membership or activity is entitled to a basic award of not less than £2,650, (April 1991) before any reduction is made. This figure is increased usually each April.[21]

The compensatory award

The compensatory award recompenses the worker for the financial loss suffered as a result of being dismissed, including expenses incurred and loss of benefits.[22]

Although ITs enjoy wide discretionary powers, it has been made clear that the object is to compensate fully, but not to award a bonus.[23] The IT has a duty to consider five different elements of the compensatory award.[24]

Loss of wages

Loss of wages is calculated from the effective date of termination (see p150) until the hearing date and is calculated net of tax and national insurance contributions. It consists of the amount the worker would have earned, including regular overtime and bonuses.[25] However, if the employer can show that such overtime has diminished or ceased, the award will be reduced.[26] Where the worker was dismissed without notice or payment in lieu of notice, s/he will be awarded the net wages to which s/he would have been entitled during the notice period less any net earnings from a new job.[27]

The manner of dismissal

Although the loss must be pecuniary (hurt feelings are thus excluded) it has been held that if the manner of dismissal causes emotional upset to the worker so that s/he will take longer to find a new job, this loss may be included in the compensatory award.[28]

Future loss of earnings

The worker must provide evidence of his/her likely future loss. The IT will estimate how long it thinks the worker will remain unemployed as a result of the dismissal and how much the worker would have earned had s/he remained in the old job. If the worker has obtained a new job at a lower rate of pay, the IT will estimate how long s/he is likely to be earning less, and award the difference.

If the worker has not found a new job, the IT, in assessing how long s/he is likely to remain unemployed, will take into consideration the worker's age[29] and personal characteristics,[30] the availability of work in the locality,[31] and the likely duration of the lost job.[32] Owing to the speculative nature of this part of the award, it is important to present compelling and persuasive evidence; this should include the opinion of the local job centre or other job agencies and the efforts made to secure employment.

In assessing what the worker would be earning, the IT must take account of anticipatory increases, including anticipated overtime increases.[33] The award will be greater where the increase is certain rather than probable. Backdated pay increases may be included in the compensatory award.[34]

Loss of benefits

The compensatory award includes loss of benefits in respect of both the immediate and the future loss period. The following have been taken into consideration by ITs:
- entitlement to holiday pay;[35]
- tips or other gratuitous payments which would have been earned during the compensatory period;[36]
- the loss of a company car which is assessed by reference to the AA annual guidelines;[37]
- cheap loans (ie the value in comparison with bank loans);[38]
- accommodation if it is free or subsidised;[39] and
- medical insurance which is assessed by reference to the cost to the worker of acquiring the same medical protection.[40]

Loss of statutory rights

Loss of long notice entitlement, maternity rights, and the right to claim unfair dismissal should be reflected in the compensatory award. The loss of right to claim unfair dismissal is worth £100[41] and the loss of long notice entitlement is based on a figure of half of the entitlement to statutory notice calculated as a net sum.[42]

Loss of pension rights

This is by far the hardest to quantify but at the same time can be the most valuable. In order to attach a realistic value to the loss of pension rights there have been a number of guideline documents. The ITs, for a number of years, have used the government's Actuary Department guidelines which were first produced in 1980 and revised in 1989.[43] There have been two recent guidelines which are now being applied. The most relevant has been drawn up by a committee of IT chairs and is entitled *Compensation for Loss of Pension Rights*. As with all guidelines, it is speculative and so the ITs have been encouraged to adopt a 'broad brush' approach when assessing loss of pension rights. As long as one of the guidelines has been followed, this will normally be sufficient.

Reduction of the award

The compensatory award can be reduced on account of contributory fault if the worker's conduct was culpable or blameworthy.[44] The decision to reduce the award and the degree of contribution is discretionary and can be challenged only if it is perverse.

If the dismissal was unfair due to the employer's failure to comply with the procedural requirements but s/he can demonstrate at the hearing that a reasonable employer would have dismissed the worker after following the appropriate procedure, the compensatory award can be reduced to a few weeks' pay to reflect the period that the procedural requirements would have taken to perform.[44A]

The award can be further reduced if the worker has failed to mitigate his/her losses, eg by getting a new job. In applying this rule the IT must identify what steps should have been taken, the date when they should have been taken and the likely consequence. If a consequence is a lower wage, the IT will award the difference.[45]

Any sum paid as an ex gratia sum or in excess of the statutory redundancy payment will be off-set against the compensatory award.[46]

The maximum compensatory award is presently £10,000 (April 1991). This figure is applied after the calculation of the compensatory award including any deduction for contributory fault – not *before* any such reduction was made.[47]

The special award

If the worker is dismissed because of union membership, for taking part in a trade union activity, or is selected for redundancy because of union membership or because of a refusal to join a union, then there is an automatically unfair dismissal and a special award will be made of 104 weeks' pay without an upper limit to a week's pay and must be not less than £13,180 and not more than £26,290.[48] If the worker seeks a re-employment order and the employer refuses to comply with it although it is practicable to do so, the special award is 156 weeks' pay, without any upper limit to a week's pay and must not be less that £19,735.

The award will be reduced if the worker's conduct before the dismissal was such that it would be just and equitable, if the worker prevented a re-employment order being complied with, or if s/he refused an offer of re-employment.[49] If the basic award was reduced on the ground of age (the year of retirement), the special award will be reduced by the same proportion.[50]

The worker must have applied for a re-employment order in order to receive a special award.[51]

The additional award

If a re-employment order is made and the employer fails to comply with it either entirely or partially, the IT must make an additional award unless the employer can satisfy the IT that it was not practicable to comply. Where the dismissal is an act of discrimination the award will be between 26 and 52 weeks' pay. In all other cases it will be between 13 and 26 weeks' pay subject to a maximum of £198 a week (April 1991). Thus, in discrimination cases the additional award is between £5,148 and £10,296 and in all other cases between £2,574 and £5,148 (April 1991).

Recoupment

If the IT makes a compensatory award, it must deduct unemployment benefit and income support (the regulations still refer to supplementary benefit) from the compensatory award.[52] The Department of Employment is notified by the IT as to the award made, and the department will serve on the employer a recoupment notice detailing the state benefits paid. The employer pays this sum to the department and the balance is paid to the worker. However, if the case is settled before the hearing, the recoupment provisions do not apply. It is therefore in the interests of both parties to settle and to reach an agreement as to compensation, bearing in mind that there will no recoupment on this settlement. However, be careful that the settlement is for a single figure and does not itemise the specific claims that are being settled such as notice pay, holiday pay, wages etc as the recoupment provisions would then apply.

CHAPTER ELEVEN

Race and sex discrimination remedies

When an IT has made a finding of unlawful discrimination, it may make such of the following as it considers just and equitable:[1]
- a declaration of the rights of the parties in respect of the matter to which the complaint related;
- a recommendation;
- an order for compensation, except for unintentional indirect discrimination.[2]

Recommendations

The IT may recommend that, within a specified period of time, the employer take action to obviate or reduce the adverse effect of the act of discrimination proved.[3] If 'without reasonable justification' the employer fails to comply with the recommendation, the IT can award compensation or additional compensation, save where the act concerned was unintentional indirect discrimination.[4] The IT cannot insist on a recommendation being carried out.

Examples of recommendations are that the employer makes a full written apology to the worker, that s/he removes discriminatory documents, warnings, adverse reports etc from the worker's personnel file, or that s/he notes on it that the worker has been discriminated against previously.

It seems that the IT is hampered in what it can recommend. In *Noone v North West Thames Regional Health Authority (No 2)*,[5] the IT recommended that if another post of consultant microbiologist became available, the health authority should seek the secretary of state's permission to dispense with the normal NHS advertising requirements and offer the post to Dr Noone. The CA rescinded the recommendation because it undermined fair recruitment procedures to the detriment of the

NHS, the professions concerned with it, the public and would-be applicants for the post.

Two other recommendations proposed by the health authority were substituted. These were that the health authority draw to the attention of any future appointments committee considering an application by Dr Noone the provisions of the RRA 1976 and remind them that Dr Noone's previous application had failed on the ground of race. It is unclear whether the Court of Appeal was particularly persuaded by the status of the NHS and its regulations on appointments or whether an IT cannot make any recommendation that a worker be appointed to the next suitable vacancy.[6]

Note that the IT cannot make general recommendations as to good practice in the workplace, for example that an equal opportunities policy is introduced or that there is monitoring or training of staff. Neither can it recommend a pay rise as this should be covered by an award of compensation.

Sometimes settlement can be negotiated as to action which an employer is willing to undertake. Not only will this not be subject to the above limitations, but it will also be enforceable.

The award of compensation

If the IT orders compensation, it must do so on the basis of what could be ordered by a county court,[7] ie the ordinary measure of damages payable in tort. Although the IT may select which of the three remedies it orders, according to what is 'just and equitable', any financial award it chooses to make must not be limited by such considerations.[8] An award of compensation should therefore comprise all reasonably foreseeable loss arising from the act of discrimination including past and future loss of earnings, loss of opportunity and injury to feelings.[9]

Loss of earnings may be claimed where the discrimination is dismissal or refusal to promote to a higher paid post. Where a candidate is not short-listed for interview, an IT may award compensation representing loss of opportunity, so that the potential loss of earnings will be reduced by a percentage representing the likelihood of the candidate actually obtaining the job had s/he not been discriminated against.

Financial limit

The total award is subject to the same financial limit as the current limit for the compensatory award in unfair dismissal.[10] An IT held that the statutory maximum does not apply in cases of sex discrimination to state employees where it is an inadequate remedy contrary to EC law, but this has been overturned by the Court of Appeal.[11]

Where several acts of discrimination are proved, each will attract a separate award, so that the total may exceed the maximum. However, where the act of discrimination is dismissal or occurred on grounds of both race and sex, the total compensation under the RRA 1976, SDA 1975 or EPCA 1978 (compensatory award) can not exceed the compensatory award for unfair dismissal.[12] Where the act of discrimination also amounts to unfair dismissal, the basic and additional awards apply as normal, except that the latter will be between 26 and 52 weeks' pay.

Injury to feelings

Until 1988, the average award for injury to feelings was extremely low. Two major decisions of the Court of Appeal in that year established that the proper range of awards should lie between £500 and £3,000. It is important to remember that both awards were made in the light of the ceilings on the compensatory award applicable at that time.

In *Alexander v The Home Office*,[13] a West Indian prisoner was deprived of work in the prison kitchen on the ground of his race. The Court of Appeal increased the county court judge's award from £50 to £500, saying that:

'For the injury to feelings, however, for the humiliation, for the insult, it is impossible to say what is restitution and the answer must depend on the experience and good sense of the judge and his assessors. Awards should not be minimal, because this would tend to trivialise or diminish respect for the public policy to which the Act gives effect. On the other hand . . . to award sums which are generally felt to be excessive does almost as much harm.'[14]

Since the Court of Appeal relied on the judge's finding that Mr Alexander 'had not suffered any substantial injury to his feelings', £500 should be regarded as the minimum appropriate award for injury to feelings.

In *Noone v North West Thames Regional Health Authority*,[15] the Court of Appeal accepted that Dr Noone suffered 'severe injury to her feelings' in failing to obtain a consultant post. Nevertheless, it considered the IT's award of £5,000 as too high in relation to the compensatory award ceiling of £7,500 at that time and substituted an award of £3,000 for injury to feelings.

Aggravated and exemplary damages

The Court of Appeal in *Alexander* suggested that aggravated and exemplary damages may be awarded in addition to the injury to feelings award.[16] Aggravated damages are additional compensation for injury to feelings where a worker's sense of injury is 'justifiably heightened by the manner in which or motive for which' the employer did the wrongful act. Exemplary damages do not relate to the worker's loss or injury, but are solely punitive for the employer's 'anti-social behaviour'.

Exemplary damages can be awarded only in rare circumstances,[17] eg where central or local government powers were exercised in the act of discrimination or where the employer calculated that it was cheaper to discriminate than not to. Where the employer has behaved particularly badly, this is likely to affect the degree of injury to feelings. Indeed in *Alexander*, the Court of Appeal said:

'even where exemplary or punitive damages are not sought, nevertheless compensatory damages may and in some cases should include an element of aggravated damages where, for example, the defendant may have behaved in a high-handed, malicious, insulting or oppressive manner in committing the act of discrimination'.

Discrimination involving sexual harassment is particularly likely to attract an award of aggravated damages,[18] although the ITs have awarded compensation under this head in a range of circumstances. The employer's manner of conducting a case including the hearing also is relevant.

Tribunal practice in making awards for injury to feelings has varied over the last few years. Sometimes umbrella awards are made for injury to feelings generally. At other times, awards have been divided between injury to feelings and aggravated damages. Since *Noone*, there have been several awards of more than £3,000. Awards for victimisation, although increasing, still tend to be low.

Indirect discrimination

No award of compensation may be made in respect of indirect discrimination if the employer proves that the requirement or condition was not applied with the intention of treating the worker unfavourably on grounds of race, sex or marital status.[19] The necessary nature of the employer's intention is unclear, especially given the case-law on what must be shown by way of 'intention' in order to prove direct discrimination.

In *Orphanos v Queen Mary College*,[20] the House of Lords made no award of compensation because, although there was an intention to discriminate against non-EC residents, there was no intention to discriminate on racial grounds. This would seem to indicate that it is not enough to show that an employer intends to treat men and women or people of different racial groups differently, but that s/he intends to do so on the ground of race or sex, ie that s/he has a discriminatory motive. *Orphanos* seems to work on the assumption that damages are always payable in direct discrimination because direct discrimination necessarily entails a bad motive. Following *R v Birmingham* and *James v Eastleigh BC* (see p92 above), *Orphanos* may be wrong.

Costs

Costs may be awarded against either party on the same basis as in unfair dismissal actions. However, costs are far more frequently awarded against unsuccessful workers in discrimination cases than against unsuccessful employers, even though it must almost always be unreasonable for an employer to defend proceedings where s/he has knowingly discriminated and certainly in cases of sexual harassment. Costs may also be awarded against individual respondents.[21]

CHAPTER TWELVE

Running an unfair dismissal case

Preliminary steps

At the outset it should be established what the worker wants to achieve. If the worker wants the job back or a good reference or payment of outstanding wages, holiday or notice pay, the worst thing to do is to start unfair dismissal proceedings. Nothing is more likely to annoy the employer.

If the priority is to get the worker's job back, negotiations with the employer should start immediately, possibly with the intervention of an ACAS conciliation officer[1] or some other party, eg another worker. The greater the delay in starting negotiations, the less likelihood of success.

If a worker simply wants a good written reference or payment of money owed, a telephone call or polite letter should be the first step. Only if the employer refuses should the worker threaten IT proceedings.

As soon as a worker comes for advice, the adviser should work out and diarise the last day for lodging an originating application (IT1). The worker should also make a note. Once IT proceedings are started, they move very quickly. It can take as little as two months from the date the IT1 is lodged to the hearing. If information and documents need to be gathered, this must be started immediately. All time limits and dates for chasing up requests made to the employer should be scheduled.

Collecting information before lodging the IT1

Before starting the claim, the adviser should get all relevant documents in the worker's possession, eg a statement of the main terms and conditions of employment and/or contract of employment, staff handbook, works rules, letter of appointment, letter of dismissal, P45 (which should state the last date worked), pay slips, warning letters and appraisal reports. There may well be other relevant documents.

It is very important to obtain all documents which may form the 147 employment contract (see p1 above). If the worker signed any statement, document or letter during employment, it is essential to see this prior to lodging the IT1 if at all possible. Employers get workers to sign statements only if they contain terms favourable to the employer, eg a mobility clause (the right to move the worker to another workplace) or a flexibility clause (the right to alter a worker's hours or shifts).

The terms of the contract will be particularly vital in relation to a constructive dismissal claim (see p43 above), where the worker must show a significant and fundamental breach of contract. If, eg, the worker relies on a change of workplace as such a breach but the contract contains a mobility clause, there will be no breach of contract and the claim will fail.

Once all the worker's documents are gathered, the adviser should take a full statement of all the material facts, concentrating on the reason for dismissal and the events immediately preceeding it. The final disciplinary hearing leading to dismissal is usually very important and the worker should write a near verbatim account while his/her memory is relatively fresh.

Probe the worker on the statement, particularly on the weaknesses. The names and addresses of possible witnesses to significant incidents and in relation to any warnings should be collected. It is usually easier to establish names and addresses at an early stage than months later when a witness order is needed.

The worker should sign and date the statement and keep a copy. It should be explained that the statement is only for private use as the adviser's working document. However, if the worker has a complete mental block at the IT, in some circumstances this statement may be produced. The statement is also useful when negotiating, as an understanding of the facts, and thereby the issues, allows negotiation from a position of strength.

Written reasons for the dismissal – EPCA s53

Before starting the claim, the worker should write to the employer requesting written reasons for the dismissal and copies of relevant documents which the worker does not have. When a worker has no contractual documents, it is sometimes uncertain whether any exist. The employer should therefore be asked at least for a statement of the main terms and conditions of employment which ought to have been given to the worker.

The first letter to the employer is important. As well as requesting information which will be instrumental in the conduct of the case and its final outcome, it creates an initial impression on the employer which may encourage settlement later on.

Every worker who qualifies to claim unfair dismissal is also entitled to receive on request an adequate and truthful statement of the reasons for dismissal.[2] The employer must supply the reasons within 14 days of the worker's request. In order to prove that a request was made, it is best to make it in writing and send it recorded delivery.

If the employer unreasonably refuses to supply written reasons within 14 days or supplies reasons which are inadequate or untrue, the worker is entitled to compensation of two weeks' gross pay.[3] There is no ceiling to this figure. An employer who fails to supply reasons within 14 days due to a genuine oversight, but supplies them when s/he realises the oversight will not be held to have unreasonably refused.[4] It is not enough for an employer to acknowledge the request within the 14 days and supply reasons later unless, for example, the person taking the decision to dismiss was on holiday.

The written reasons must be adequate so that it is clear to the worker and to anyone else why the worker was dismissed and which of the potentially fair reasons under EPCA s57 (see chapter 4) the employer relies on.[5]

The purpose of the right is to make the employer state truthfully the reason for dismissal. Any statement given by the employer is admissible in unfair dismissal proceedings and will be important in determining the fairness of the dismissal.[6] In deciding whether to award compensation under EPCA s53, the IT is not concerned as to whether the reasons given were intrinsically good or bad.[7] If the reason was bad, the dismissal will be unfair, but there will be no award under s53.

The time limit for a claim for failure to supply adequate and true reasons is the same as for unfair dismissal. Even if reasons are supplied within 14 days, a s53 claim should always be added to the unfair dismissal claim. One can never be sure what will emerge during the unfair dismissal hearing as to the truth of the reasons given.

The originating application (IT1)

The time limit for lodging an unfair dismissal claim is within three months from dismissal, which is far shorter than that for any other civil claim. The time limit is strictly enforced with an extension only in exceptional circumstances.

The period of three calendar months runs from the effective date of termination (EDT). If the EDT is 20 May, the claim must be presented on or before midnight on 19 August.[8] For time-limit purposes, the EDT means:

- when the contract is terminated by notice, the date that the notice expires;[9]
- when the contract is terminated without notice, the date on which termination takes effect.[10] With a summary dismissal for gross misconduct, this will be the last day worked. However, where there is no gross misconduct and notice is required, if the employer pays money in lieu of notice, the EDT can be ambiguous. Either the employer has terminated the contract of employment with immediate effect and paid in lieu of notice, or the employer has terminated the contract as from the end of the notice period, but does not require the worker to attend work in the interim.[11] The dismissal letter may indicate which is the case. Usually when the employer pays in lieu of notice, the EDT is the last day actually worked[12] and it is safest when calculating time limits to work from this date.

A useful rule of thumb is to present the claim within three months of the last day actually worked. By doing this, the claim will always be in time.

Late application

Exceptionally, the IT will admit a late claim provided it was not reasonably practicable to present the claim in time, and it was presented within such further period as the IT considers reasonable.[13] It is for the worker to show that it was not reasonably practicable to present the claim in time.[14] Ignorance of the law or of facts will be an acceptable excuse only if, tested objectively, 'a reasonable worker' would not be expected to know of the law[15] or be put on enquiry because of the facts.[16] It is getting increasingly difficult to make claims out of time.

If the worker is pursuing an internal appeal s/he must still lodge the claim in time, even if the internal appeal is still unresolved.

It is no defence that the worker's adviser, whether legally qualified or not, failed to tell the worker the time limit. The worker's remedy is then against the adviser for negligence. This is so whether the adviser is a solicitor,[17] trade unionist[18] or Citizens Advice Bureau worker.[19]

Even if the worker shows that it was not reasonably practicable to present the claim in time, s/he must do so within a further reasonable period. The worker must act promptly once s/he discovers that the claim is out of time.[20]

Presentation of the IT1

The IT1 should be sent to the Central Office of the Industrial Tribunals at the address on the IT1 form. It should be addressed to the Secretary to the Industrial Tribunals. In an emergency, when it is necessary to deliver the IT1 by hand on the last day, it can be presented to any regional office.[21] It is permissible to fax a claim to the IT in an emergency. A list can be obtained from the Department of Employment. The Central Office will allocate the claim to the appropriate regional office. Future correspondence will be with the regional office and addressed to the Assistant Secretary to the Industrial Tribunal.

Drafting the IT1

IT1 forms can be obtained from the Department of Employment, job centres and most advice centres. The IT1 form need not be used for the originating application as long as all the necessary information is contained in a letter or statement namely:

- the worker's name and address. The worker is called the 'Applicant';
- the employer's name and address. The employer is called the 'Respondent'; and
- the grounds of the application and particulars of the relief sought. The worker must state why s/he thinks s/he has been unfairly dismissed. An extensive statement is not necessary as long as sufficient detail is given for the employer to resist the claim.[22]

It is important to remember that the IT1 will be the first document read by IT members before the hearing starts and will give them an important early impression of the merits of the case which can be difficult to shake afterwards. It is therefore foolish to write only a very brief statement. The IT1 should state fully all the material facts (without going into laborious detail) and attach copies of any documents which the worker would like the members to note at the outset. If there are obvious weaknesses in the case, they cannot be hidden and it is best to refer to them in the IT1 and offer as convincing an explanation as possible.

It is unnecessary to refer to the law in the IT1, but it helps when completing the form to bear in mind the relevant law and therefore what issues are relevant or irrelevant. For example, if the employer is a large company, this should be stated in the IT1, since the tribunal must consider fairness in the light of the employer's size and administrative resources (see p47 above). If the employer is small, this will not help the worker and should not be mentioned in the IT1.

It is best to complete the IT1 bearing in mind what the employer must do for a dismissal to be fair. The worker can then draw attention to what the employer ought to have done but did not. For example, in a conduct case, it is of little assistance to focus on the worker's innocence of the misconduct or to refer to matters occurring after dismissal, eg the police's decision to drop charges. What is relevant is the employer's genuine and reasonable belief at the time of dismissal and reasonable investigations into the worker's guilt. The IT1 should focus on these points.

The employer's defence (IT3)

The Central Office of Industrial Tribunals sends the employer a copy of the IT1 and s/he replies, usually on an IT3 form. The employer must indicate whether s/he intends to resist the claim and if so, on what grounds.[23] The employer must prove that dismissal was for one of the potentially fair reasons and that it actually was fair to dismiss for that reason.[24] The employer must give sufficient particulars of the grounds for the defence[25] and if no grounds are set out in the IT3, a letter should be written to the IT pointing this out.

The IT3 should be supplied by the employer within 14 days of receiving the copy IT1, but the late submission of an IT3 does not affect the IT's jurisdiction. In practice therefore, the time limit is very loosely enforced. An employer will not be allowed to defend the action if s/he has submitted no IT3 by the time of the hearing. If an employer first produces an IT3 at the hearing itself or very shortly before, the IT has a discretion whether to allow it in. Quite often the tribunal will give leave for the late IT3 but grant an adjournment of the hearing, ordering the employer to pay the worker the wasted costs caused by the late adjournment.

When the IT3 is received, all the information in it should be checked, listing what points are not accepted. For example, it may be necessary to get another worker to give evidence on length of service, or bank statements to prove wages, if these are in dispute. If the employer's reasons for justifying the dismissal are vague or unclear, it may be wise to ask for more particulars and for relevant documents.

Interlocutory matters

Further and better particulars of the IT3

The IT can order the worker and employer to supply further and better particulars of the IT1 or IT3 respectively.[26] The IT can make an order on its own initiative or at the request of either party.

If further particulars of the IT3 are wanted, a letter should be written to the employer asking for these within a specified time limit, usually 14 days. It is a good idea to send a copy of the letter to the IT in case the employer later denies having received it. If the employer fails to comply with the request, the IT should be asked, in writing, for an order.[27] The employer should always be asked to supply the particulars voluntarily first.[28]

The IT will usually order the employer to supply some or all of the requested particulars within a further time limit. If the employer fails to comply with the order, the IT should be informed. It has power to strike out all or part of the IT3, which will prevent the employer from defending the claim or the relevant part of the claim.[29]

All that can be asked for is more details or 'particulars' of the employer's defence as set out in the IT3.[30] Completely unrelated questions cannot be asked, as they can in a questionnaire under the RRA or SDA (see pp162–165 below). Clarification on essential points should always be requested, in order to be fully prepared. For example, if previous warnings are mentioned, ask for details as to what they related to and when they were given.

A request for an order will be considered by the duty chair at the IT. The IT tends to be very reluctant to order particulars and frequently amends the request. So the temptation to ask for too many particulars should be avoided unless it is necessary because of the vagueness of the IT3. An IT's refusal to make an order is not appealable unless the worker's case is clearly prejudiced.

Discovery

'Discovery' is the method by which the worker can obtain documents which are in the employer's possession. Strictly speaking, an order for discovery only obliges the employer to produce a list of the requested documents. This is combined with an order for inspection, which allows the documents to be seen and copies taken at the worker's expense. In practice, the IT often simply asks the employer to send copies to the worker. This is useful as it saves copying costs and the employer can always be asked to bring the originals to the hearing. You should note that the IT does not in fact have the power to order that copies be sent.

The same process should be adopted in seeking discovery as for further and better particulars. Indeed, particulars and discovery are usually requested in the same letter.[31] Only when the employer does not comply with a voluntary request should an order be sought. An employer's failure to comply with the IT's order will be treated in the same way as failure to supply ordered particulars.

Which documents?

All courts prefer documents to witnesses and the IT is no exception. Cases are often won or lost on the strength of the documents before the IT and it is essential that all relevant documents are available at the hearing.

Unlike with most civil litigation, the parties are under no general duty to produce all relevant documents in their possession. An adviser must therefore specifically ask for what s/he wants and thinks that the employer has. The employer does not have to produce documents which will help a worker's case unless withholding certain documents in the light of a specific request would mislead the worker as to whether they existed.[32]

The IT is readier to order discovery than particulars although it will not allow wide-ranging and speculative requests. The test is whether the documents are relevant for the fair disposal of the case or in order to save costs.[33] A document is relevant if it advances the worker's case or damages the employer's case.[34] The case-law on what documents are relevant is particularly developed in relation to discrimination cases (see p168 below).

In unfair dismissal cases it is usually relevant to seek discovery of all contractual documents or statements of terms and conditions and any personnel file and written warnings relied on. It is always a good idea to request 'any other relevant documents on which the employer will rely at the hearing'. The IT will usually order this category of documents and it prevents the employer surprising the worker with unseen documents at the hearing.

Letters between the parties or to ACAS concerning possible settlement of the claim must not be disclosed on discovery or put before the IT unless the party concerned expressly agrees.[35]

Witness orders

A worker can apply for a witness order requiring the attendance of any person as a witness if that person can give relevant evidence which is necessary (because it is disputed) and s/he will not attend voluntarily.[36]

A request for an order should be sent to the IT in good time for the hearing, setting out the name and home or work address of the witness. It should very briefly summarise why the evidence is relevant and necessary and state that the witness is not prepared to attend the hearing voluntarily. The IT will then send the worker or his/her representative a witness order, which it is that person's responsibility to ensure is delivered to the witness. There is a financial penalty if the witness fails to attend, unless the witness successfully applies to the IT before the hearing for the order to be set aside.

An order should be obtained only if the witness is co-operative, but wants to be able to tell his/her employer that s/he is not attending the hearing voluntarily. A witness who is forced to attend without giving his/her public or private consent is invariably a bad witness. It will also be hard to get a statement from an unwilling witness in advance of the hearing.

Hearing dates and adjournments

Each party must receive at least 14 days' notice of a hearing date unless s/he agrees to less. Some ITs simply send the parties notification of the hearing date. If the date is inconvenient, an adjournment should be requested immediately. Normally this will be successful. Other ITs send out pre-listing letters, ie they ask the parties to indicate what dates within a given period are impossible. Once a date has been fixed, it is extremely hard to get an adjournment, even with both parties' consent, unless, eg a key witness is ill.

If a request for an adjournment of the hearing is needed, an attempt should be made to get the employer's consent first. The IT will contact the employer in any event and the chances of a postponement are better if there is no objection.

Consolidation

Where similar issues of fact or law are concerned, the IT may order that cases be considered together. The IT can do this of its own accord or on application by either party. Each party will have the opportunity to argue for or against consolidation and consideration should be given to whether tactically it would help the individual cases. The commonest instances of consolidation are for multiple redundancy or equal pay claims.

Pre-hearing reviews

Either of its own accord or at the request of either party, the IT may hold a pre-hearing review. This is an informal hearing before a full IT panel, where each party's representative may make oral or written representations. The IT will decide, solely on the basis of the representations and the IT1 and IT3, whether there are reasonable prospects for the success of the claim (or defence).

If the IT thinks that there are no reasonable prospects of success, it will require a deposit of up to £150 from a party as a condition of proceeding further (Employment Act 1989 s20). This deposit will be used as security against costs being awarded to the other party.

Prior to the coming into force of this provision of the Employment Act 1989, an IT had the more limited power of giving a 'costs warning' at a pre-hearing assessment. This, like the deposit, was to deter a warned party from going ahead. Even where a deposit has been required, costs may presumably still be awarded against that party if unsuccessful.

Since verbal and documentary evidence is not allowed at the pre-hearing review, the IT will rarely require a deposit if evidence is clearly central to the case or if there is substantial disagreement about the key facts. This should be borne in mind when attending a pre-hearing.

Preparation for the hearing

If possible a joint bundle of documents should be agreed with the employer and the adviser should try to persuade him/her to copy the four bundles for the IT's use (three IT members and the witness box). Otherwise, the worker's representative should prepare his/her own bundle. The bundle should be numbered.

A representative should finalise a statement or 'proof' from the worker containing all relevant information in a sensible order. This is a private document for the representative and the worker to ensure that there is no misunderstanding between them. The worker should also bring to the hearing details of all efforts to secure new employment, eg letters, copies of advertisements, details of employment agencies contacted and expenses. If the worker wins, the IT will want to know that s/he has made genuine efforts to obtain another job and mitigate his/her loss (see p140 above). The IT clerk will also want to know details of the unemployment benefit office where the worker has signed on.

Each witness should also be told where and when to attend the IT and statements should have been obtained from each of them.

The adviser should prepare for his/her role as representative and in particular note down the key points on which s/he wants to cross-examine the employer's witnesses. S/he ought to be able to anticipate what the employer will say at the hearing.

Before the hearing

If an adviser has not run a case before, it is a good idea to visit another IT hearing to see what happens. The worker may find this useful too. Arrive before 10am when the hearings start and ask the clerk at reception what would be the most appropriate case to watch. The clerks are usually very helpful if asked for assistance.

On the day of the hearing

On the day of the hearing, arrive early and visit the employer in the respondents' waiting room to sort out any last-minute problems and to see what witnesses are there. The worker's representative should give the employer's representative copies of any cases that will be discussed in the closing speech.

On arriving at the IT, the clerk must be given the name of the worker's witnesses and, if asked, the clerk will say who are the employer's. The names and references of any cases to be referred to in closing should also be given to the clerk. S/he will probably ask whether the witnesses will swear or affirm. If witnesses require any holy book other than the New Testament, the clerk should be told at this point.

The time before the hearing starts can be used to clear up last-minute queries and to calm the worker and witnesses.

Cases often settle on the morning of the hearing, so the representative should have in mind terms of settlement. If part of the settlement would be an agreed reference, which is common, a draft should have been prepared in advance.

The hearing

The original intention was for the hearing of unfair dismissal claims to be simple and informal. The rules encourage the IT to avoid formality and strict rules about evidence.[37] Unfortunately ITs vary enormously in their practice, from far too informal to the strict formalities of civil courts. As the IT has a wide discretion to conduct hearings as it likes, there is not much that can be done except be prepared for anything. Always call the chair 'Sir' or 'Madam' and remain seated.

If the worker's claim is prejudiced by the IT's conduct, eg continuous interruptions from the panel or refusing to allow certain evidence to be called, this can be a ground of appeal. An appeal can also be made if it is felt that the IT is biased or any member has a conflict of interest, eg has some connection with the employer. If it is intended to appeal on any of these points, an objection must first be raised in the IT. Ensure that a note is made of the objection. Only object if it is felt that it is really necessary, as it will alienate the IT and appeals are difficult.

At the start of the hearing, the IT will deal with preliminary matters such as arguments about the documents or matters of jurisdiction, although the latter will usually have been resolved at a separate preliminary hearing. The IT usually informs the parties at this stage as to how it wants the hearing conducted.

The order of events

If there is a dispute as to whether there was a dismissal, the worker goes first. Otherwise the employer starts.[38] The party starting will usually make an opening statement, although there is no longer a right to do so. This statement should last no longer than five to twenty minutes and should simply outline the claim, what are the key issues in dispute and the main questions of law. The key documents should be identified. Nothing said in opening is evidence and too much detail should not be given as the worker and other witnesses might not remember to say everything in their evidence.

Assuming the employer starts, after the opening speech, s/he will call his/her witnesses. The employer (or employer's representative) will then ask questions of the first witness. The representative must not 'lead' the witness, ie must not ask a question in such a way that it tells the witness what the answer should be. However, if the facts to be established are not in dispute by the other side, the representative can lead. Whether there are any facts that can be agreed should be checked with the other side before the hearing. If this has been done, it is wise to indicate to the IT that leading questions are being put because the facts are agreed.

The witness's evidence to his/her own representative is called 'evidence in chief'. After it is finished the worker's representative can then ask questions. This is called cross-examination. After that, the employer's representative can ask a few more questions, simply clearing up anything that arose in cross-examination. This is called re-examination. The IT panel then usually questions the witness.

The same process is followed with each witness. After all the employer's witnesses have given evidence, the worker is immediately called to give evidence and then any of the worker's witnesses. The worker's representative does not have an opening speech.

The closing speech

Each party has a right to make a closing speech.[39] Normally the party which started, addresses the IT last. The length of the speech depends on the complexity of the case, but the IT should not be bored.

The main point of the closing speech is to relate the key points of evidence to the relevant law. If the employer's representative has the last word, the worker's should anticipate and deal with the employer's strong points in his/her closing speech.

The IT should be reminded of the main issues and related evidence. Where there is a conflict of evidence, it can be suggested why the IT should prefer the worker's witness. To ensure that the IT addresses its mind to certain key issues, it should expressly be invited to make findings of fact on those matters. It may even be helpful to circulate a skeleton argument, ie a list of the main legal and factual issues which are expanded in the closing speech, eg that provisions of the ACAS Code of Practice have been breached.

If any reported cases are refered to, remember that only the decision of the most senior court on a particular issue is important. On the whole, it is not necessary to read extracts from the case-law unless there is an unusual or difficult legal issue. The IT will be familiar with the main cases and legal principles and a key authority may just be referred to by name. If references are made to reported cases, advisers should make sure that they fully know and understand them.

The decision

The IT's decision is usually unanimous, although it may be by a majority.[40]

The IT must give full written reasons in cases under the RRA 1976, SDAs, EqPA or related to trade union activities, but otherwise may choose whether to give full or summary reasons. It says at the top of the decision which it is. Full written reasons are necessary for an appeal. Therefore be careful to ask for full reasons at the end of the hearing or within 21 days of the summary reasons being sent.[41]

Most often the IT hears and decides whether the dismissal was unfair and holds a subsequent hearing on the question of compensation. Delays in fixing the compensation hearing can cause financial distress to the worker and may also deprive him/her of the benefit of interest on an unpaid award.

Appeals and reviews

Any appeal must be made within 42 days of the date when the decision was sent to the parties. The IT may also be asked to review its decision within 14 days on specified grounds,[42] eg because a crucial new case has just been reported, because the IT made a mathematical error in calculating compensation or the interest of justice requires it.

Workers often cannot understand that they may not automatically appeal when they lose. An appeal to the EAT is not a fresh rehearing of the entire case. It is a legal argument between the representatives for each party, largely based on the pleadings and the IT's decision. Normally the IT's notes of oral evidence will only be glanced at by the EAT, if at all.

The appeal is confined to errors of law. Where there is no legal error, the worker must show that the IT's decision on the factual evidence was perverse, ie that no reasonable IT could possibly come to the same decision. It is very hard to show this and the EAT is reluctant to interfere with the IT's discretion.

Costs

Unlike most civil courts, the IT does not usually order that the unsuccessful party pays the costs of the winner.[43] However, the IT may order costs if:

- the hearing was adjourned at the request of one party, when it can order costs of the adjournment,[44] or
- a party has acted frivolously, vexatiously or otherwise unreasonably in bringing or conducting the proceedings.[45]

Costs may or may not be awarded regardless of whether or not there was a costs warning.

The IT may order one party to pay some or all of the other party's costs. If the worker is ordered to pay the employer's costs, the amount of costs the employer claims to have incurred must be taxed, ie independently adjudicated, unless agreed.[46] The employer's estimate of his/her costs should not be agreed unless it seems very low.

In practice costs tend to be awarded against a party who withdraws at the last moment without any explanation or who fails to attend the hearing without notifying the IT in advance. Costs may also be awarded if the case turns out to be completely hopeless and unreasonable or if the worker's representative greatly prolongs the hearing by bringing up entirely irrelevant matters.

Settlement[47]

An ACAS officer is attached to every claim for unfair dismissal or unlawful discrimination and has a statutory duty to promote a settlement. The ACAS officer usually contacts each party by telephone and one can choose whether to use him/her as an intermediary or negotiate direct with the employer. To find out which ACAS officer is allocated to the case, telephone the ACAS central office with the case number.

The ACAS officer has no duty to advise on the merits of the claim and there is no need to enter a discussion. There is also a risk that what is said to ACAS about the worker's case may be passed on to the employer's representative.

There are many advantages in settling a claim, as it avoids the risk of losing, the unpleasantness of the hearing, the recoupment provisions and may be the only way to negotiate a good reference as a term of the settlement.

A settlement agreement reached through ACAS is binding and effective even if it is not recorded on the COT3 form.[48] The COT3 form is used to record the settlement terms and is signed by the worker and employer or their representatives. If a settlement is reached in direct negotiation with the employer's representative, both must inform ACAS. The ACAS officer then notifies the IT.

Care should be taken that the worker fully understands the implications and meaning of any settlement before an agreement is concluded. If possible, only the particular IT claim should be settled. In practice, many employers insist on a wider settlement, ie that in return for payment of the specified sum, the worker waives any other claim arising out of the contract of employment or its termination. One should ensure that any industrial injury claims and pension benefits are expressly excluded from such a settlement. ACAS officers usually suggest this exclusion in their standard wording.

It is advisable to specify in the COT3 a date for payment and to incorporate the terms of any agreed reference.[49]

RUNNING A CASE: KEY POINTS

- Winning unfair dismissal cases is all about evidence. In running a case, advisers should try and get as much relevant evidence as they can, including witnesses.
- ITs are frequently persuaded by good documentary evidence.

Witnesses are often treated with suspicion as they are considered to be more unreliable than documents.

- If there is a potentially good witness, an order can be obtained from the IT to have that worker at the hearing.
- It is essential that there is a detailed written statement taken from the worker as soon after the dismissal as possible. The worker can write down his/her own statement. Once the statement is completed it should be dated and signed.
- In most cases it is important to get further and better particulars of the employer's case and inspection of the employer's documents before the hearing.
- It is crucial for the worker to detail all efforts made to look for new employment, and to keep a list of all expenses incurred. The duty is on the worker to get another job as soon as possible even if it is not as well paid.
- Every case is allocated an officer from ACAS. Most of what is told to this officer will get back to the employer. The ACAS officer is there to try to settle the case and will get in touch in respect of a possible settlement.
- There are a number of advantages in settling claims. The most important is that the settlement can, and should, include an agreed written reference. This reference should be set out in writing as part of the settlement. A settlement also has the advantage of avoiding the recoupment of benefits by the DSS.
- Remember, if an adviser is representing a worker at the IT and his/her name is on the record, everything will be sent to the adviser and not to the worker, including the hearing date. Remember to keep the worker informed.
- At the hearing, always make a note of the questions asked by the IT members and make sure that they are dealt with during the hearing and also in the closing speach. This is particularly true of the questions asked by the chair of the IT.

CHAPTER THIRTEEN

Running a race or sex discrimination case

In running discrimination cases, the basic principles are similar to those of unfair dismissal, dealt with in chapter 12 above. This chapter should be read in conjunction with that and highlights the procedural and technical differences that arise in cases under the RRA 1976 and SDAs.

The questionnaire

Effective use of the special questionnaire procedure under RRA 1976 s65 and SDA 1975 s74 offers an important opportunity to obtain information from which inferences may later be drawn. There are several advantages of the procedure over the more limited potential of a request for further and better particulars of the IT3:
- any questions can be asked, not those limited to clarification of what is already in the IT3;
- questions may concern matters of evidence; and
- a questionnaire submitted at a very early stage can help decide whether a case should be pursued at all and, if so, how it should be formulated.

Time limits

A questionnaire must be served on the employer within three months after the act of discrimination,[1] unless an IT1 has already been presented, in which case the questionnaire must be served within 21 days of the date of presentation. The IT has a discretion to grant leave for service of a questionnaire out of time,[2] but it may take the opportunity to reduce the permissible questions.

Provided the time limits are adhered to, the questions and answers are admissible as evidence at the hearing. The EAT has said that it is a 'sensible and necessary part of the procedure that a worker can ask leave to serve a follow-up questionnaire after the initial one, provided that notice is given to the employer of the request for leave so that s/he can argue that any question is 'unnecessary or too wide or oppressive'.[3] It may also be possible to elicit follow-up information via a request for further particulars of the IT3 or discovery.

It is arguable that answers to a questionnaire served out of time without leave would be admissible as evidence in any event, although only of weaker hearsay value unless containing admissions contrary to the employer's interests. However, it is most unlikely that an adverse inference would be drawn from failure to answer a late questionnaire.

Procedure

Questionnaires are best submitted on the standard forms,[4] although in emergencies it is sufficient to accompany the questions with a statement of the alleged unlawful treatment on a letter headed as appropriate 'Race Relations (Questions and Replies) Order 1977 SI No 842' or 'Sex Discrimination (Questions and Replies) Order 1975 SI No 2048'. The questionnaire should be sent by recorded delivery to the employer.

Unlike with particulars and discovery, the IT cannot make an order compelling the respondent to answer the questionnaire. Many employers do not realise this and it is worth fostering the illusion by requesting an answer within 14 days of service. The only sanction is the IT's ability to draw an inference from the failure to reply or from an evasive reply. If the employer does not reply after a chasing letter or if s/he replies selectively, an open letter should be written, stating that the failure to reply adequately will be drawn to the attention of the IT which will be invited to draw an adverse inference.

Drafting the questionnaire

Since an IT may draw an inference only if the employer had no reasonable excuse for failing to answer a questionnaire adequately and if it is just and equitable to do so,[5] it is important not to hand the employer an easy excuse by drafting an unclear or unreasonable questionnaire.

Employers often say they cannot answer the questions because they do not understand in what way they are alleged to have discriminated. This objection is illogical and runs counter to one of the main purposes of the procedure – to assist in the formulation of the claim. Unfortunately it is an objection which frequently wins sympathy in the IT and therefore the statement at para 2 of the questionnaire form should clarify the allegations as far as possible.

The grounds set out eventually in the IT1 should be identical to para 2 of the questionnaire. Certainly no key facts should be omitted from either statement as the worker is likely to be cross-examined on any difference between the statements and any difference between either statement and his/her oral evidence.

If the information requested in the questionnaire is too wide-ranging and/or difficult to collate, it will irritate the IT and provide an easy excuse for the employer not to answer. Either the extent of the requested statistics should be confined from the outset to the minimum necessary, or at a later stage the employer can be offered the opportunity of providing more limited information if s/he raises this objection. In particular, it should be carefully considered over what period, at what intervals and within what geographical or departmental area to request statistics.

Where the employer objects that statistics are not kept, it can be asked whether information is kept on computer or, with smaller employers, suggest a head-count. Either at the outset, or after an employer objects that certain information is confidential, it should be agreed that names and addresses of other workers be deleted.[6]

Race and colour are vague concepts which usually require clarification. To avoid misunderstanding or deliberate evasion in response to questionnaires under the RRA 1976, it should be specified under which 'racial categories' information is to be provided. For example, where there is any doubt as to whether the employer discriminates solely against African/Caribbeans or against all non-whites or only against workers born abroad, the questions should cover all the options.

The questionnaire should be sent as early as possible so that there is time before the hearing to follow up the information provided. Also, if an IT is to draw an adverse inference from an employer's failure to answer a lengthy questionnaire adequately, it should be served sufficiently in advance of the hearing for the employer to be expected to collate the information.

The originating application (IT1)

The time limit

The IT1 must be presented within three months of the act of discrimination,[7] although the IT's discretion to allow a claim out of time if it is just and equitable is wider than for unfair dismissal claims. If a claim is late, it should be argued that discrimination is a particularly serious issue and someone should not lightly be deprived of a hearing.

The act of discrimination is not always easy to identify, so one must be alert about the time limit. Time usually runs from when a decision not to promote or appoint is made or communicated, or from when a warning is given, and not from the end of any appeal or grievance procedure. However, if the failure of the grievance procedure or appeal was itself on grounds of race or sex, then that is a further act of discrimination from which another three-month period runs.

In some cases, discrimination continues over a period of time sometimes up to the date of leaving employment.[8] The time for lodging an IT1 then runs from the end of that period.

Advisers should try not to rely on showing continuing discrimination for time-limit purposes as it is sometimes hard to distinguish it from a single act of discrimination with continuing effects. For example, a failed promotion attempt resulting in continued employment at a lower grade and wage is not in itself continuing discrimination.[9] If a worker is out of time, s/he should make another attempt at promotion on which it may be appropriate to base a claim. On the other hand, if an employer maintained a rule that only workers of a particular race or sex would be promoted to certain posts, that would be continuing discrimination.

In *Calder v James Finlay Corporation Ltd*,[10] a woman was twice refused a mortgage subsidy from her employer which was available to men. The EAT said that although the unsuccessful requests took place more than three months prior to her claim, the rules of the scheme barring women constituted a discriminatory act extending throughout Mrs Calder's employment until she left. Similarly, in *Barclays Bank v Kapur and Others*,[11] the employer kept in force 'a discriminatory regime' throughout the workers' employment in that their past service in banks in Africa was not credited towards their pensionable service. The IT had jurisdiction to hear the claim even though the workers entered the discriminatory scheme several years earlier, which was when the decision not to include their service was taken.

Drafting the IT1

If unfair dismissal is being claimed in addition to discrimination, this should be added in a separate paragraph specifying in which way the dismissal was unfair, to clarify that it is recognised that it is a different issue.[12] All key matters on which the worker will rely should be mentioned concisely in the grounds of application.

In indirect discrimination, because of the uncertainty as to which pool the IT will approve, it is probably best to express the claim in broad terms.

Naming individual respondents

In the questionnaire and in the IT1, individuals may be named as respondents, as well as the employing organisation. The latter should always be named, but whether the former are added depends on several considerations:
- It usually ensures that the named individuals will give evidence at the hearing, so the desirability of their attendance must be considered.
- It ensures that the claim succeeds against somebody if the employing organisation might escape liability because the perpetrators of the discrimination acted outside the course of their employment or because the employer took all reasonably practicable steps to prevent the discrimination happening (see pp115–116). If the claim succeeds against the employer and named individuals, the award will usually be enforceable in its entirety against any of the respondents.
- Where there has been intentional discrimination, costs may be awarded against an individual respondent for unreasonably defending the proceedings.[13] This is valuable because, where – as is common – the employer supports and funds the individual's case, it can be implied that s/he has underwritten the individual's costs,[14] including those ordered against the individual. However, where the individual is not joined as respondent, unless it can be argued that the principle in RRA 1976 s32 and SDA 1975 s41 extends to vicarious liability for the conduct of proceedings, the employer could avoid a costs order by claiming that s/he was entitled to rely on statements from the individual that s/he (the individual) had not discriminated.
- Individuals should be named as respondents only if there is a strong case against them, as the IT will be reluctant to make a specific finding against them. Caution should be used in naming more than one individual since ITs react badly to any suggestion of a conspiracy.

Written reasons for dismissal

Where the alleged act of discrimination is dismissal, a worker should always request written reasons under EPCA s53 provided s/he had sufficient service (see p148 above). In discrimination cases this may be a particularly significant piece of evidence. Even if the reply is received within the 14 days, one should always add a s53 claim to the IT1 since, if the discrimination is proved, the worker is bound to receive an award for untrue reasons.

Interlocutory matters

Further and better particulars of the IT3

The considerations and procedure are the same as for unfair dismissal. However, in discrimination cases it is especially important to secure as much information as possible of the employer's defence and this opportunity should not be lost. Although questions cannot be as free-ranging as on the questionnaire (see above), the advantage is that the IT can be asked to order the employer to reply.

Discovery

Discovery is a crucial part of the information-gathering process in most discrimination cases. The IT will not permit wide, trawling exercises for helpful evidence or a general request for all relevant documents[15] and what will be relevant and useful needs to be thought out (see checklist p183 below). If documents are necessary for disposing fairly of a case or for saving costs, the IT should order their disclosure, even if they are confidential. Where there is a problem about confidentiality, the IT can look privately at the documents to see if they are necessary and to decide whether the same information can be obtained in any other way.[16]

If an IT refuses discovery of something important, one should write asking the same chair to review the decision, quoting the relevant test.[17] It may be best to request an oral hearing and to give notice to the employer of the request.

The IT can order disclosure of relevant statistics provided that they do not relate solely to the question of the employer's credit, but go to an issue in the case, eg whether the employer, intentionally or otherwise, operated a discriminatory policy which manifested itself on other occasions and may have manifested itself in respect of the present complaint.[18]

Discovery is concerned with disclosure of documents. However, for the sake of convenience, the IT can order that the employer supply a digest of information contained in bulky documents. In this way, information generally only available from a questionnaire can be made the subject of an order for discovery. However, where the statistical information is known to the employer but is not contained in existing documents, the IT cannot order the employer to draw up such a schedule.[19]

Original documents should always be inspected, as tampering is not uncommon in discrimination cases, and a request should also be made that the originals be brought to the hearing.

Evidence

Statistics

In indirect discrimination cases, statistics need to be gathered to show adverse impact within every likely pool for comparison. The statistics must relate to those within and those outside the relevant race or sex group and within the possible pools.

One of the difficulties with indirect discrimination cases is that statistics are rarely available to meet the exact purpose. Where directly relevant statistics are not available, other statistics or evidence, from which the relevant facts may be inferred, should be used. For example, statistics may be unavailable as to how many people of each sex actually have childcare responsibilities. However, statistics as to the economic activity of women[20] show that this declines dramatically at child-bearing age, unlike for men between 18 and 33 years. The obvious inference is that this is due to childcare responsibilities.

Statistics on any workplace pool can be obtained on the questionnaire, eg by asking how many of the existing workforce, by reference to sex and marital status, work part-time or full-time or how many women left after having children.

The CRE and EOC should be consulted as to what statistics can be obtained from various sources, eg the Low Pay Unit, the Child Poverty Action Group, the TUC, trade unions and university research departments, libraries, the Joint Council for the Welfare of Immigrants and community groups. The EOC and CRE will advise on available reports and statistical sources and the CRE and Runnymede Trust have specialist libraries. The EOC publishes a useful annual booklet, 'Women and Men in Britain'. The Department of Employment's *Gazette* summarises workforce surveys and is available in most libraries, as are the Labour Force Surveys and General Household Surveys which contain detailed statistics on patterns of full-time and part-time work by single and married men and women.[21] Research reports such as 'The Black Nurse: an endangered species'[22] on the position of black workers in the NHS are useful for direct and indirect discrimination cases. Local authority social services should have statistics on childcare facilities and take-up.

Where there is no statistical or research evidence precisely on the point required, verbal evidence from 'experts' or respected members of the community may be useful.

Witnesses

The principles are the same as in other IT cases. However, there is little doubt that independent witnesses in discrimination cases – particularly if they are of a different sex or race to the worker – can vastly increase the chances of success. If witnesses are called on any point of detail, the adviser should check what they will say if asked whether they believe unlawful discrimination has taken place. Although this is only a matter of their opinion, it will harm the worker's case if his/her witness considers that discrimination has not occurred.

The IT will pay special rates for official or unofficial interpreters. It is usually unhelpful to use an unofficial interpreter, especially one known to the worker.

Other evidence

Sometimes other evidence may be wanted. For example, if the worker saw her GP because of stress, during or after her employment, a medical report could be useful to show 'detriment' and also be relevant to the injury to feelings award.[23] Or in a recruitment case, if a job centre or recruitment agency was involved, it should be asked what job description the employer supplied. If the MSC was involved, obtain the employer's authorisation to get the job card. The reverse of the card will show who else applied for the job.

Interlocutory hearings

Some ITs always propose interlocutory hearings in discrimination cases. Their purpose is usually to clarify the issues, to sort out what discovery and particulars should be ordered and to estimate the length of hearing. The request for discovery and particulars should be served well before the interlocutory hearing, so that an order can be requested. It is also useful to mention any unanswered items in the questionnaire, since, although the IT cannot make an order, the chair may well encourage the employer to reply.

Many employers take the opportunity to seek clarification of the case against them and the adviser should go prepared for some tricky questions. The IT may insist on knowing whether direct or indirect discrimination is being claimed or on every incident of discrimination on which the worker relies being set out. The latter can be very awkward as, although the major incidents will have been pleaded in the IT1, quite often the worker will come out with additional, more minor, examples of less favourable treatment during the main hearing. If taken by surprise at the interlocutory hearing, do not attempt to answer on the spot and ask for 14 days to supply voluntary particulars.

The hearing

Preparing the worker

It should be clearly explained to the worker what has to be proved and that the issue is not fairness. In particular, it should be stressed that it is necessary to prove that the reason for what happened was the worker's race or sex. Advise the worker to keep to the relevant incidents, not to quote weak examples or accuse irrelevant people of racism or sexism. Certain cross-examination techniques are very common and the worker should be warned. In particular, s/he is likely to be asked in respect of all key persons for the employer whether they are racist or have discriminated. Explain the legal significance of saying that someone may have discriminated and that it is not the same as saying that someone is prejudiced. If the legal issues are not explained, the worker may find that as a result of being pinned down at the outset, s/he unwittingly makes concessions or gives evidence which (wrongly) appears to contradict how the case has been set out. On the other hand, be careful not to confuse the worker.

Most discrimination hearings are traumatic experiences, whatever the results, so the worker should bring along a friend or relative, especially where s/he may otherwise be the only woman or black person in the room. Sexual harassment cases will be particularly unpleasant and the worker should be warned about possible lines of cross-examination (see p115 above).

Opening

As the burden of proof is on the worker, usually the worker's witnesses go first and his/her representative has the advantage of giving an opening speech. Many ITs have deep reservations about the concept of discrimination and the proper role of the law. The opening speech may be the best opportunity to address any misconceptions, either as to the law or as to the extent of discrimination in society. It may also be a useful tactic briefly to remind the IT of some of the research findings as to the extent of discrimination in employment.[24] The closing speech is too late.

In most direct discrimination cases, it is worth reminding the IT at the outset that in order to succeed, prejudice need not be demonstrated, nor need unlawful discrimination be a conscious or intentional act. It could also usefully be reminded that the standard of proof is only the balance of probabilities. Even though it is serious to allege discrimination against an employer, it is equally serious to fail to find discrimination where it has occurred.[25]

Where a discrimination claim is combined with one of unfair dismissal, it is unclear who should start and the IT has the right to govern its own procedure. For the reasons set out above, it is usually worth arguing for the right to start. Sometimes, however, it may be best to let the employer start, for example where the worker will make a bad witness but the employer has clearly breached procedures. If the worker starts in such a case, the IT may form an adverse view early on which distracts it from the employer's conduct.

Strategy

Employers' representatives frequently object at the beginning of a hearing that they do not know what case they have to meet and in what way they are alleged to have discriminated. ITs sometimes go along with this approach and require workers' representatives to commit themselves to precise allegations, even when the case is clearly pleaded and no request for clarification has been made at interlocutory stages. The adviser should therefore be prepared to answer the following sort of question put at the start of the hearing:

- Is it alleged that the worker was discriminated against because s/he is of African national origin or because s/he is black?
- Precisely who are you alleging discriminated against the worker? In promotion cases, which members of the selection panel are you alleging discriminated?
- In what way did the employer discriminate? What is every matter relied on?

The difficulty with the last question is that the worker will be confined to every matter that s/he can remember to list at the outset. In respect of the first two questions, the issues should be kept open by putting matters in the alternative. Some ITs recognise that in a promotion case, for example, the worker cannot know how a decision was made, who influenced whom, who may have been prejudiced, who may have unconsciously discriminated etc, and permit the worker simply to say it was some or all of the panel. If an IT insists on the worker saying which of a selection panel discriminated, unless one panel member clearly had a decisive influence, it may be best to name all panel members, reserving the right to drop the allegations against some. The worker's representative may also wish to register a formal protest against being forced to take a position, to safeguard the possibility of a later appeal.

As a general rule, it is best to run cases in a low key way. Fierce cross-examination and use of emotive words such as 'racist' will usually alienate the IT. In the opening speech, the IT's expectations should not be needlessly raised. It may be planned to reveal overt prejudice, but legally this need not be shown, so do not promise more than may be possible to deliver. The IT may find it easier to accept that senior managers have acted with benevolent motives or through a desire to have someone who 'fits in' rather than through racial or sexual hostility.

In most cases, it is not certain whether the act of discrimination was conscious or unconscious, intended or not. The IT must not be relied on to understand what unconscious discrimination is or that it can happen. Many ITs still look for indications of deliberate discrimination (whether the motives were good or bad) and focus on the honesty and sincerity of the employer's witnesses. This issue must be taken on explicitly. It should be explained that an employer may not be aware that s/he has discriminated and that the proper approach for the IT to take in determining discrimination cases – ie whether inferences can be drawn from the primary facts (see p127 above) – does not require it to make a finding as to whether the unlawful discrimination was conscious or not.

On the whole, the fewer people that have to be proved discriminatory or prejudiced, the better, except where the main point is that a whole workplace was hostile towards workers of a particular race or sex. Unless there is extremely strong evidence, probably in the form of a direct witness, any suggestion of a conspiracy or policy in the employing organisation to discriminate should be avoided.

As a final note of caution, in running the case, be careful not to lose sight of the main issues in a mass of detail.

Dismissals

Where an unfair dismissal claim is also before the IT, it usually entails quite different considerations, unless the claim is purely that the dismissal was unfair by reason of being discriminatory. The issues should be kept separate in the opening and closing speeches.

Where the worker does not have sufficient service to qualify for claiming unfair dismissal, ITs tend to be very suspicious, seeing the discrimination claim as an attempt to circumvent the qualifying period under the EPCA. Great care must be taken when running such a case not to deal with issues which relate solely to fairness. Even so, in some circumstances it may be appropriate to argue that matters such as the employer's failure to follow disciplinary procedures, inadequate grounds for dismissal, failure to consult etc, are also matters from which an inference of less favourable treatment may be drawn.

No case to answer

At the end of the evidence of the worker and his/her witnesses, the employer may ask the IT to reject the case at that stage on the basis that the worker has not made out a prima facie case for the employer to answer. The IT should be reminded of the decision in *JSV Oxford v DHSS*,[26] that only in the most exceptional cases should the employer not be called to give an explanation. If the IT dismisses the case at that stage, there is a likely basis for appeal.

Some ITs deal with the matter instead, by warning the worker as to costs of proceeding further. Regardless of whether the IT actually gives a costs warning, workers' representatives should be aware of the danger of an ultimate award of costs if the IT seems sympathetic to the suggestion that there is no case to answer.

Costs

Costs are awarded on the same basis as in unfair dismissal cases although they seem seem to be awarded more readily against unsuccessful workers in discrimination cases. Because of the greater length of the latter, costs tend to be larger. There is little that can be done about this except to keep the issues within reasonable bounds and to be aware that if a case is clearly going badly, points should not be laboured. If a costs award has to be argued, point out the matters which called for an explanation from the employer and could only be obtained in the forum of an IT hearing.

Costs can be awarded regardless of whether there was a previous costs warning. In fact costs warnings are infrequent in discrimination cases and many ITs are reluctant to hold pre-hearing reviews because they recognise that discrimination is overwhelmingly a matter of evidence, which can be tested only at hearing.

APPENDICES

Running IT cases:
checklists and samples

Timetable for the basic procedure

1 Interview worker, take statement, check all documents, check time limits.

2 Request written reasons for dismissal and await reply.

3 Start case by sending IT1 to the Secretary of the Tribunals at the Central Office of the Industrial Tribunals (COIT). IT1 must arrive within the time limit.

4 COIT will send an acknowledgement with a case number and regional office. From then on, correspondence with the IT goes to the Assistant Secretary at the regional office.

5 COIT will send the IT1 to the employer and will send a copy of the employer's IT3 to the worker's representative. Expect this 2–3 weeks after the acknowledgement.

6 When the IT3 is received, write to the employer asking for further and better particulars of the IT3 and for discovery. Set a time limit, usually 14 days. Send a copy to the IT for information.

7 If the information is not received, write to the IT and ask for an order. The IT will send any order it makes to the employer and a copy to the worker's representative.

8 If the employer does not supply the information as ordered, write to the IT asking that the employer be requested to show cause why it should not be struck out.

9 The IT will list the case for hearing.

10 An ACAS officer will be allocated to the case at the start and will ring the worker's representative and the employer. Negotiation can be through ACAS or direct with the employer. Once an agreement is concluded, it becomes binding when each side has confirmed it with ACAS. ACAS then tells the IT that the case has been settled.

11 ACAS will send a COT3 form for signature. This contains the agreed terms of settlement. Make sure that the worker at all stages knows the terms. If there is no settlement, the case will go to hearing. Any settlement agreed on the day of

the hearing does not go to ACAS, but the IT should be asked to make an order in the agreed terms.

12 In good time for the hearing, write to the IT to request any witness orders that are wanted. Then serve these on the witnesses.

13 Prior to the hearing, prepare trial bundles, preferably in agreement with the employer.

14 At the end of the hearing, the IT will give its decision or reserve judgment and write to the parties later.

15 The IT will either hear evidence relating to liability and compensation all at once or, more usually, will hear just liability and then have a hearing on compensation if the worker wins. Be prepared for both.

16 Remember time limits for review and appeal after the decision if unsuccessful. If successful, interest runs on compensation not paid within 42 days of the decision.

Variations:

a) The IT may hold a pre-hearing review, usually at an early stage, at which a deposit may be required.

b) The IT may hold a preliminary hearing on issues of jurisdiction at an early stage which is prepared for and conducted like a full hearing except that it is confined to the preliminary issue.

c) The IT may hold an interlocutory hearing or hearing for directions with the representatives at any stage, just to sort out what needs to be done, eg particulars and discovery.

d) RRA and SDA cases – the questionnaire is sent within the time limits, before or after the IT1 is lodged. Chasing letters are sent if necessary.

e) Equal value cases under the EQPA – similar, but procedure relating to the independent expert is different. In particular, a preliminary hearing is held prior to the appointment of the expert.

Initial interview with worker seeking advice on dimissal

1 Check what worker wants.

2 Check whether correct contractual/statutory notice was given or pay in lieu (unless gross misconduct).

3 Check whether any outstanding wages or holiday pay due.

4 Check date of dismissal and time limits for possible IT claims. Inform worker and diarise.

5 Check whether worker qualifies for unfair dimissal (continuous service, status as employee, whether s/he was 'dismissed').

6 Check possibility of unlawful race or sex discrimination (no continuous service required). Consider other forms of discrimination (gay workers/ disability/AIDS etc).

7 Where minimum wage rates apply (eg most catering and retail workers) check pay level.

8 Where likely, eg where there is a sex discrimination issue, check for unequal pay under EqPA.

9 Check pay-slips. If worker was given none, consider claim for failure to give itemised pay statements. Ask tax authorities and DSS to investigate contributions record so that credited contributions can be requested if necessary. Consider risk of illegal contract.

10 Obtain all relevant documents from worker and take full statement.

11 Write initial letter to employer requesting written reasons for dismissal and moneys due.

Interview of worker with discrimination claim

The following list suggests points that should be established by an adviser when interviewing a worker with a potential race discrimination claim. It can be adapted for sex discrimination cases. The suggestions are for guidance only and must not be followed rigidly. In each case, the facts and what needs to be proved must be carefully considered.

– Ask the worker why s/he thinks s/he was dimissed/disciplined/not promoted or appointed. This helps establish whether the worker believes it is race discrimination, although it may be necessary to ask more overtly. It also helps draw out any non-discriminatory explanation for the employer's conduct.

– Establish what is the worker's nationality or national origin (as relevant under the RRA 1976); what 'racial' group it is that the employer is discriminating against.

– Ask what makes the worker think s/he has been discriminated against. This is a good question to draw out evidence indicating discrimination. Ask whether there is a direct comparison with a white worker on the relevant incident.

– Establish all acts of discrimination within the last three months (eg failed promotion applications; unfair appraisals; warnings; dismissal). These can be the basis of the claim.

– Establish all acts of discrimination or evidence of prejudicial attitudes throughout the worker's employment. (Although these cannot form the basis of a claim if more than three months ago, they can be supporting evidence for the main claim.)

– Expressly ask the worker whether any racist remarks were made by any relevant manager, either directly to the worker or in his/her hearing. Ask whether relevant managers demonstrated prejudice in any other way, eg by differential treatment of staff according to their 'race'.

- Ask whether the worker ever alleged race discrimination and whether that can be proved. Ask for details and the employer's reaction. (This is relevant to credibility of the worker, and of the employer if no action was taken, and to any victimisation claim.)

- Establish who made the relevant decisions and what is the decision-making hierarchy; establish whether any discriminatory patterns among the workforce can be attributed to the same decision-makers (eg the expression of prejudice by a senior manager is relevant only if that manager has some control over this worker's fate). Avoid 'conspiracy theories', ie accusing too many senior managers and staff of racism.

- Assess whether there are non-racial explanations for events, eg the person promoted above the worker was better qualified or was married to the appointing officer, or the worker was unpopular for reasons unconnected with his/her 'race'.

- Try to establish patterns. Patterns in the way the worker has been treated by certain persons in the past compared with how white staff are treated, and in the way other staff of the same 'racial' group are treated and their position in the workforce.

- Establish now rather than later if there are any holes in the patterns, eg if the managers accused have in the past made senior appointments of persons in the same 'racial' group as the worker, or if black workers are generally highly placed in the employing organisation. Also look at who appointed/promoted the worker in the past and why, if the same manager is now discriminating.

- Ask if the employer has an equal opportunities policy.

- Establish whether direct or indirect discrimination or both is possible.

- Establish whether victimisation took place, ie whether the worker alleged discrimination in the past and/or during incidents leading to dismissal and/ or in any disciplinary hearing prior to dismissal.

- Watch out for sex discrimination – in addition to or instead of race discrimination.

- Establish evidential strength – witnesses, documents, and matters from which inferences could be drawn.

- Establish what information could be usefully obtained on a questionnaire. Ask worker about distribution (and treatment – promotions/dismissals etc) of workers of different racial groups in the workforce.

- Establish what the worker wants (particularly if still employed).

RRA questionnaire – failed job application/promotion

Sample questionnaire in case of direct or indirect race discrimination in failed job application after interview. These questions would not be suitable for a small informal employer.

1 Please supply full details of the job for which the Complainant applied, including duties, responsibilities and pay. Please supply a copy of the job description and contract.

2 Please state the criteria for the selection of an appointee to the post for which the Complainant applied and, in respect of each of these, please state:
   a) when it was devised or agreed and by whom;
   b) whether it was put in writing and, if so, when;
   c) whether it was mandatory that applicants should comply with the said criterion or simply a factor taken into consideration.

3 Please state in detail your procedures for advertising the said post and where and when advertisements appeared.

4 Please list all applications received for the said post, by reference to race,* academic qualifications, previous experience and whether internal or external candidates.

5 Please denote which of those listed at 4 above were (a) short-listed, (b) interviewed and (c) offered the job.

6 Please state who was responsible for short-listing and the criteria applied.

7 Of each of those interviewed including the Complainant, please state:
   a) the date of the interview;
   b) the name and position of each member of the interview panel;
   c) whether each member of the panel had at any stage received equal opportunities training and if so, what and when;
   d) the name and position of each person making the decision whether or not to appoint and whether there was any difference of opinion;
   e) precisely why the application failed or succeeded as the case may be.

8 Please give the name of any other person consulted in any way or advised of the decisions to appoint or not to appoint interviewees, and please state their role.

9 Why was the Complainant's application unsuccessful?

10 Were there any notes or standard interview forms completed by each appointment committee member at every interview? If yes, please forward copies of all notes and forms relating to all interviewees including the Complainant.

11 Please state by reference to race* and job title the number of employees of the Respondents as at [appropriate date].

---

* For 'race' please state under the following categories: colour, nationality, national origin.

12 Please state by reference to race,* job title, date of appointment and place of work, the number of persons in the Respondent company appointed from outside or promoted from within, to the position for which the Complainant applied or above, within the five years prior to the date of this questionnaire.

13 Please denote which of the above appointments/promotions were made by panels including any of the members of the Complainant's interview panel. Please identify which panel member.

14 Please state whether the Respondents operate an equal opportunities policy and if so, please supply a copy. Please state how the policy was applied to the Complainant.

---

* For 'race' please state under the following categories: colour, nationality, national origin.

SDA questionnaire – retirement

Questionnaire in case of sex discrimination, by reason of dismissal, of a woman at an earlier retirement age than a man.

Facts:

Date of dismissal: 1.6.89
Age of Complainant: 60 years as at 1.6.89
Occupation: Accounts clerk in a large company

Questions under paragraph 6:

1 Please state by reference to (a) job title and (b) sex, all staff employed by the Respondents as at 1.6.89 in the following departments:
   a) accounts department;
   b) other departments.

2 Of the above, please state:
   a) the date when employment with the Respondents commenced;
   b) the date of birth, or, where unknown, the age of all staff of the age of 59 and above as at 1.6.89.

3 Please state by reference to (a) job title, (b) sex, (c) date of birth, (d) commencement date and (e) termination date, all staff whose employment terminated between 1.6.84 and 1.6.89 at the age of 59 or above.

4 Please state the normal retirement age, if any, for (a) men and (b) women staff.

5 Please state the contractual basis for requiring the Complainant to retire at 60.

6 Please state who made the decision to terminate the Complainant's employment at 60. Please name anyone else consulted.

7   Please state whether the Respondents operate an equal opportunities policy. If so, please give details.

SDA questionnaire – pregnancy

Questionnaire in case of sex discrimination in a dismissal, apparently on grounds of pregnancy.

Questions under paragraph 6:

1   Why was the Complainant dismissed?

2   Who took the decision to dismiss the Complainant? Was anyone else consulted?

3   When was the decision to dismiss the Complainant taken?

4   State by reference to (a) job title, (b) sex, (c) marital status, (d) number and age of children, (e) whether or not pregnant at the date of dismissal, (f) date employment with the Respondents started, (g) date of dismissal, (h) absence record and (i) reason for dismissal, all employees dismissed during the three years prior to the Complainant's dismissal.

5   In relation to all employees away from work through sickness or other reasons for more than a total of one month in any 12-month period, state (a) sex, (b) reason for absence, (c) dates of absence and (d) disciplinary action taken.

6   What tasks do you think the Complainant could not do as a result of being pregnant?

7   Do the respondents operate an equal opportunities policy? If so, please give details.

RRA request for discovery

Sample request for discovery in a case of alleged race discrimination in promotion or job application where the complainant failed to obtain a post after interview.

1   All notes made at any time by the members of the short-listing and interview panels relating to the candidates who applied for and were appointed to the post.

2   All documents including application forms which were before the short-listing and interview panels for the said post.

3   Any memorandum or report written to or by any member of the interview panel relating to each of the said appointments.

4   All references written on behalf of the Applicant and the successful candidate.

5   Any other notes, memoranda, letters or documents relating to the selection process for the post.

6   The advertisements placed for the post.

7   Any rules or regulations governing procedures for the appointment of employees of the Respondents.

8   Any documents relating to the Respondents' equal opportunities policy.

9   All other documents on which the Respondents intend to rely at the hearing.

Sample letter chasing questionnaire replies

Address the letter to the employer's representative, if known, and otherwise to the chief executive or managing director.

Dear Madam/Sir,

Thank you for your reply to the questionnaire dated 21 January, seven weeks after it was sent to the Health Authority.

I am concerned that the Health Authority has not answered questions 13–15 inclusive. It must be possible from conducting a simple 'head count' to answer question 13. Matters raised in question 14 and certainly in question 15 must be within the memory of senior staff, at least in part.

I would remind you of the provisions of section 65 of the Race Relations Act 1976. The industrial tribunal is entitled to draw an adverse inference from a late or evasive answer to a questionnaire. I will be drawing this letter to the attention of the tribunal at the hearing and I would ask the Authority to reconsider its position.

Yours faithfully,

Unfair dismissal *and* direct and indirect race discrimination

IT1 grounds of application

1   The Respondents operate a chain of fast-food restaurants in central London. The Applicant worked as manager at various branches since his engagement in 1984. At the time of his dismissal, the Applicant was working at the Piccadilly branch.

2   The Applicant is of Algerian national origin.

3   On 5 July 1990, the Applicant was told that his employment would be terminated by reason of redundancy on the closure of his branch on 17 July.

4   The Applicant was not consulted at any time prior to his dismissal as to the possibility of employment at any of the Respondents' other restaurants. Other staff in the Applicant's branch who were white and of British national origin were redeployed within the Respondents' organisation.

5   During a conversation in May 1990, the Respondents' area manager told the Applicant that the Respondents had started to 'professionalise' their operation and bring in managers with catering qualifications from recognised UK colleges.

6 Having regard to the size and administrative resources of the Respondents, the Applicant's dismissal was unfair. The Applicant was unfairly selected for redundancy. Further, the Respondents failed to consult with the Applicant concerning the possibilities of alternative employment and failed to offer such employment.

7 Further, the Applicant was dismissed on the ground of his race contrary to Race Relations Act 1976 s1(1)(a).

8 Further or in the alternative, the Applicant was subjected to indirect discrimination in his dismissal contrary to Race Relations Act 1976 s1(1)(b) in that the Respondents applied a condition of retaining his services that he hold a UK catering qualification.

Questionnaire questions

1 Why was the Applicant dismissed?

2 Who took the decision to dismiss the Applicant and when?

3 When did the Respondents take the decision to close the Piccadilly restaurant?

4 In relation to all staff employed at the Piccadilly restaurant as at 1 July 1990, please state their race,* job title, date of engagement by the Respondents, whether dismissed on closure of the branch, and if redeployed, where.

5 Please provide a list of all the Respondents' branches as at 17 July 1990.

6 Please list all vacancies within the Respondent's organisation in the posts of manager, deputy manager, assistant manager or supervisor, between 1 May 1990 and 1 November 1990.

7 Please state all dismissals from 17 July 1987 to date by reference to (a) race,* (b) job title and (c) reason for dismissal.

8 In relation to all appointments or promotions made to the posts of branch supervisor and above from 17 July 1987 to date, please state (a) race,* (b) job title, (c) whether external appointment or internal promotion, (d) branch to which appointed and (e) academic and catering qualifications held.

9 In relation to all existing employees as at 17 July 1990 in post as supervisor or above, please state (a) their race,* (b) job title, (c) date of engagement and (d) any catering qualifications held.

10 Do the Respondents have an equal opportunities policy? If so, please supply a copy.

---

* For 'race' please state under the following categories: colour, nationality, national origin. Please indicate which are Algerian.

IT1 – conduct

Grounds of application

1 The applicant commenced employment on 1 November 1981 as a kitchen porter at the respondent's restaurant situated at 35 Wellington Street,

London WC2. The applicant was promoted on three separate occasions and at the time of his dismissal he was employed in the capacity of head chef.[1]

2 At no time during the currency of the applicant's employment did he receive any written or verbal warnings as to his conduct or capability.[2]

3 On 26 May 1990 at about 3pm the applicant had cause to complain to a waitress about an order which was not removed from the service lift. This service lift is the method by which food prepared in the kitchen can be transferred from the basement to the restaurant on the ground floor.

4 The applicant had told the waitress 'not to leave the bloody food in the service lift'. This was not said in an aggressive, loud, or offensive manner and such language was commonplace among the staff and managers in the restaurant.[3]

5 The assistant manager overheard the conversation and told the applicant not to speak to other members of staff in this manner. There was no apparent explanation for the assistant manger's intervention which was both offensive and abusive. At the conclusion of this conversation the assistant manager left the kitchens.

6 In or about October 1989, (when the menu prices were increased in the respondent's restaurant) the applicant sought an increase in his salary. The applicant repeated this request thereafter on a number of occasions. As a consequence of these request, the respondent's management, and in particular the assistant manager, subjected the applicant to similar demonstrations of capricious and arbitrary conduct as set out in paragraph 5 above.[4]

7 At about 5.50pm on 26 May 1990 the manager came down to the kitchen and told the applicant that he was being dismissed for being abusive to the assistant manager. The applicant endeavoured to discuss the incident with the manager but was told that there was no point as he had been dismissed. The applicant asked the manager to speak to two of the other members of the kitchen staff who had been present in the kitchens on 26 May 1989 but he refused to do so.[5]

8 The applicant was told to leave the restaurant immediately, that he had been dismissed and not to return to the restaurant.

9 The applicant's dismissal was unfair in that:[6]
   a) The respondent did not have reasonable grounds for believing that the applicant had been in fundamental breach of contract.
   b) The respondent failed properly or adequately to investigate the applicant's dismissal and refused him any opportunity to advance an explanation for the conversations which ensued, contrary to the requirements of the rules of natural justice.
   c) In the circumstances, no reasonable employer would have dismissed the applicant.

IT1 – capability

Grounds of application

1   The respondent operates some 30 hotels throughout the United Kingdom. In addition to the respondent's centralised personnel department, each of the hotels has a personnel department which forms part of the respondent's administrative resources.[7]

2   The applicant commenced employment on 1 January 1981 at the respondent's Pepy's Hotel situated in Sartor Road, London w1 as a porter and remained employed in this capacity until his dismissal on 23 November 1990.

3   On 23 November 1990, without prior warning or consultation, the applicant was notified of his summary dismissal by letter dated 22 November 1990 sent to his home address. The reason given for his dismissal in this letter was his 'prolonged absence from work on account of sickness'.

4   The applicant wrote to the respondent appealing against his dismissal in accordance with the respondent's disciplinary and grievance procedure. The respondent notified the applicant by letter dated 1 December 1990 that there was no point in having a meeting as the decision had been made 'at the highest level'.[8]

5   The applicant's dismissal was unfair as the respondent failed to:
   a) take all reasonable steps as was necessary to ascertain the applicant's true medical condition and in particular the likely date of his return to work;[9]
   b) consult and discuss fully with the applicant his medical condition and the consequence for his future employment;[10]
   c) consider and/or discuss with the applicant the possibility of alternative employment elsewhere within the respondent company;[11]
   d) allow the applicant access to the respondent's disciplinary and/or grievance procedure contrary to the rules of natural justice and in breach of contract.

6   The applicant seeks an order for reinstatement and/or re-engagement.

Assessment of compensation for unfair dismissal

Ben Hugh was dismissed on 9 April 1991 for being persistently late for work. He had been with the company for seven years and at the time of dismissal was aged 35. His gross pay was £200 per week and his average take-home pay £155.

He received six weeks' net pay in lieu of notice (£930) and an ex gratia payment of £1,386. Owing to the nature of his dismissal, the DE has suspended his unemployment benefit and he is not entitled to income support.

Ben accepts that he is partly to blame for his dismissal and therefore that his award will probably be reduced by 25% due to contributory fault.

Ben's case is due to be heard in the IT on 15 July 1991. He has two letters from local job agencies informing him that, based on their data, he is unlikely to secure similar employment for at least six months from that date.

BASIC AWARD (£198 × 7)		£1,386
Less: (a) Unreasonable refusal of reinstatment		—
(b) Conduct before dismissal		—
(c) Redundancy award/payment		£1,386
Net basic award (A)		—

COMPENSATORY AWARD (maximum £10,000)

Prescribed element

Loss of wages to date of hearing (14 × £155)	£2,170
Less: (a) Earnings/money in lieu	£930
(b) Any balance of (i) and (ii) not deducted from C below	—
Sub total	£1,240
Less: Contributory fault 25% × £1,240	£310
Conduct before dismissal	—
Total prescribed element (B)	£930

Future loss

(1) Future loss of wages (after deduction for mitigation) (26 × £155)	£4,030
Other loss	
(2) Loss of other benefits* (before and after hearing) – company car	£480
(3) Loss of statutory rights	£100
(4) Loss of long notice entitlement (½ × 6 × £155)	£465
(5) Loss of pension rights	—
(6) Loss of national insurance payments (26 × £5)	£130
(7) Expenses incurred in job hunting	—
(8) Compensation for breach of EPCA s53	—
Total (1) to (8)	£5,205
Less: (i) Any payment from employer	—
(ii) Excess of redundancy payment	—
(iii) Contributory fault 25% × £5,205	£1,301
Total future and other loss (C)	£3,904

ADDITIONAL AWARD
Worker not re-employed	—
Total (D)	—

Totals A	—
B	£930
C	£3,904
D	—
	£4,834
Less recoupment	—
FINAL TOTAL	£4,834

---

* Other benefits might include tips, loans, holiday pay, free or subsidised food or accommodation, medical insurance. For a detailed discussion of the assessment of compensation, see May 1991 *Legal Action* 11.

Claim for underpayment of wages in the county court

IN THE LOUGHTON COUNTY COURT

BETWEEN

BOB SPENCE   plaintiff

and

GORE ENTERPRISES LTD   defendant

T/A JENKINS RESTAURANT

PARTICULARS OF CLAIM

1   The plaintiff was employed by the defendant as a waiter at its licensed restaurant situated at 212 The Willows, Jenkinsvale, Cambridge.[1]

2   The plaintiff was continuously employed for the period 4 January 1988 until 22 March 1988 inclusive.[2]

3   The plaintiff worked 60 hours a week and in consideration was paid £75 by the defendant.[3]

4   The plaintiff's employment was governed by the provisions of the Wages Act 1986, and the Licensed Residential and Licensed Restaurant Wages Council Orders made thereunder.[4]

5   By virtue of the aforementioned provisions, the plaintiff was entitled to be paid not less than £141.00 a week.

6   The defendant in breach of contract underpaid the plaintiff by £66 a week.

AND THE PLAINTIFF CLAIMS

1   12 weeks of the underpayment at £66 a week = £792.00.

2   Interest pursuant to section 69 of the County Courts Act 1984 at 15% per annum amounting to £_____ and continuing thereafter at the rate of £_____ per day from the date hereof until judgment or sooner payment.

3   Costs.

Unfair dismissal case study

The statement of Carol Else

1 Since leaving Huyton Catering College in 1972 I have worked in a number of hotels and restaurants as a sous chef. In September 1976 I was working as the head chef of the Kyverdale restaurant.[1]

2 On 14 September 1976 I received a letter from Brian Gerrard of the American Steak House offering me a job as head chef at the Felstead restaurant. This was the company's smallest restaurant. Over the next 12 years I worked at several of the company's other restaurants. Each move was a promotion (more prestigious premises) coupled with an increase in pay. My last move was on 19 August 1988 when I was made the head chef of the Johnson restaurant, the most prestigious and best restaurant in the group.

3 The company, American Steak House, has 150 restaurants throughout the United Kingdom, a substantial number of them are situated in London. The company also has a large head office at 153 Shaftesbury Avenue, London which includes a personnel department headed by Brian Gerrard and employing 25 full-time workers.

4 I never had any time off work for sickness during the 14 years of my employment nor any warnings about my work. I remember Brian Gerrard telling me at my last annual appraisal that he wished all the workers had the same commitment to the company as I did.

5 In April 1990 at the time of the annual appraisal and pay increase I was told that I would get £25,000 a year salary as well as a company car. I had been asking for a company car for some time as I often worked late and had no alternative but to catch a taxi home on those occasions. I was told that it would take about a month to get the car.

6 On 20 May 1990 I had an audit meeting. At this meeting I asked Brian Gerrard about my company car. He told me to stop going on about it as I was becoming 'too expensive for the company'. The company had a reputation of being tight with money especially where workers were concerned. I decided that I was not going to let them get away with this and continued to pester Brian Gerrard every time I saw him about my car.

7 On 9 September 1990 I was asked to attend a meeting with Brian Gerrard. I thought the meeting was about a new trainee programme which the company was implementing. It had been arranged for a number of weeks, as Ms Hillman the managing director of the company was also attending and it had been in her diary for at least eight weeks.

8 At the meeting I was told that I was being dismissed on the ground of redundancy because of the economic climate. I was devastated. I had no prior warning that I might be losing my job. I still do not understand why they should dismiss their longest serving worker.

9 I tried to enter into a discussion about my dismissal, seeking an explanation for this decision. They kept saying that I had been made redundant and that I should not take it personally. I was given a letter by Brian Gerrard which contained a brief statement that my dismissal was on the ground of redundancy, my P45 form, and my final pay slip. I was told that I was not required to work out my notice and that I would be paid 12 weeks' pay in lieu of notice, and £2,000 as an ex gratia payment. I asked about my holiday pay, I was told that as I had never been given a written contract, I was not entitled to any accrued holiday pay on dismissal. I was told that holidays were always at the discretion of management and as I had been paid £2,000 I would not get any holiday pay. I had four weeks owing to me which I was going to take at Christmas.

10 I asked whether there were any other job for me in the company but Brian Gerrard said that there was nothing suitable. By the end of the meeting I was very angry. As I left, I said the letter was not good enough and that I wanted the real reasons for my dismissal in writing to be sent to my home address.

11 I was so shocked by my dismissal that I went to see my GP that same evening. It was the first time that I had seen my GP for nearly 10 years. She prescribed me tablets to take for my nerves and for shock. It was the first time that I had been sacked in all my working life.

12 I remember telephoning Ms Hillman on 10 September 1990 asking for a meeting but she told me there was no point as the decision would stand. She did say that she would give me a very good reference as soon as I asked for one.

13 About two weeks after my dismissal I saw Brian Gerrard's secretary in Berwick Street market. She told me that my dismissal had not been a complete surprise to her as she remembered writing to the finance company cancelling the application for my company car. This she thought was in the first week of May. She felt so strongly about the way that I had been treated that she told me that she would be prepared to go to court with me.

14 Since my dismissal I have been trying without success to secure other employment. I saw a full-page advert in the Hotel and Catering magazine for five different jobs at the American Steak House, and I could have done any of them. It was then that I realised that I was not wanted by the company. You can imagine how I felt. This was in the October 1990 edition. I have also signed-on at a number of specialist agencies.[2]

Signed _____   5 October 1990.[3]

Letter of dismissal

American Steak House Ltd
153 SHAFTESBURY AVENUE, LONDON W1

Ms Carol Else
12 Wesley Place
Hackney
London E8   9 September 1990

Dear Carol,

Further to our meeting today with myself and Ms Hillman the managing director, I very much regret that I have to confirm that your position as head chef is now redundant.

You have been given 12 weeks' pay in lieu of your notice entitlement and in the circumstances you are not required to attend work during this period.

I will endeavour to find you suitable alternative employment within the company. Should any position or vacancy arise we will notify you.

May I take this opportunity to thank you for the considerable service you have given to this company.

Yours faithfully

Brian Gerrard
Personnel manager

Initial letter to the employer

London Employment Project
12 MALVERN ROAD, LONDON E8 3LT

Brian Gerrard, Personnel Manager
The American Steak House Ltd
153 Shaftesbury Avenue, London W1   12 September 1990

Dear Sir,

Re: Carol Else

I act on behalf of the above named in respect of all matters pertaining to her employment at the American Steak House Ltd, and the termination thereof.

In order that I can advise my client further in respect of her several claims against the company, please supply the following:

1   My client's main terms and conditions of employment or her contract of employment. In particular will you supply me with the following particulars:
    a)   My client's contractual right to holiday pay, with sufficient particulars to calculate her entitlement to accrued holiday pay on the termination of her

employment. Your attention is drawn to section 1(3)(d)(i) of the Employment Protection (Consolidation) Act 1978.

b) My client's disciplinary and grievance procedure.[4]

2 All other documents which purport to vary my client's contract of employment.

3 Details of the company's customary arrangement or agreed redundancy selection procedure.[5]

4 The written reasons for my client's dismissal. As you are no doubt aware, if the reasons given in purported compliance of this request are inadequate or untrue, the company will have failed to discharge its legal obligation. The reasons were requested by my client on 9 September 1990. Your attention is drawn to section 53 of the said Act.[6]

5 All monies which are owed to my client including her holiday pay and her redundancy payment.

My client will be seeking an order for reinstatement or re-engagement as her primary remedy before the industrial tribunal. To this end please supply me with all vacancies within the company, the terms and conditions attributable to each job and the salary, so that my client can consider applying for the vacancy.[7]

Please supply the above information within the next fourteen days.

Yours faithfully

Jacquie Sparky

The London Employment Project

FOR OFFICIAL USE ONLY

Received at COIT

Case No.

Code

Initials

ROIT

Application to an Industrial Tribunal

Please read the notes opposite before filling in this form.

1 Say what type of complaint(s) you want the tribunal to decide *(see note opposite)*. 8

1 Whether the applicant has been unfairly dismissed.

2 Whether the respondent has unreasonably refused to supply the written reasons for dismissal.

3 A declaration and an order for repayment of holiday pay unlawfully deducted.

2 Give your name and address etc. in CAPITALS *(see note opposite)*

~~Mr/Mrs~~
~~Miss~~/Ms   Carol ELSE

Address
        12 Wesley Place
        London E8

Telephone

Date of birth   19.08.48

3 Please give the name and address of your representative, if you have one. 9

Name   Jacquie Sparky

Address   The London Employment Project
        12 Malvern Road
        London E8 3LT

Telephone   437 4455

4 Give the name and address of the employer, person or body (the respondent) you are complaining about *(see note opposite)*

Name   The American Steak House Ltd

Address
        Shaftesbury Avenue
        London W1

Telephone

Give the place where you worked or applied for work, if different from above.

Name   Johnson Restaurant

Address

Telephone

5 Please say what job you did for the employer (or what job you applied for). If this does not apply, please say what your connection was with the employer.

IT 1 (Revised August 1986)   Please continue overleaf ◢

6 Please give the number of normal basic hours you worked per week.

Hours 65 per week

7 Basic wage / salary £ 25,000 per year

Average take home pay £ per

Other bonuses / benefits 10 £ company car, meals, travel per

8 Please give the dates of your employment *(if applicable)*

Began on 14 September 1978

Ended on 9 September 1990

9 If your complaint is **not** about dismissal, please give the date when the action you are complaining about took place (or the date when you first knew about it).

Date

10 Give the full details of your complaint *(see note opposite)*

Please see attached sheet.

11 Unfair dismissal claimants only (Please tick a box to show what you would want if you win your case).

[X] Reinstatement: to carry on working in your old job as before

[ ] Re-engagement: to start another job, or a new contract, with your old employer

[ ] Compensation: to get an award of money

You can change your mind later. The Tribunal will take your preference into account, but will not be bound by it.

Signature: Date:

Dd 8040082 100m 11 86 H.D.B. Ltd. 3657

Details of complaint

1 The respondent is a public company operating 150 restaurants throughout the United Kingdom. A substantial number of these restaurants are situated in or around London. In addition to the administrative and personnel functions performed by each of the managers, the respondent has a large personnel department situated at head office employing some 25 full-time employees.[11]

2 The applicant commenced employment on 14 September 1976 with the respondent as a chef at its Felstead restaurant. Thereafter, the applicant was promoted on several occasions and at the time of her dismissal she was employed as the head chef of the respondent's Johnson restaurant which is the most prestigious in the group.[12]

3 At no time during the currency of the applicant's employment did she receive any written or verbal warnings as to her conduct or capability.[13]

4 On 9 September 1990 the applicant was first informed that she was being dismissed on the ground of redundancy at a meeting convened by the respondent's managing director Ms Hillman, and the personnel manager Brian Gerrard. At no time prior to this meeting had the applicant been consulted as to her impending dismissal nor had she been informed as to the nature or purpose of this meeting. The applicant was told at this meeting that she was not to return to work.[14]

5 At the conclusion of this meeting the applicant was handed a letter dated 9 September 1990, a copy of which is hereto attached.

6 The applicant's dismissal was unfair in that:[15]

a) The dismissal of the applicant was not attributed wholly or mainly to a redundancy situation. The duties which the applicant performed pursuant to her employment contract had neither diminished nor ceased.

b) The respondent failed to consult with the applicant prior to the meeting on 9 September in respect of her impending dismissal notwithstanding both statutory and common law obligations to do so.

c) The respondent unfairly selected the applicant for dismissal in contravention of what is currently regarded as a fair selection criterion. The applicant was the longest serving employee.

d) Having regard to the nature of the respondent's undertaking, and its size and administrative resources, the respondent failed adequately to seek or to offer the applicant alternative employment.

7 At the conclusion of the meeting on 9 September 1990 the applicant sought the written reasons for her dismissal. To date the respondent has unreasonably refused to comply with this request. The applicant seeks a declaration as to the reasons for dismissal and compensation.[16]

8   The respondent unlawfully and without authority deducted four weeks' holiday pay from the applicant's final wage. The applicant seeks a declaration that this sum has been unlawfully deducted and an order for repayment of this sum.[17]

9   The applicant seeks an order for reinstatement and/or compensation.

Signed _____   Dated 28 September 1990.

Industrial Tribunals

Case number:
24234/90/LS

Notice of Appearance by Respondent

---

1 Please give the following details
Mr ☐ Mrs ☐ Miss ☐ Ms ☐

Other title The American Steak House Ltd
(*Or give the name of the company or organisation*)

Name
Address 153 Shaftesbury Avenue
London W1

Telephone

---

5 If a representative is acting for you,
please give his/her name and address
(NOTE: *All further communications wil be sent to him or her, not to you*)

Name David Hart
Address Ince, Webb & Co
Knighton House, 13 Edwards Street
London EC2H 1PE

Telephone 071-232 7201
Reference DH

---

2 Do you intent to resist the application made by Carol ELSE

YES ☑   NO ☐

---

3 Was the applicant dismissed?
YES ☑   NO ☐
If 'YES', what was the reason?

---

4 Are the dates of employment given by the applicant correct?
YES ☑   NO ☐
If 'NO', please give the correct dates
Began on
Ended on

---

6 Are the details given by the applicant about wages/salary or other payments or benefits correct?
YES ☑   NO ☐

If 'NO', or if details were not given, please give the correct details:

Basic wage/salary
£ _____ per _____

Average take home pay
£ _____ per _____

Other bonuses/benefits
£ _____ per _____

---

7 Maternity rights cases only
When the applicant's absence began did you have more than five employees?
YES ☐   NO ☐

Please continue overleaf

IT3

The notice of appearance

1   In September 1990 the kitchen at the Johnson restaurant was reorganised and decisions regarding menu planning, costing, standards, gross profits and budgets were, in future, to be dealt with by Ms Hughes, the executive director, who was based at the Rusty restaurant.

2   In the early summer of 1990 it was also decided that the kitchen of the Johnson restaurant would be used as a development for senior chefs de partie and junior sous chefs at the Rusty restaurant (the largest of the respondent's restaurants) to develop their management skills. These persons were to assume responsibility for running the kitchen but would report directly to Ms Hughes.

3   As soon as the decision was made, a meeting was arranged between the applicant, Brian Gerrard the personnel manager and Lucy Hillman the managing director of the respondent company. This took place on 9 September 1990. The applicant was told of the reorganisation of the kitchen and how in future it would be used as a development for senior chefs in the respondent company. This meant that there was no need for a head chef at the Johnson restaurant and in consequence thereof the position had been made redundant following the reorganisation of the kitchen. Brian Gerrard told the applicant that every effort would be made to find her alternative employment.

4   There has been no suitable alternative employment available since this date.

Request for further and better particulars

London Employment Project
12 MALVERN ROAD, LONDON E8 3LT

David Hart
Ince, Webb & Co, Solicitors
Knighton House, 13 Edwards Street
London EC2H 1PE   12 November 1990

Re: Carol Else v American Steak House Ltd
    Case Number 24234/90/LS/A

Please will you forward to this office within the next 14 days[18] the following further and better particulars of the notice of appearance:

OF 'In the early summer of 1990 it was also decided that the kitchen of the Johnson restaurant would be used as a development for senior chefs de partie and junior sous chefs at the Rusty restaurant. . .'

PLEASE STATE

1   The precise date in the early summer when it was decided that the Johnson restaurant would be used for this alleged development, who made the decision, and who else was present at the time.[19]

OF 'The position had become redundant following the reorganisation of the kitchen'.

PLEASE STATE

1   The names of all other members of staff who were dismissed on the ground of redundancy as a consequence of this reorganisation.[20]

OF 'Every effort was made to find her alternative employment within the company'.

PLEASE STATE

1   The efforts made to secure the applicant alternative employment, who was responsible for this exercise, and the manner and extent of the enquiries made.[21]

OF 'There has been no suitable alternative employment available since this date'.

PLEASE STATE

1   Each and every vacancy within the company, the position and salary attributable to the position;[22]

2   Each and every vacancy which had been considered unsuitable for the applicant for the period 1 May 1990 until and including 2 December 1990.

Please will you also supply me, within 14 days, with the following documents:

1   A list of all chefs employed by the company on 1 May 1990, 1 September 1990 and 1 December 1990, their location and the date on which they commenced employment.[23]

2   A list of all job vacancies for kitchen staff within the company from 1 May 1990 until 1 December 1990, the job title, place of employment and the salary.[24]

3   All notes, minutes or memoranda of all meetings at which the reorganisation of the kitchen of the Johnson restaurant was discussed.[25]

4   Copies of all documents which purport to evidence the applicant's contract of employment.[26]

5   All other documents on which you intend to rely at the hearing.[27]
    If you are unable to supply the above within the next 14 days, please contact this office in order that a further extension of time can be agreed.[28]

Yours faithfully,

Ms Jacquie Sparky
The London Employment Project
cc Regional Office of the Industrial Tribunal[29]

Request for order for further and better particulars

London Employment Project
12 MALVERN ROAD, LONDON E8 3LT

The Assistant Secretary of the Tribunals
London South Tribunal
93 Ebury Bridge Road, London SW1   12 December 1990

Dear Sir/Madam,

Re: Industrial Tribunal Application 24234/90/LS/A
    Carol Else v American Steak House Ltd

On 12 November 1990 I requested from the respondent's solicitors further and better particulars of the notice of appearance and discovery of certain documents. A copy of this request is attached.

Notwithstanding the time limit given, there has been no reply nor a request for an extension of time. Please will you exercise your discretion and make an order for those matters sought in my letter of 12 November 1990. It is essential for my client's case to have this information, to establish that she has been unfairly dismissed.

Yours faithfully,

Jacquie Sparky
The London Employment Project

Request for witness order

London Employment Project
12 MALVERN ROAD, LONDON E8 3LT

The Assistant Secretary of the Tribunals
London South Tribunal
93 Ebury Bridge Road, London SW1   18 December 1990

Dear Sir/Madam,

Re: Industrial Tribunal Application 24234/90/LS/A
    Carol Else v American Steak House Ltd

I apply to the tribunal for a witness order for the following person to attend the hearing listed for 14 February 1991.

Margaret Spillar
23 Miller Court
London EC3

Margaret Spillar is employed by the respondent as a secretary to the personnel manager. She can give evidence in respect of the respondent's decision to dismiss the applicant.

Margaret Spillar is not prepared to attend volutarily as she is still in the employ of the respondent.[30]

Yours faithfully,

Jacquie Sparky
The London Employment Project

Further and better particulars of defence

Ince, Webb & Co.
Knighton House, 13 Edwards Street, London EC2H 1PC

Jacquie Sparky
The London Employment Project
12 Malvern Road, London E8 3LT   15 January 1991

Dear Madam,

Re: Case Number 24234/90/LS/A

In reply to the industrial tribunal order of 2 January 1991 for further and better particulars of the notice of appearance:

OF 'In the early summer of 1990 it was also decided that the kitchen of the Johnson restaurant would be used for the development for senior chefs de partie and junior sous chefs at the Rusty restaurant. . .'

PLEASE STATE

1   The precise date in the early summer when it was decided that the Johnson restaurant would be used for this alleged development, who made the decision, and who else was present at the time.

REPLY

The decision was made at a meeting on 10 May 1990 attended by Brian Gerrard and Lucy Hillman. It was a decision reached as part of a reorganisation of the company which was felt to be in the best future interest of all concerned.

OF 'The position had become redundant following the reorganisation of the kitchen'.

PLEASE STATE

1   The names of all other members of staff who were dismissed on the grounds of redundancy as a consequence of this reorganisation.

REPLY

No other person was dismissed.

OF 'Every effort was made to secure the applicant alternative employment within the company'.

PLEASE STATE

The efforts made to secure the applicant alternative employment, who was responsible for this exercise, and the manner and extent of the enquiries made.

REPLY

After 9 September 1990 Brian Gerrard personally dealt with this matter. He decided to offer the applicant any future vacancy at head chef level in the larger restaurant. There was no point offering her any other position as she would not have accepted such an offer.

OF 'There has been no suitable alternative employment available since this date'.

PLEASE STATE

1   Each and every vacancy within the company, the position and salary attributable to the position.

REPLY

The respondent is a large organisation and the turnover of staff in the industry is high. There were many vacancies for other positions within the company, but they were not suitable. The respondent did not take these positions into consideration as they were not relevant.

Yours faithfully,

David Hart

Terms of settlement

The respondent undertakes:

to pay the applicant on or before 2 March 1991 the sum of £7,500 in full and final settlement of all claims that she has arising out of her employment and the termination thereof, save for any claim for personal injury;[31] and

to supply the following reference and only this reference, if requested for the same, and not to depart from it unless with the express permission of the applicant. If the reference is requested in writing, to supply the same on headed notepaper, dated and duly signed.[32]

'Carol Else has been employed by American Steak House Ltd since September 1976 until her dismissal on the ground of redundancy on 9 September 1990. She was promoted on several occasions and at the time of her dismissal was employed as the senior head chef. Throughout her employment we found her to be honest, hard working and enthusiastic. She had a pleasant personality and was liked by the other members of staff, as well as by management. We have no hesitation in recommending her for future employment in a similar capacity.'[33]

The applicant undertakes to withdraw her application to the industrial tribunal on receipt of the above sum, and in the meanwhile the case is adjourned generally.[34]

Wages councils and wages inspectorate offices

Wages councils

Retail trades (non-food)
Licensed non-residential
Retail food and allied trades
Licensed residential establishment and licensed restaurant
Clothing manufacturing
Unlicensed place of refreshment
Hairdressing undertakings
Laundry
General waste materials reclamation
Toy manufacturing
Aerated waters
Boot and shoe repairing
Hat, cap and millinery
Retail bespoke tailoring
Made-up textiles
Linen and cotton handkerchief & household goods & linen piece goods
Rope twine and net
Perambulator and invalid carriage
Fur
Button manufacturing
Sack and bag
Ostrich and fancy feather & artificial flower
Cotton waste reclamation
Coffin furniture and cerement making

Wages inspectorate offices

BIRMINGHAM
Cumberland House
200 Broad Street
Birmingham B15 1SP
021–631 3300

BRISTOL
The Pithay
Bristol BS1 2NQ
0272-273710
EDINBURGH
127-129 George Street
Edinburgh EH2 4JN
031-220 2777
LEEDS
City House
Leeds LS1 4JH
0532-438232
LONDON
Clifton House
83-117 Euston Road
London NW1 2RE
071-387 2511
MANCHESTER
2nd Floor
Alexandra House
14-22 Parsonage Gardens
Manchester M3 2JS
061-832 6506
NEWCASTLE-UPON-TYNE
Broadacre House
Market Street East
Newcastle-upon-Tyne NE1 6HQ
091-232 1881

Glossary

Admissible evidence

Evidence to the IT may be in documents or oral. Some forms of evidence will not be allowed by the IT and are termed inadmissable. The IT operates very lax rules of evidence. Most forms of evidence will be admissible although some may not be given much weight, eg hearsay, written unsworn statements from absent witnesses, incomplete or unclear tape recordings.

Applicant

This is the formal term for the worker in IT proceedings.

Breach of contract

This means breaking or not complying with one of the agreed terms of a contract (of employment).

Burden of proof

This refers to which party (employer or worker) has the responsibility of proving matters, such as whether a dismissal took place or whether unlawful discrimination happened. The party with the burden of proof cannot simply make an allegation and ask the other party to disprove it.

Complainant

This is another legal term for the worker, used in the questionnaire procedure under the SDA or RRA.

Discovery

This is the process of one party disclosing relevant documents to the other.

Ex parte

This is when a procedural step is taken by one party in the IT without notifying the other party. Requests for interlocutory orders are usually made ex parte and not on notice.

Fact – questions of fact; fact findings

If something is a question of fact for the IT, it means that the issue is decided on the facts of the particular case as opposed to on the law alone. A fact finding is the IT's decision as to where the truth lies between two conflicting pieces of evidence.

Indirect discrimination
This has a specific legal meaning under the RRA and SDA (see pp93 ff).

Interlocutory
This refers to all procedural matters between lodging the claim and the hearing.

Jurisdiction
The IT may adjudicate only on certain claims brought by certain workers. These are matters 'within its jurisdiction'. The IT has no discretion to decide claims outside its jursdiction, eg where a worker has insufficient qualifying service.

Lodging documents
This usually refers to lodging the IT1 or lodging trial bundles at the IT. It simply means delivering the relevant document to the IT by whatever means.

Notice of appearance
This is the employer's reply or defence, usually written on an IT3 form.

Obiter
This is where a higher court makes a statement of legal principle or interpretation, on which the decision in that particular case does not depend. It is therefore not a binding precedent but is of persuasive authority.

On notice
This is where a party takes a procedural step in the IT having informed the other party, as opposed to ex parte.

Originating application
This is the worker's document which starts the IT proceedings, usually written on an IT1 form.

Pleadings; to plead
Pleadings are the documents which set out each party's case, ie the IT1, IT3 and any further and better particulars. To plead something is to put it into any of these documents.

Pre-hearing review
This is a hearing before the IT without any verbal or written evidence, where the IT decides, on the basis of the pleadings and what the party's representatives say, whether the claim or defence (as the case may be) has reasonable prospects of success. If not, it requires a deposit of up to £150 as a condition of proceeding further.

Precedent
The courts decide cases by applying and interpreting the law to given facts. There is a hierarchy of courts and tribunals for employment law purposes, ie House of Lords, Court of Appeal, High Court, EAT, IT. Each level of court/tribunal is compelled to follow legal principles and interpretations set by higher level courts unless a case can be 'distinguished' on its facts. Where no higher level decision

exists, the courts (except the IT) follow the interpretation of other courts of the same level. Precedent may also be referred to as 'authority'.

Preliminary hearing

This a full hearing with evidence before the IT on a preliminary issue which can be separated from the main claim. It is usually on a matter of jurisdiction, eg whether a worker has sufficient continuous service to claim unfair dismissal.

Presenting the IT1

An IT1 is presented at the IT when it is received at the COIT.

Respondent

This is the legal term for the employer in IT proceedings.

Serving proceedings

This is delivering/sending documents to the other party.

Summary dismissal

This occurs when a worker's conduct is sufficiently grave as to justify immediate termination of the employment contract without notice. The worker is not entitled to either notice or pay in lieu of notice when summarily dismissed.

Notes

INTRODUCTION

1 Employment Protection (Consolidation) Act 1978 (EPCA) s153(1).
2 Ibid s1 (see p4).
3 *Stubbes v Trower, Still & Keeling* [1987] IRLR 321, CA.
4 EPCA s1.
5 *Lister v Romford Ice and Cold Storage Co* [1957] 1 All ER 125, HL and *Mears v Safecar Security* [1982] IRLR 183, CA.
6 *Woods v WM Car Services (Peterborough)* [1982] ICR 693, CA.
7 *Western Excavating (EEC) v Sharp* [1978] ICR 221, CA.
8 *Wigan BC v Davies* [1979] ICR 411, EAT.
9 *Post Office v Strange* [1980] IRLR 515, EAT.
10 *FC Gardiner Ltd v Beresford* [1978] IRLR 63, EAT.
11 *Boston Deep Sea Fishing & Ice Co v Ansell* (1888) 39 ChD 339, CA.
12 *Hivac Ltd v Park Royal Scientific Instruments* [1946] 1 All ER 350; Ch 169, CA.
13 *Faccenda Chicken Ltd v Fowler* [1986] IRLR 69, CA.
14 *Hudson v Ridge Manufacturing Co* [1957] 2 All ER 229.
15 Employers' Liability (Defective Premises) Act 1969.
16 *British Aircraft Corporation v Austin* [1978] IRLR 332, EAT.
17 Vicarious liability. The worker may have to indemnify the employer.
18 EPCA s55(2)(c). Depends on whether the worker qualifies for unfair dismissal rights.
19 Those who work between eight and 16 hours must normally wait five years.
20 EPCA s1.
21 Where the employer and any associated employer employs fewer than 20 workers at the time when the worker commenced employment, s/he need not provide the disciplinary procedure: Employment Act 1989 s13(3) came into force 26 February 1990.
22 EPCA s4.
23 Ibid s11.
24 *Eagland v British Telecommunications* [1990] IRLR 328, EAT.

CHAPTER 1

1 *Gillies v Richard Daniels Co* [1979] IRLR 457 and see p43 below.
2 Wages Act (WA) 1986 Pt I and see p12 below.

3 If the worker works less than 16 hours per week but more than eight hours, this statement must be supplied within five years of the commencement of employment.
4 EPCA s1(3)(a).
5 Ibid s1(3)(b).
6 Ibid s8.
7 WA 1986 Pt II and the Agricultural Wages Act 1948.
8 WA 1986 s16.
9 *Collier v Sunday Referee Publishing Co* [1940] 4 All ER 234; 2 KB 647.
10 *Miles v Wakefield MDC* [1987] IRLR 193, HL.
11 Truck Act 1831 s1.
12 Truck Act 1831.
13 Truck Amendment Act 1887 and Truck Act 1896.
14 Truck Amendment Act 1887 s2.
15 *Bound v Lawrence* [1892] 1 QB 226.
16 Payment of Wages Act 1960 s2.
17 Ibid s3.
18 WA 1986 s11.
19 Ibid s3.
20 Ibid s4(2).
21 EPCA s153(1).
22 WA 1986 s8(1) and (2).
23 Ibid s2.
24 Ibid s2(1).
25 Ibid s4.
26 *Bristow v City Petroleum* [1987] IRLR 340, HL.
27 WA 1986 s2(2).
28 Ibid s8(1) and (2).
29 Ibid s9(1).
30 Ibid s9(3).
31 Ibid s9(4).
32 Ibid s30(3).
33 Ibid s30(2) and see p38 below.
34 Ibid s7(1)(a).
35 Ibid s7(1)(d).
36 Ibid s7(1)(e).
37 Ibid s7(1)(f).
38 Ibid s1(1)(a).
39 Ibid.
40 Ibid s1(3)(b).
41 Ibid s1(1)(b). *Pename Ltd v Paterson* [1989] IRLR 195, EAT.
42 WA 1986 s1(2).
43 Ibid s1(5).
44 Ibid s8(3).
45 *Delaney v Staples* [1991] IRLR 112, CA.
46 *Kournavos v JR Masterton & Sons* [1990] IRLR 119, EAT.
47 *Greg May (CF & C) v Dring* [1990] IRLR 19, EAT.
48 WA 1986 s5(4).

49 Ibid s5(2).
50 Ibid s5(3).
51 *Reid v Camphill Engravers* (1990) 404 IRLIB 14, EAT.
52 WA 1986 s5(2)(b).
53 EPCA s67.
54 See p150 below.
55 Trade Boards Act 1909.
56 Wages Councils Act 1945.
57 Employment Protection Act 1975.
58 WA 1986 s14(1)(c).
59 Ibid s12.
60 Ibid s26(1).
61 Ibid s15(2).
62 See appendix 4.
63 WA 1986 s16(1).
64 Ibid s19(8)(a).
65 Ibid s15(3).
66 Ibid s20(6).
67 There are 71 inspectors responsible for about 25,000 establishments each.
68 M Turner and T Kibling 'Private Prosecutions under the Wages Act 1986 Pt II' October 1987 *Legal Action* p12.
69 WA 1986 s20(7).
70 Ibid s5(3) and *Reid v Camphill Engravers* n51.
71 WA 1986 s16(2).
72 Ibid s19(1).
73 Ibid s19(4). Level 3 fine is currently £400.
74 WA 1986 s21(1)(b). Level 5 fine is currently £2,000.
75 The only exception is agricultural workers covered by the Agricultural Wages Act 1948.
76 EPCA s1(3)(d)(i).
77 WA 1986 Pt I.
78 6 April 1983. Social Security and Housing Benefits Act 1982 Pt I.
79 Statutory Sick Pay (General) Regulations 1982 SI No 894 (SSP Regs).
80 Social Security Act 1975 s15.
81 SSP Regs reg 2.
82 Social Security and Housing Benefits Act 1982 s2.
83 SSP Regs regs 17, 18 and 19.
84 *Mears v Safecar Security* [1982] IRLR 183, CA.
85 EPCA s1(3)(d)(ii).
86 Ibid s8.
87 *Coales v John Woods & Co (Solicitors)* [1986] IRLR 129, EAT.
88 EPCA s8.
89 Ibid s9.
90 Ibid s11(8).
91 *Scott v Creager* [1979] ICR 403; IRLR 162, EAT.
92 See C Underhill and T Kibling 'Further effects of tax avoidance and evasion' February 1987 *Legal Action* 15.

CHAPTER 2

1 Equal Pay Act 1970 (EqPA) s1(6).
2 Cf *Leverton v Clwyd CC* [1989] IRLR 28, HL, on the meaning of 'common terms and conditions'.
3 *O'Sullivan v J Sainsbury plc* (1990) 393 IRLIB 12, IT.
4 See below p86.
5 *Macarthy's v Smith (No 2)* [1980] IRLR 209, CA. *Albion Shipping Agency v Arnold* [1981] IRLR 520; [1982] ICR 22, EAT.
6 EqPA s1(2)(a) and (4).
7 Ibid s1(2)(b) and (5).
8 Ibid s1(2)(c), added by the 1983 Regulations.
9 *Pickstone and Others v Freemans* [1988] IRLR 357, HL.
10 *Murphy and Others v Bord Telecom Eireann* (1988) 19 EOR 46; [1988] IRLR 267, ECJ where a woman's work was in fact found to be of higher value than her male comparator's, even though she was paid less.
11 *Bromley and Others v H & J Quick* [1988] IRLR 249, CA.
12 As defined by EqPA s2A(3).
13 EqPA s1(2)(b) and see above.
14 Ibid s2A(1) and (2).
15 *Avon CC v Foxall and Others* [1989] IRLR 435; ICR 407, EAT.
16 *Arnold v Beecham Group Ltd* [1982] ICR 744; IRLR 307, EAT.
17 Cf *Dibro Ltd v Hore and Others* [1990] IRLR 129, EAT, which is unclear as to whether the claim is blocked.
18 EqPA s2A(1).
19 See p26 below.
20 Industrial Tribunals (Rules of Procedure) Regulations 1985 SI No 16 Sch 2 'Complementary Rules of Procedure' reg 8(2E).
21 Ibid Sch 2 regs 7A and 8 govern the parties' rights in relation to the preparation and admissibility of the expert's report.
22 *Lloyds Bank v Fox and Others* [1989] IRLR 103, EAT.
23 *Tennant Textile Colours v Todd* [1988] IRLR 3; (1988) 23 EOR 39, NICA.
24 *Hayward v Cammell Laird Shipbuilders* [1988] IRLR 257, HL.
25 *Barber v GRE Assurance Group* [1990] IRLR 240, ECJ.
26 See pp26–28 below on the s1(3) defence and its proper interpretation.
27 See wording of ECJ's judgment in *Barber* n25.
28 [1987] IRLR 26; ICR 129, HL.
29 [1986] IRLR 317, ECJ.
30 Ibid.
31 This is the same test as governs what is justifiable indirect discrimination under the Race Relations Act 1976 or Sex Discrimination Act 1975; see p98 below.
32 [1989] IRLR 439; (1989) 28 EOR 43, EAT.
33 *Rainey v Greater Glasgow Health Board* n28.
34 [1988] IRLR 333; ICR 391, EAT.
35 N32. This may be only obiter given the actual findings in the case.
36 Cf *Boyle v Tennent Caledonian Breweries* [1978] IRLR 321, EAT. *NCB v Sherwin and Another* [1978] IRLR 122; ICR 700, EAT.

37 *Handels-og Kontorfunktionaerernes Forbund i Danmark v Dansk Arbejdsgiverforening (acting for Danfoss)* [1989] IRLR 532, ECJ.
38 See p29 below.
39 See p29 below.
40 This is also the case under Art 119, where the basis of the pay system is not apparent to workers and where there is a statistical imbalance between the wages of men and women; cf *Danfoss* n37.
41 *Pickstone and Others v Freemans* n9.
42 [1982] IRLR 111; [1988] ICR 420, ECJ.
43 *Hammersmith and Queen Charlotte's Special Health Authority v Cato* [1987] IRLR 483; [1988] ICR 132, EAT.
44 *Barber* n25.
45 *Sec State Employment v Levy* [1989] IRLR 469, EAT, at the time of writing, on appeal to the CA.
46 *Rinner-Kühn v FWW Spezial-Gebäudereinigung GmbH* [1989] IRLR 493, ECJ.
47 See p118 below on retirement.
48 *Bilka-Kaufhaus GmbH v Weber von Hartz* n29.
49 *Barber* n25.
50 See pp90 and 93 below.
51 See section on part-time working, p109 below.
52 N29. See also *Jenkins v Kingsgate (Clothing Productions) (No 2)* [1981] IRLR 388, EAT.
53 See p26 for more detail of this definition.
54 N46.
55 Ibid.
56 For a justification of what the government might put forward see (1989) 28 EOR 41.
57 *Kowalska v Freie und Hansestadt Hamburg* [1990] IRLR 447, ECJ.
58 EqPA s2(5).
59 [1988] IRLR 20, EAT.
60 *Stevens and Others v Bexley Health Authority* [1989] IRLR 240, EAT.
61 When Art 119 came into effect.

CHAPTER 3

1 Trade Union and Labour Relations Act 1974 s1.
2 Employment Protection Act 1975 s2(1).
3 Employment Act 1980 s3(8)(a) and (b).
4 Ibid s6.
5 Employment Act 1982 s20.
6 SDA 1986 s3(1). Also see p38 below.
7 Employment Act 1989 s15.
8 Ibid s13 inserting EPCA s2A.
9 Employment Protection Code of Practice (Disciplinary Practice and Procedures) 1977 para 1.
10 The Industrial Relations Code of Practice 1972, Industrial Relations Act 1971 ss2–4.
11 N9.

12   Ibid para 10.
13   Employment Act 1980 s3(8).
14   *Polkey v AE Dayton Services* [1987] IRLR 503; [1988] ICR 142, HL. *West Midlands Co-operative Society v Tipton* [1985] IRLR 116; [1986] ICR 192, HL.
15   *Stevenson Jordan & Harrison v MacDonald & Evans* [1952] 1 TLR 101, CA.
16   EPCA s153(1).
17   Ibid.
18   [1983] IRLR 369; ICR 728, CA.
19   [1984] IRLR 240; ICR 612, CA.
20   *Massey v Crown Life Insurance Co* [1978] ICR 590; IRLR 31, CA.
21   *Ready Mixed Concrete (South East) v Minister of Pensions and National Insurance* [1968] 2 QB 497.
22   EPCA s64(1)(b), SDA 1986 s3(1).
23   *Waite v GCHQ* [1983] ICR 653; IRLR 341, HL.
24   See p118 below on sex discrimination and retirement.
25   EPCA s141(2).
26   *Wilson v Maynard (Shipbuilding Consultants) AB* [1977] IRLR 491; [1978] ICR 376, CA.
27   EPCA s141(5).
28   *Wood v Cunard Line* [1990] IRLR 281, CA.
29   EPCA s146(3).
30   Ibid s138(3).
31   Ibid s138(4).
32   State Immunity Act 1978 s1(1).
33   Ibid s4(3).
34   EPCA s144(2). *Goodeve v Gilson's* [1985] ICR 401, CA.
35   EPCA s142(1).
36   Ibid s142(3).
37   *Open University v Triesman* [1978] IRLR 114; ICR 524, EAT.
38   EPCA s55(2)(b).
39   Ibid s142(1).
40   *Tomlinson v Dick Evans U Drive* [1978] ICR 639; IRLR 77, EAT.
41   *Newland v Simons & Willer (Hairdressers)* [1981] IRLR 359; ICR 521, EAT.
42   *Coral Leisure v Barnet* [1981] ICR 503; IRLR 204, EAT.
43   EPCA Sch 13 para 3.
44   Ibid Sch 13 para 5.
45   Or eight, as the case may be.
46   EPCA Sch 13 para 9(1)(d) and (2).
47   Ibid Sch 13 para 9(1)(b).
48   Ibid Sch13 para 9(1)(a) and (2).
49   Ibid Sch 13 para 9(1)(c).
50   See p161 below.
51   EPCA s151(3).
52   Ibid Sch 13 para 1(3).
53   Ibid s55(4).
54   *Nicoll v Nocorrode* [1981] IRLR 163; ICR 348, EAT.
55   See pp149–150 below.

56 *Fox Maintenance v Jackson* [1977] IRLR 306; [1978] ICR 110, EAT.
57 SI No 1704.
58 Ibid reg 5(1).
59 *Litster and Others v Forth Dry Dock and Engineering Co* [1989] IRLR 161; ICR 341, HL. However, the worker must still be employed immediately before the transfer where the dismissal was due to an economic, technical or organisational reason entailing changes in the workforce.
60 Transfer of Undertakings Regs 1981, n57, reg 2(1).
61 Ibid reg 3(2).
62 EPCA s55(2)(a).
63 *Morris v London Iron & Steel Co* [1987] ICR 855; IRLR 182, CA.
64 *J&J Stern v Simpson* [1983] IRLR 52, EAT.
65 *Sothern v Franks Charlesly & Co* [1981] IRLR 278, CA.
66 *Sovereign House Security Services v Savage* [1989] IRLR 115, CA.
67 *Barclay v City of Glasgow DC* [1983] IRLR 313, EAT.
68 EPCA s55(2)(b).
69 *BBC v Dixon* [1979] IRLR 114; ICR 281, CA.
70 *Martin v MBS Fastenings (Glynwed) Distribution* [1983] IRLR 198, CA.
71 EPCA s55(2)(c).
72 *Western Excavating (EEC) v Sharp* [1978] IRLR 27; ICR 221, CA.
73 A 'fundamental breach' may also be called a 'repudiatory breach'.
74 *Industrial Rubber Products v Gillon* [1977] IRLR 389, EAT.
75 *Ford v Milthorn Toleman* [1980] IRLR 30, CA.
76 *Derby CC v Marshall* [1979] IRLR 261; ICR 731, EAT.
77 *Courtaulds Northern Spinning v Sibson* [1988] IRLR 305; ICR 451, CA.
78 *Lewis v Motorworld Garages* [1985] IRLR 465; [1986] ICR 157, CA.
79 For fuller treatment of ways to handle an employer's unilateral variation of the contract see T Lewis and M Westgate 'Unilateral change of contractual terms by employers' July 1989 *Legal Action* p13.
80 See eg *Bevan v CTC Coaches* (1989) 373 IRLIB 10, EAT.
81 EPCA s56 and p75 below.
82 See p54 below.
83 *Burton, Allton & Johnson v Peck* [1975] IRLR 87, QBD.
84 EPCA s140(1), *Igbo v Johnson Matthey Chemicals* [1986] ICR 505; IRLR 215, CA and p56 below.
85 EPCA s57(1).
86 Ibid s57(2)(a).
87 Ibid s57(2)(b).
88 Ibid s57(2)(c).
89 Ibid s57(2)(d).
90 Ibid s57(1)(b).
91 *Gilham and Others v Kent CC (No 2)* [1985] ICR 233; IRLR 18, CA.
92 *Abernethy v Mott, Hay & Anderson* [1974] ICR 323; IRLR 213, CA.
93 *Hotson v Wisbech Conservative Club* [1984] ICR 859; IRLR 422, EAT.
94 See below, sections dealing with each reason and relevant issues.
95 *Post Office v Fennell* [1981] IRLR 221, CA.
96 *W&J Wass v Binns* [1982] IRLR 283; ICR 486, CA.
97 N14.

98 See p140 below on compensation.
99 *British Leyland (UK) v Swift* [1981] IRLR 91, CA.
100 *Power Packing Casemakers v Faust* [1983] ICR 292; IRLR 117, CA.
101 EPCA Sch 13 para 24. *Express and Star v Bunday* [1987] IRLR 422; [1988] ICR 379, CA.
102 Ibid.
103 EPCA s62.
104 *Hindle Gears v McGinty and Others* [1984] IRLR 477, EAT.
105 *Coates v Modern Methods and Materials* [1982] ICR 763; IRLR 318, CA.
106 *Williams v Western Mail & Echo* [1980] IRLR 222; ICR 366, EAT.
107 *Hindle Gears v McGinty* n104.
108 EPCA Sch 9 para 2(1).
109 Ibid s60.
110 *Brown v Stockton-on-Tees BC* [1988] IRLR 263; ICR 410, HL.
111 EPCA s58.
112 Trade Union and Labour Relations Act 1974 s30(1).
113 Rehabilitation of Offenders Act 1974 s4(3)(b).
114 *Gateway Hotels v Stewart* [1988] IRLR 287, EAT. *Litster v Forth Dry Dock* n59. Transfer of Undertakings Regs 1981, n57, reg 8.
115 EPCA s59(a).
116 Ibid.
117 Ibid s59(b).
118 *Henry v Ellerman City Liners* [1984] IRLR 409; ICR 57, CA. *Surflex Ltd v Thomas and Others* [1987] IRLR 435, EAT.
119 *Surflex Ltd v Thomas and Others* n118.
120 *Axe v British Domestic Appliances* [1972] IRLR 58; [1973] ICR 133, NIRC.

CHAPTER 4

1 EPCA s57(2)(a).
2 Ibid s57(4)(a).
3 Ibid s57(4)(b).
4 *Brown v Hall Advertising* [1978] IRLR 246, EAT.
5 *McPhie and McDermott v Wimpey Waste Management* [1981] IRLR 316, EAT.
6 *Alidair Ltd v Taylor* [1978] IRLR 82; ICR 455, CA.
7 *Abernethy v Mott, Hay & Anderson* [1974] ICR 323; IRLR 213, CA.
8 *Bristow v ILEA* (1979) EAT 602/79.
9 See p56 below.
10 *Rolls-Royce v Walpole* [1980] IRLR 343, EAT.
11 *International Sports Co v Thompson* [1980] IRLR 340, EAT.
12 *Lyncock v Cereal Packaging* [1988] IRLR 510; ICR 670, EAT.
13 *Spencer v Paragon Wallpapers* [1976] IRLR 373, EAT.
14 Access to Medical Reports Act 1988.
15 *Polkey v AE Dayton Services* [1987] IRLR 503; [1988] ICR 142, HL.
16 *East Lindsey DC v Daubney* [1977] IRLR 181; ICR 566, EAT.
17 Ibid.
18 *Garricks (Caterers) v Nolan* [1980] IRLR 259, EAT.
19 *Spencer v Paragon Wallpapers* n13.

20 See p42 above on dismissal under the EPCA.
21 See p124 on disability, below.
22 *Tayside RC v McIntosh* [1982] IRLR 272, EAT.
23 See pp93 ff below.
24 *Evans v Bury Football Club* (1981) EAT 185/81.
25 This may be a capability issue, see p52 above on health.
26 Ibid.
27 See wrongful dismissal, summary dismissal and gross misconduct, above.
28 *British Home Stores v Burchell* [1978] IRLR 379; [1980] ICR 303, EAT. See also pp46–48 below on the reasonableness test.
29 *Singh v London Country Bus Services* [1976] IRLR 176, EAT.
30 *John Lewis & Co v Smith* (1981) EAT 289/81.
31 *Bartholemew v Post Office Telecommunications* (1981) EAT 53/81.
32 *Engineering Services v Harrison* (1977) EAT 735/77.
33 *British Home Stores v Burchell* n28. *Weddel & Co v Tepper* [1980] ICR 286; IRLR 96, CA.
34 *Monie v Coral Racing* [1980] IRLR 464; [1981] ICR 109, CA. *Whitbread & Co v Thomas* [1988] IRLR 43; ICR 135, EAT.
35 *British Home Stores v Burchell* n28.
36 EPCA s57(3).
37 *Parker v Clifford Dunn* [1979] ICR 463; IRLR 56, EAT.
38 *Scottish Special Housing Association v Linnen* [1979] IRLR 265, EAT.
39 Employment Protection Code of Practice (Disciplinary Practice and Procedures) 1977.
40 *Khanum v Mid-Glamorgan Area Health Authority* [1978] IRLR 215; [1979] ICR 40, EAT.
41 See also p120 below on offences affecting gay men which have no heterosexual equivalent.
42 *CA Parsons & Co v McLoughlin* [1978] IRLR 65, EAT.
43 *Taylor v Parsons Peebles* [1981] IRLR 119, EAT.
44 *Greenwood v HJ Heinz & Co* (1977) EAT 199/77.
45 *LB Ealing v Goodwin* (1979) EAT 121/79.
46 *Monie v Coral Racing* n34.
47 *Post Office v Fennell* [1981] IRLR 221, CA.
48 See p52 above.
49 *International Sports Co v Thompson* n11.
50 See ACAS Advisory Handbook *Discipline at Work* 1987 on the importance of these considerations.
51 *Post Office v Stones* (1980) EAT 390/80.
52 *Rampart Engineering v Henderson* (1981) EAT 235/81.
53 *London Transport Executive v Clarke* [1981] ICR 355; IRLR 166, CA.
54 See pp42–45 above on what is dismissal under the EPCA.
55 *Morrish v Henlys (Folkestone)* [1973] 2 All ER 137; ICR 482, NIRC.
56 *Redbridge LBC v Fishman* [1978] IRLR 69; ICR 569, EAT.
57 *Horrigan v Lewisham LBC* [1978] ICR 15, EAT.
58 *Cresswell v Board of Inland Revenue* [1984] 2 All ER 713; IRLR 190, ChD.
59 *Ellis v Brighton Co-operative Society* [1976] 419, EAT.
60 *McAndrew v Prestwick Circuits* [1988] IRLR 514, EAT.

61 *UCATT v Brain* [1981] ICR 542.
62 See above on capability/health dismissals and *Strathclyde RC v Syme* (1979) EAT 233/79.
63 *Mathewson v RB Wilson Dental Laboratory* [1988] IRLR 512, EAT.
64 This would be a dismissal for 'some other substantial reason'.
65 *Norfolk CC v Bernard* [1979] IRLR 220, EAT.
66 Industrial Relations Act 1971.
67 EPCA s81(2)(a).
68 Ibid s81(3).
69 *H Goodwin v Fitzmaurice* [1977] IRLR 393, EAT.
70 EPCA s81(2)(a).
71 *Lesney Products & Co v Nolan and Others* [1977] IRLR 77, CA.
72 *Stevenson v Teeside Bridge and Engineering* [1971] 1 All ER 296.
73 *Jones v Associated Tunnelling Co* [1981] IRLR 477, EAT.
74 *Managers (Holborn) v Hohne* [1977] IRLR 230, EAT.
75 *O'Brien v Associated Fire Alarms* [1968] ITR 182; [1969] 1 All ER 93, CA.
76 EPCA s81(2)(b).
77 *Association of University Teachers v University of Newcastle* [1987] ICR 317; [1988] IRLR 10, EAT.
78 *McRae v Cullen & Davison* [1988] IRLR 30, NICA.
79 *Nelson v BBC (No 1)* [1977] IRLR 148; ICR 649, CA.
80 *Robinson v British Island Airways* [1977] IRLR 477; [1978] ICR 304, EAT.
81 *Lesney Products & Co v Nolan and Others* n71.
82 See p70 below.
83 *Gimber & Sons v Spurrett* [1967] ITR 308.
84 See p137 below on remedies and p118 on discrimination and redundancy pay.
85 See p66 below for overlap.
86 EPCA s81(5).
87 *Kitching v Ward* [1967] ITR 464; (1967) 3 KIR 322, DC.
88 *Havenhand v Thomas Black Ltd* [1968] 2 All ER 1037; ITR 271, DC.
89 EPCA s84.
90 Ibid s84(3).
91 *MacFisheries v Willgloss* [1972] ITR 57, NIRC.
92 *Smith v City of Glasgow DC* [1987] ICR 796; IRLR 326, HL.
93 See p36 above.
94 Industrial Relations Code of Practice 1972 para 46.
95 *Freud v Bentalls* [1982] IRLR 443; [1983] ICR 77, EAT.
96 Employment Protection Act 1975 s99.
97 Industrial Relations Code of Practice 1972 para 65.
98 See p47 above on *Polkey v AE Dayton Sevices*.
99 See p50 above.
100 *Bessenden Properties v Corness* [1974] IRLR 338; [1977] ICR 821, CA.
101 See pp93 and 112 below.
102 EPCA s57(3).
103 *Williams and Others v Compair Maxam* [1982] IRLR 83; ICR 156, EAT.
104 *Thomas & Betts Manufacturing Co v Harding* [1980] IRLR 255, CA and p47 above.
105 *Elliott v Richard Stump Ltd* [1987] ICR 579; IRLR 215, EAT.

106 *Avonmouth Construction Co v Shipway* [1979] IRLR 14, EAT.
107 Industrial Relations Code of Practice 1972 para 46(ii).
108 *Vokes Ltd v Bear* [1973] IRLR 363, EAT.
109 *Appleyard v FM Smith (Hull)* [1972] IRLR 19, IT.
110 *Sutcliffe & Eaton v Pinney* [1977] IRLR 349, EAT.
111 EPCA s57(1)(b).
112 *Gilham v Kent CC (No 1)* [1985] IRLR 16, CA.
113 For failing to meet EPCA s57(1).
114 *Lesney Products & Co v Nolan* n71.
115 *Hollister v National Farmers Union* [1979] ICR 542; IRLR 238, CA.
116 *Banerjee v City and East London Area Health Authority* [1979] IRLR 147, EAT.
117 *Chubb Fire Security v Harper* [1983] IRLR 311, EAT.
118 *Polkey v AE Dayton Services* n15 and p47 above.
119 *RS Components v Irwin* [1973] ICR 535; IRLR 239, NIRC.
120 *Skyrail Oceanic v Coleman* [1981] ICR 864, CA.
121 See p62 above.
122 See p120 above on discrimination against gay men.
123 *Skyrail Oceanic v Coleman* n120.
124 *Turner v Vestric Ltd* [1980] ICR 528; [1981] IRLR 23, EAT.
125 Transfer of Undertakings (Protection of Employment) Regulations 1981 SI No 1794 reg 8.
126 *Wheeler v Patel* [1987] IRLR 211; ICR 631, EAT.
127 *McGrath v Rank Leisure* [1985] ICR 527; IRLR 323, EAT.
128 For a fuller guide see three articles on pregnancy and maternity IRLIB 376–378 May/June 1989.
129 See p107 below.
130 EPCA s33(3)(a).
131 Ibid s33(3)(b). The usual rules apply, ie two years at 16 hours per week, five years at eight hours per week.
132 Although this may affect her statutory maternity pay.
133 EPCA s33(3)(d).
134 The test is similar to that for submitting a late application for unfair dismissal. See *Nu-Swift International v Mallinson* [1978] IRLR 537; [1979] ICR 157, EAT.
135 EPCA s33(5).
136 Ibid s33(3A) and (3B).
137 EPCA s47(1).
138 *Crawford v Wandsworth Council for Community Relations* (1985) EAT 657/85.
139 EPCA s45(1).
140 Ibid s153(1).
141 Ibid s47(3).
142 Ibid.
143 Ibid s45(1).
144 Ibid ss56 and 86.
145 Ibid.
146 Ibid Sch 2 para 2(1).
147 Ibid s45(3) and Sch 2 para 2(2).

148 Ibid s56A(1) and (3).
149 Ibid s56A(3).
150 *Lavery v Plessey Telecommunications* [1983] IRLR 202; ICR 534, CA.
151 Ibid. *Lavery* is probably wrong on this: see commentary in (1989) 377 IRLIB 6.
152 EPCA Sch 2 para 6.

CHAPTER 5

1 EPCA s53.
2 Ibid s4.
3 See p124 below for free help and aids for employers of disabled workers.

CHAPTER 6

1 See p22 above for the ambit of the EqPA. Also note SDA 1975 s8.
2 RRA 1976 s47(10), SDA 1975 s56A(10).
3 *West Midlands Passenger Transport Executive v Singh* [1988] IRLR 186 at paras 15 and 25.
4 *Pickstone v Freemans* [1988] IRLR 357; ICR 697, HL. *Litster v Forth Dry Dock and Engineering Co* [1989] IRLR 161; ICR 341, HL. *Finnegan v Clowney Youth Training Programme* [1990] IRLR 299, HL.
5 *Marshall v Southampton and South-West Hampshire Area Health Authority* [1986] IRLR 140; ICR 335. The European Court of Justice said it was necessary that a state employee could invoke the directive to prevent the state taking advantage of its own failure to comply with EC law.
6 *Marshall* n5.
7 *Johnston v Chief Constable of the Royal Ulster Constabulary* [1986] IRLR 263; [1987] ICR 83, ECJ.
8 *Foster v British Gas* [1990] IRLR 353, ECJ.
9 Ibid.
10 *Barber v GRE Assurance Group* [1990] IRLR 240, ECJ.
11 SDA 1975 s82(1), RRA 1976 s78(1).
12 Cf RRA 1976 s8 and SDA 1975 s10 for what is considered to be employment in an establishment in GB.
13 RRA 1976 s14, SDA 1975 s15.
14 RRA 1976 s13 as amended, SDA 1975 s14 as amended.
15 Ie the equivalent of RRA 1976 s4(1)(a), SDA 1975 s6(1)(a).
16 RRA 1976 s32, SDA 1975 s41.
17 See pp115–116 below for more detail.
18 RRA 1976 s16, SDA 1975 s17.
19 RRA 1976 s3(2).
20 *Orphanos v Queen Mary College* [1985] IRLR 349, HL.
21 *Bogdeniec v Sauer-Sundstrand Ltd* (1988) 383 *IDS Brief* 7, IT.
22 *Gwynedd CC v Jones & Doyle* (1986) 336 *IDS Brief* 15, EAT.
23 *Mandla v Lee* [1983] IRLR 209; ICR 385, HL.
24 *CRE v Dutton* [1989] IRLR 8, CA.
25 *Dawkins v The Crown Suppliers (PSA)* (1989) 25 EOR 6, IT. Note that this was a majority decision at IT level and cannot be relied upon.

26 *Nyazi v Rymans* (1988) EAT 6/88.
27 For indirect discrimination see pp90 and 93 below.
28 *CRE v Dutton* n24.
29 But note that the case-law has not fully examined whether discrimination against a racial/ethnic group on purely religious grounds will always fall within the RRA 1976. Cf *LB Tower Hamlets v Rabin* (1989) 406 *IDS Brief* 12, EAT.
30 See pp93 ff below for definition of indirect racial discrimination.
31 SDA 1975 ss6 and 10, RRA 1976 ss4 and 8.
32 RRA 1976 s6.
33 Ibid s4(3).
34 See *Heron Corporation v Commis* [1980] ICR 713, EAT.
35 *Jeremiah v Ministry of Defence* [1979] 3 All ER 833; IRLR 436, CA. Here, men were required to work in a dustier part of the factory than women.
36 *De Souza v The Automobile Association* [1986] IRLR 103; ICR 514, CA.
37 SDA 1975 s2.
38 SDA 1975 s5(3) and RRA 1976 s3(4).
39 See chapter 9 below for relevant evidence to prove direct discrimination.
40 See p107 below.
41 See *Schmidt v Austicks Bookshops* [1977] IRLR 360; [1978] ICR 85, EAT; see also EOR *Discrimination Case Digest* no 3 p2 on 'appearance' and D Pannick *Sex Discrimination Law* (Oxford University Press, 1985) pp183–187 (which argues that *Schmidt* is wrong).
42 *Owen & Briggs v James* [1982] ICR 618; IRLR 502, CA.
43 The key cases on this are *R v Birmingham CC ex p EOC* [1989] IRLR 173, HL and *James v Eastleigh BC* [1990] IRLR 288, HL.
44 *Hafeez v Richmond School* (1981) COIT 1112/38.
45 *Din v Carrington Viyella* [1982] IRLR 281; ICR 256, EAT.
46 *James v Eastleigh BC* n43.
47 *R v Birmingham CC ex p EOC* n43.
48 See *R v Birmingham CC ex p EOC* n43 and *James v Eastleigh BC* n43 by a 3:2 majority.
49 *West Midlands Passenger Transport Executive v Singh* n3. See also, in passing, *Baker v Cornwall CC* [1990] IRLR 194, CA. Unfortunately, the facts of *Birmingham* and *James* are concerned only with conscious, non-malicious discrimination. Indeed a close reading of *James* reveals that even the majority did not readily envisage unconscious forms of discrimination.
50 Published in 1985 as part of the CRE's statutory duty to review the working of the RRA 1976, but not implemented.
51 *Clarke v Eley (IMI) Kynoch* [1982] IRLR 482; [1983] ICR 165, EAT. *The Home Office v Holmes* [1984] IRLR 299; ICR 678, EAT.
52 *Francis v British Airways Engineering Overhaul* [1982] IRLR 10, EAT.
53 *Kingston and Richmond Health Authority v Kaur* [1981] IRLR 337; ICR 631, EAT.
54 *Perera v Civil Service Commission* [1983] IRLR 166; ICR 428, CA. *Meer v LB Tower Hamlets* [1988] IRLR 399, CA.
55 And it is possibly a wrong interpretation of the legislation, but will stand until there is a HL decision.
56 *Meer v LB Tower Hamlets* n54.

57   See p181 below for sample questionnaire.
58   See pp29–30.
59   *Clarke v Eley (IMI) Kynoch* n51.
60   Ibid.
61   *Raval v DHSS and the Civil Service Commission* [1985] IRLR 370; ICR 685, EAT.
62   *Clarke v Eley (IMI) Kynoch* n51.
63   *Mandla v Lee* n23. *Price v The Civil Service Commission* [1977] IRLR 291; [1978] ICR 27, EAT.
64   *Mandla v Lee* n23.
65   *Price v The Civil Service Commission* n63.
66   Ibid.
67   Ibid but see p111 below on *Clymo v Wandsworth LBC* [1989] IRLR 241; ICR 250, EAT on this point.
68   Question 6 in *Raval v DHSS* n61.
69   *Pearse v City of Bradford MC* [1988] IRLR 379, EAT. *Price v The Civil Service Commission* n63.
70   RRA 1976 s3(4), SDA 1975 s5(3).
71   *Kidd v DRG (UK)* [1985] IRLR 190; ICR 405, EAT.
72   *Orphanos v Queen Mary College* n20.
73   *R v Sec State Education ex p Schaffter* [1987] IRLR 53, QBD.
74   Although the High Court in *Schaffter* said that it was relevant to the Equal Treatment Directive if, in absolute numbers, substantially fewer women than men could comply with a requirement.
75   *Schaffter* n73.
76   *Greencroft Social Club and Institute v Mullen* [1985] ICR 796, EAT.
77   *Ojutiku and Oburoni v MSC* [1982] IRLR 418; ICR 661, CA.
78   *Hampson v Dept Education and Science* [1989] IRLR 69, CA.
79   *Bilka-Kaufhaus GmbH v Weber von Hartz* [1986] IRLR 317; [1987] ICR 110, ECJ. *Rainey v Greater Glasgow Health Board* [1987] IRLR 26; ICR 129, HL.
80   Ibid. NB these were equal pay cases. *Hampson* n78.
81   *Hampson* n78. This is now the key case on what is justifiable. It imports the concept of 'proportionality' or balance from EC and US law.
82   Employment Act 1989 ss11–12. Note that employers' liability for injury is, as a consequence, restricted.
83   SDA 1975 (Exemption of Special Treatment for Lone Parents) Order 1989 SI No 2140. This order makes *Training Commission v Jackson* (1990) 398 IRLIB 16, EAT of academic interest, since it concerns indirect discrimination in married women's access to childcare payments for employment training.
84   See p132 below on burden of proof.
85   *Cobb v Sec State Employment and MSC* [1989] IRLR 464, EAT.
86   *Aziz v Trinity Street Taxis* [1988] IRLR 204; ICR 534, CA.
87   Ibid. The CA overruled the EAT, which had thought that the consideration was whether the applicant was less favourably treated than another worker, who had done the same protected act, might have been.
88   RRA 1976 s2(a) and (b).
89   Ibid s2(c) and (d).
90   *Grant and Others v Knight and City of Bradford MC* (1990) 394 IRLIB 14, IT.

91   *Cornelius v University College of Swansea* [1987] IRLR 141, CA.
92   N86.
93   RRA 1976 s2, SDA 1975 s4.

CHAPTER 7

1   RRA 1976 s5(1), SDA 1976 s7(1).
2   RRA 1976 s5(4), SDA 1975 s7(4).
3   [1989] IRLR 150, EAT.
4   SDA 1975 s7(2)(b)(i) and (ii).
5   RRA 1976 s5(3), SDA 1975 s7(3).
6   *Tottenham Green Under Fives' Centre v Marshall* [1989] IRLR 147; ICR 214, EAT.
7   *LB Lambeth v CRE* [1990] IRLR 231, CA.
8   *Tottenham Green* n6.
9   *LB Lambeth v CRE* n7.
10   *Tottenham Green* n6. *LB Lambeth v CRE* n7.
11   *LB Lambeth v CRE* n7.
12   RRA 1976 s5(4), SDA 1975 s7(4).
13   See sections for exceptions to liability.
14   RRA 1976 s63, SDA 1975 s72.
15   *Hampson v Dept Education and Science* [1990] IRLR 302, HL.
16   SDA 1975 s51(2).
17   RRA 1976 s4(3).

CHAPTER 8

1   *Turley v Allders Stores* [1980] ICR 66; IRLR 4, EAT.
2   [1985] IRLR 367; ICR 703, EAT.
3   *Curl v Air (UK)* (1988) 22 EOR 44, IT.
4   *Webb v EMO Air Cargo (UK)* [1990] IRLR 124, EAT, on appeal to CA.
5   Ibid.
6   SDA 1975 s2(2).
7   *Handels-og Kontorfunktionaerernes Forbund i Danmark (acting for Mrs Hertz) v Dansk Arbejdsgiverforening (acting for Aldi Marked)* [1991] IRLR 31, ECJ. *Dekker v Stichting Vormingscentrum voor Jonge Volwassenen Plus* [1991] IRLR 27, ECJ.
8   Look out for *Webb v EMO (Air Cargo)* n4 which is on appeal to the CA.
9   [1984] IRLR 299; ICR 678, EAT.
10   [1989] IRLR 241; ICR 250, EAT. See (1989) 25 EOR 34 for detailed analysis of *Clymo* and *Industrial Law Journal* vol 18 no 4 p244.
11   [1990] IRLR 181, NICA.
12   See pp93-99.
13   *The Home Office v Holmes* n9. *Briggs v North Eastern Education and Library Board* n11.
14   This clearly contradicts *Holmes,* and the EAT was wrong to say that *Holmes* envisaged cases where full-time working might be part of the job itself.
15   *Briggs* n11.

16   Despite the wide meaning of 'can comply' established by *Price v Civil Service Commission* and *Mandla v Lee*, pp95–96 above.
17   *Greater Glasgow Health Board v Carey* [1987] IRLR 484, EAT.
18   *Clarke v Eley (IMI) Kynoch* [1982] IRLR 482; [1983] ICR 165, EAT, see p96 above.
19   See pp29–30 on equal pay and EC law.
20   SDA 1975 s6(1)(a).
21   [1986] IRLR 134; ICR 564, Court of Session.
22   [1990] IRLR 3, EAT.
23   N21.
24   RRA 1976 s4, SDA 1975 s6 set out types of behaviour covered by the statutes.
25   RRA 1976 s4(2)(c), SDA 1975 s6(2)(b).
26   *Jeremiah v Ministry of Defence* [1979] 3 All ER 833; IRLR 436, CA.
27   N21.
28   *Bracebridge Engineering v Darby* n22.
29   [1986] IRLR 103, CA at 107.
30   *Wileman v Minilec Engineering* [1988] IRLR 144; ICR 318, EAT.
31   *Snowball v Gardner Merchant* [1987] IRLR 397; ICR 719, EAT.
32   *Wileman* n30.
33   *De Souza* n29.
34   *Irving v The Post Office* [1987] IRLR 289, CA, applying tortious principles.
35   Ibid.
36   N22.
37   RRA 1976 s32(3), SDA 1975 s41(3).
38   *Balgobin and Francis v LB Tower Hamlets* [1987] IRLR 401; ICR 829, EAT.
39   A useful comparison may be made with the way in which the case-law has interpreted a similar phrase in relation to permitting late applications in unfair dismissal cases.
40   See p43 above.
41   [1978] IRLR 27; ICR 221, CA.
42   N22.
43   Eg *Straker v McDonald's Hamburgers* (1990) EOR *Discrimination Case Digest* no 3 p7.
44   See p38 for effect on what is the normal retirement age for unfair dismissal purposes.
45   See p28 above.
46   *Hammersmith and Queen Charlotte's Special Health Authority v Cato* [1987] IRLR 483; [1988] ICR 132, EAT.
47   *Barber v GRE Assurance Group* [1990] IRLR 240, ECJ.
48   *Sec State Employment v Levy* [1989] IRLR 469, EAT. But after *Barber*, n47, such payments are probably covered.
49   Brought in to comply with Directive 86/378/EEC. Social Security Act 1989 also applies to other employment-related benefit schemes.
50   See (1989) 405 *IDS Brief* 'Retiring and pension age' for greater detail on the law in this area as at that date.
51   *Bilka-Kaufhaus GmbH v Weber von Hartz* [1986] IRLR 317; [1987] ICR 110, ECJ.
52   *Barber* n47.

53 As mentioned above, this area of law is difficult and developing.
54 Although the contractual position is not conclusive.
55 *LM Boychuk v HJ Symons Holdings* [1977] IRLR 395, EAT.
56 *Saunders v Scottish National Camps Association* [1981] IRLR 277, Court of Session.
57 See Phil Greasley *Gay Men at Work* (Lesbian and Gay Employment Rights, 1986) and Paul Crane *Gays and the Law* (Pluto Press, 1982).
58 *Wiseman v Salford CC* [1981] IRLR 202, EAT.
59 See Department of Employment/Health and Safety Executive booklet *AIDS and employment*.
60 See *Turner v Vestric Ltd* [1980] ICR 528; [1981] IRLR 23, EAT on how an employer should approach a breakdown in working relationships betwen employees.
61 EPCA s63.
62 See *Bliss v South East Thames Regional Health Authority* [1985] IRLR 308; [1987] ICR 700, CA on requiring a surgeon to undergo a medical examination.
63 Only 27% in 1986. In 1990 *Equal Opportunities Review* reported that only 24% of employers, with 20 employees or more, met the quota. There have been only 10 prosecutions since 1947 and none in the last 10 years.
64 Companies Act 1985 Sch 7 sets out the issues to be covered.
65 Disabled Persons (Registration) Regulations 1945 SR&O No 938.
66 S8A.
67 *Post Office v Husbands* (1980) EAT 432/80. See also *Seymour v British Airways Board* [1983] IRLR 55; ICR 148, EAT.
68 *Hobson v GEC Telecommunications* [1985] ICR 777, EAT.
69 See *O'Brien v Prudential Assurance Co* [1979] IRLR 140, EAT.

CHAPTER 9

1 *Khanna v Ministry of Defence* [1981] IRLR 331; ICR 653, EAT. *Chattopadhyay v Headmaster of Holloway School* [1981] IRLR 487; ICR 132, EAT. *Baker v Cornwall CC* [1990] IRLR 194, CA.
2 *Noone v North West Thames Regional Health Authority* [1988] IRLR 195, CA.
3 As in *Dornan v Belfast CC* [1990] IRLR 179, NICA.
4 *West Midlands Passenger Transport Executive v Singh* [1988] IRLR 186, CA.
5 See below for a discussion of inferences.
6 *JSV Oxford v DHSS* [1977] IRLR 225, EAT.
7 *Hampson v Dept Education and Science* [1989] IRLR 69; ICR 179, CA.
8 *Cobb v Sec State Employment and MSC* [1989] IRLR 464, EAT. *Training Commission v Jackson* (1990) 398 IRLIB 16, EAT.
9 *Cobb* n8. This was the majority view, but one member of the EAT said that it was for the secretary of state to balance objectively the discriminatory effect of the condition against the reasonable needs of the MSC and that he had not done this, either when applying the condition or at the IT hearing.
10 See pp145–146 below.
11 *Khanna v Ministry of Defence* n1.
12 *Eke v Commissioners of Customs and Excise* [1981] IRLR 334, EAT.
13 *Chattopadhyay v Headmaster of Holloway School* n1.

14   N4.

15   Ibid at 188.

16   Monitoring was approved by the CA in *Singh*, n4, and by the EAT in *Carrington v Helix Lighting* [1990] IRLR 6.

17   Some issues of *Equal Opportunities Review* and the CRE and EOC should have this information.

18   *Noone* n2.

19   The Court of Appeal, in *De Souza v The Automobile Association* [1986] IRLR 103, felt able to draw this distinction.

20   *Baker v Cornwall CC* n1 at 198.

21   In *King v The Great Britain-China Centre* (1988) 22 EOR 43, a majority of the IT was prepared to infer race discrimination from an evasive answer to the questionnaire on a central point.

22   *Carrington v Helix Lighting* n16.

23   *Briggs v North Eastern Education and Library Board* [1990] IRLR 181, NICA.

24   *Cobb* n8.

25   Ibid.

CHAPTER 10

1   In less than 1% of claims is a reinstatement order made: Dept of Employment 1990.

2   EPCA s69(5).

3   *Artisan Press v Srawley and Parker* [1986] IRLR 126; ICR 328, EAT.

4   EPCA s69(5).

5   Ibid s70(1).

6   *Coleman and Stephenson v Magnet Joinery* [1974] IRLR 343; [1975] ICR 46.

7   *Enessy Co SA v Minoprio* [1978] IRLR 489, EAT.

8   *Nothman v LB Barnet (No 2)* [1980] IRLR 65, EAT.

9   EPCA s69(5)(c).

10   *W Devis & Sons v Atkins* [1977] IRLR 314; ICR 662, HL.

11   EPCA s69(1).

12   Ibid s69(4).

13   Ibid s69(6).

14   Employment Act 1975.

15   From 1 April 1991. The annual April upratings are noted in *Legal Action*, IRLIB etc.

16   EPCA s73(7B).

17   Ibid s73(9).

18   *Chelsea Football Club v Heath* [1981] IRLR 73; ICR 323, EAT.

19   EPCA s73(7A).

20   Ibid s73(6).

21   Ibid ss58 and 59(a).

22   Ibid s74(1) and (2).

23   *Norton Tool Co v Tewson* [1972] IRLR 86; ICR 501, NIRC.

24   *Tidman v Aveling Marshall* [1977] IRLR 218; ICR 506, EAT.

25   *Mullett v Brush Electric Machines* [1977] ICR 829, EAT.

26   *Everwear Candlewick v Isaac* [1974] ICR 525; ITR 334, NIRC.

27   *Tradewinds Airways v Fletcher* [1981] IRLR 272, EAT.

28 *Norton Tool Co v Tewson* n23.
29 *Isle of Wight Tourist Board v Coombes* [1976] IRLR 413, EAT.
30 *Fougère v Phoenix Motor Co* [1976] IRLR 259, EAT.
31 *Eastern Counties Timber Co v Hunt* (1976) EAT 483/76.
32 *Penprase v Mander Bros* [1973] IRLR 167, IT.
33 *York Trailer Co v Sparks* [1973] IRLR 348; ICR 518, NIRC.
34 *Leske v Rogers of Salcoates* (1982) EAT 502/82.
35 *Wilson v Tote Bookmakers* (1981) COIT 15570/81.
36 *Palmanor v Cedron Ltd* [1978] IRLR 303; ICR 1008, EAT.
37 *Gotts v Hoffman Balancing* (1979) COIT 951/115.
38 *AA schedule of estimated standing and running costs of vehicles.*
39 *UBAF Bank v Davis* [1978] IRLR 442, EAT.
40 *Butler v Wendon & Sons* [1972] IRLR 15; ITR 418, IT.
41 *Head v SH Muffet* [1986] IRLR 488; [1987] ICR 1, EAT.
42 *Daley v Dorsett (Almar Dolls)* [1981] IRLR 385; [1982] ICR 1, EAT.
43 *A suggested method for assessing loss of pension rights under an occupational scheme following a finding of unfair dismissal by an industrial tribunal.*
44 *Nelson v BBC (No 2)* [1979] IRLR 346; [1980] ICR 110, CA.
44A *Polkey v AE Dayton Services* [1987] IRLR 503; [1988] ICR 142, HL.
45 *Gardiner-Hill v Roland Berger Technics* [1982] IRLR 498, EAT.
46 EPCA s75(3).
47 *Walter Braund (London) v Murray* [1990] IRLR 100, EAT.
48 EPCA s75A.
49 Ibid s75A(4) and (5).
50 Ibid s75A(3).
51 Ibid s72(c).
52 Employment Protection (Recoupment of Unemployment Benefit and Supplementary Benefit) Regulations 1977 SI No 674.

CHAPTER 11

1 RRA 1976 s54, SDA 1975 s65.
2 RRA 1976 s57(3), SDA 1975 s66(3).
3 RRA 1976 s56(1)(c), SDA 1975 s65(1)(c).
4 RRA 1976 s56(4), SDA 1975 s65(3).
5 [1988] IRLR 530; (1989) 23 EOR 46, CA.
6 The EAT, in *British Gas v Sharma* [1991] IRLR 101; (1990) 435 *IDS Brief* 12, has interpreted *Noone* (n15) in this latter way.
7 RRA 1976 s56(1)(b), SDA 1975 s65(1)(b).
8 *Hurley v Mustoe (No 2)* [1983] ICR 422, EAT.
9 RRA 1976 s57(4), SDA 1975 s66(4).
10 RRA 1976 s56(2), SDA 1975 s65(2).
11 *Marshall v Southampton and South-West Hampshire Area Health Authority (No 2)* [1988] IRLR 325, EAT; [1990] IRLR 481, CA.
12 RRA 1976 s56(3).
13 [1988] IRLR 190, CA.
14 Ibid, May LJ at 193.
15 [1988] IRLR 195, CA.

16   Citing Lord Diplock in *Cassell & Co v Broome* [1972] AC 1027, HL at 1124.
17   *City of Bradford MC v Arora* (1991) 36 EOR 39, CA. These circumstances are set out by HL in *Rookes v Barnard* [1964] 1 All ER 367 and *Cassell & Co v Broome* n16.
18   See p170 on appropriate evidence in the IT.
19   RRA 1976 s57(3), SDA 1975 s66(3).
20   [1985] IRLR 349; 2 All ER 233, HL.
21   See p167 above on costs against individual respondents.

CHAPTER 12

1   EPCA s134(3)(b) and see p161 below.
2   EPCA s53 as amended by Employment Act 1989 s15(1).
3   EPCA s53(4)(b).
4   *Ladbroke Entertainments v Clark* [1987] ICR 585, EAT.
5   *Horsley Smith & Sherry v Dutton* [1977] IRLR 172, EAT.
6   EPCA s53(3).
7   *Harvard Securities v Younghusband* [1990] IRLR 17, EAT.
8   *Post Office v Moore* [1981] ICR 623, EAT.
9   EPCA s55(4)(a).
10   Ibid s55(4)(b).
11   *Adams v GKN Sankey* [1980] IRLR 416, EAT.
12   *Dixon v Stenor* [1973] ICR 157; IRLR 28, NIRC.
13   EPCA s67(2).
14   *Porter v Bandridge* [1978] ICR 943; IRLR 271, CA.
15   Ibid.
16   *Churchill v A Yeates & Sons* [1983] ICR 380; IRLR 187, EAT.
17   *Dedman v British Building & Engineering Appliances* [1973] IRLR 379; [1974] ICR 53, CA.
18   *Times Newspapers v O'Regan* (1976) 11 ITR 259; [1977] IRLR 101, EAT.
19   *Riley v Tesco Stores and GLCABS* [1980] IRLR 103; ICR 323, CA.
20   *Golub v University of Sussex* (1981) 13 April, unreported, CA. *James W Cook & Co (in liquidation) v Tipper and Others* [1990] IRLR 386, CA.
21   *Bengey v North Devon DC* (1976) 11 ITR 211; [1977] ICR 15, EAT.
22   *Burns International Security Services v Butt* [1983] IRLR 438; ICR 547, EAT.
23   Industrial Tribunals (Rules of Procedure) Regulations 1985 SI No 16 (IT Regs) reg 3(1).
24   EPCA s53.
25   N23.
26   IT Regs reg 4(1)(b)(i).
27   Ibid reg 12(3).
29   Ibid reg 4(4).
30   See sample request on p199.
31   See sample on p199.
32   *Birds Eye Walls v Harrison* [1985] IRLR 47; ICR 278, EAT.
33   County Court Rules Ord 14 r8.
34   *Compagnie Financière du Pacifique v Peruvian Guano Co* (1882) 11 QB 55, CA.
35   Or otherwise waives privilege.

36 *Dada v Metal Box Co* [1974] IRLR 251; ICR 559, NIRC.
37 IT Regs reg 8(1).
38 See burden of proof p78.
39 IT Regs reg 8(2).
40 For a discussion of the role of lay members and why decisions are usually unanimous, see Linda Dickens *The industrial tribunal system* (1985, Blackwell, Oxford).
41 IT Regs reg 9(5).
42 Ibid reg 10(1).
43 Ibid reg 11(1).
44 Ibid reg 11(2).
45 Ibid reg 11(1).
46 Ibid reg 11(1)(a).
47 For more detail, see N O'Brien and T Kibling 'Settling industrial tribunal claims' August 1988 *Legal Action* 9.
48 *Gilbert v Kembridge Fibres* [1984] IRLR 52, EAT.
49 See p203 for sample.

CHAPTER 13

1 Race Relations (Questions and Replies) Order 1977 SI No 842, Sex Discrimination (Questions and Replies) Order 1975 SI No 2048.
2 1977 SI No 842, n1, art 5(b); 1975 SI No 2048, n1, art 5(b).
3 *Carrington v Helix Lighting* [1990] IRLR 6, EAT.
4 RR65 and SD74 obtainable from the Department of Employment and CRE or EOC respectively.
5 RRA 1976 s65(2)(b), SDA 1975 s74(2)(b).
6 See p168 above for confidentiality in relation to discovery.
7 RRA 1976 s68, SDA 1975 s76.
8 RRA 1976 s68(7), SDA 1975 s76(6).
9 *Amies v ILEA* (1976) 121 SJ 11; [1977] ICR 308, EAT.
10 [1989] IRLR 55, EAT (sitting on 24 November 1982).
11 [1989] IRLR 387, CA; [1991] IRLR 136; (1991) 36 EOR 33, HL.
12 See p151 above for drafting an IT1 in unfair dismissal claims.
13 Industrial Tribunals (Rules of Procedure) Regulations 1985 SI No 16 reg 11.
14 *Bourne v Colodense* [1985] ICR 291; IRLR 339, CA.
15 *Nassé v Science Research Council; Vyas v Leyland Cars* [1979] IRLR 465; ICR 921, HL.
16 Ibid.
17 Ibid.
18 *West Midlands Passenger Transport Executive v Singh* [1988] IRLR 186; ICR 614, CA.
19 *Carrington v Helix Lighting* n3.
20 Contained in *Women and men in Britain* published annually by the EOC, HMSO.
21 *The regional trends survey* shows large regional variations in patterns of working women.

22 By C Baxter, National Education College, 1988. There are also regularly articles in *Nursing Times* about discrimination in the NHS.
23 See the section on remedies, p142 above.
24 See, for example, *The first report of the Home Affairs Committee on discrimination in employment* and extracts compiled in the notes for *Equal before the law?* (MOSAIC, Continuing Education Dept, BBC, 1990).
25 See G Meeran *Equal before the law?* n24.
26 [1977] IRLR 225, EAT and see p126 above on the burden of proof.

APPENDIX 1

1 If the worker has been promoted or commended during his/her employment, state this.
2 If there have been no warnings during the worker's employment, state this.
3 Anticipate the employer's case, and do not avoid dealing with awkward or difficult matters of evidence. If this is done, it reflects badly on the case. If abusive language was used, try to put it into context.
4 If there is some explanation or motive for the employer's conduct this should be stated here and/or dealt with at the hearing. The members of the tribunal have to decide at the hearing whom they believe, and motive is crucial in this decision.
5 Failure to consult and to discuss properly, or adequately with the worker the reasons for dismissal, prior to dismissal, is contrary to the rules of natural justice and will in the majority of cases render the dismissal unfair. The employer is required to have reasonable grounds for dismissing after carrying out a proper investigation, which will involve discussions with the worker and all the material witnesses. (See p57 above and *British Home Stores v Burchell* [1978] IRLR 379).
6 Set out each of the considerations which the tribunal has to address in determining the fairness of the dismissal. Never under-estimate the tribunal's capacity to get the law wrong.
7 Under EPCA s57(3), the tribunal must take into account the size and administrative resources of the employer's undertaking, when determining the fairness of the dismissal. Therefore, if the employer is a large company, ensure that this is stated in the application to the tribunal.
8 The failure to allow the worker to operate the contractual disciplinary and grievance procedures will usually render the dismissal unfair. (See p57 above and *West Midlands Co-operative Society v Tipton* [1986] IRLR 112).
9 The employer must take the necesary steps to form a balanced view of the worker's medical condition and this will involve the obtaining of medical evidence. (See p54 above and *Patterson v Messrs Bracketts* [1977] IRLR 137).
10 See p54 above and *East Lindsey DC v Daubney* [1977] IRLR 181).
11 The tribunal might expect a large employer to consider alternative employment before dismissing. (See p47 and *Carricks (Caterers) Ltd v Nolan* [1980] IRLR 259).

APPENDIX 2

1 Establish that the worker's function and place of work are covered by a wages

council order (here Licensed Residential and Licensed Restaurant Wages Council Order).

2 The period of employment must be stated.

3 In determining whether the worker has been underpaid it is necessary to set out the hours worked and the pay received.

4 Establish the worker's right to a minimum rate of pay.

APPENDIX 3

1 When taking a statement for the purpose of an unfair dismissal claim it is important to establish the previous work record (if it is good) and the qualifications that the worker has acquired. If the person has worked for a long time for one employer this should be emphasised at the tribunal hearing, particularly in cases of conduct/capability dismissals. Workers should tell the tribunal if they are well qualified, have had considerable experience in the industry, have worked for well-known employers, and held important positions in the past.

2 It is important that the worker can demonstrate that s/he has attempted to mitigate his/her losses. Prior to the hearing it will be necessary to obtain letters from specialist job agencies or the Department of Employment stating when the worker first signed on, what type of jobs s/he was prepared to do, what vacancies are available in the industry, and whether any jobs were offered.

3 It is important to get the worker to sign the statement and date it. A copy should then be given to the worker. If at the hearing s/he cannot remember something contained in the statement, the tribunal may allow the worker to be reminded as to what s/he had said in the statement or the statement could be offered as evidence. The tribunal will attach more importance to evidence given by the worker without reference to this statement, so this ploy should be used only as a last resort.

4 The employer is obliged by virtue of EPCA s1 to have supplied the worker with a statement containing these details. However, rather than asking for the statement itself, ask specifically for each of the statutory terms and conditions which are needed for the case. If there is a dispute about holiday entitlement ask for these particulars. Always ask for a copy of the employer's disciplinary and grievance procedure.

5 If a dismissal on the ground of redundancy is in contravention of the customary arrangement or agreed procedure it will be automatically unfair (see p50 above and EPCA s59(b)).

6 Even if the employer has supplied the written reasons the adviser is entitled to ask for them pursuant to EPCA s53 and it will be these reasons which the tribunal will consider. If they are different to the previous statement, both can be referred to. To apply pressure on the employer, add the statement concerning the adequate and true reasons. If the reasons were requested orally confirm this in the letter to avoid dispute later.

7 If the worker wants the job back it is important that this is made known to the employer at the earliest opportunity. It will also assist in obtaining an additional award from the tribunal (see pp135 and 141 above) if the employer was put on notice at an early stage.

8   All claims being made must be stated on the IT1 form and in the details of the complaint at para 10.

9   If a representative is put on the application all correspondence will be sent to the representative including notice of the hearing date.

10   All benefits and bonuses should be stated and if it is not possible to put a value to them either be generous in the assessment or leave the figure blank.

11   If the employer is a large company then it is imperative that this is stated on the application as the tribunal must consider, in determining the fairness of the dismissal, the size and administrative resources of the employer's undertaking (EPCA s57(3)).

12   If the worker has been promoted or commended during his/her employment state this.

13   If there have been no warnings during the worker's employment state this.

14   In determing the fairness of a redundancy dismissal the tribunal has to be satisfied that the employer properly consulted with the worker prior to dismissal unless it was utterly pointless to do so (see p67 above, the Industrial Relations Code of Practice 1972 paras 65–70 and *Polkey v AE Dayton Services* [1987] IRLR 503, HL).

15   Set out each of the considerations which the tribunal has to address in determining the fairness of the dismissal. The tribunal's capacity to get the law wrong should never be under-estimated!
     (a) EPCA s81;
     (b) See n4;
     (c) See p67 above;
     (d) See p68 above.

16   The claim for the failure to supply the written reasons must be set out in the details of the complaint.

17   Wages Act 1986 Pt I see p113 above.

18   State a time limit in which to comply.

19   It is important to try and ascertain the precise date when the decision was reached to dismiss the worker. From this date the employer would be expected to consult with the worker.

20   This information is necessary to ascertain whether the worker was the only person dismissed and, if not, the other types of workers who were dismissed.

21   The failure to find alternative employment can make the dismissal unfair. The tribunal will have to consider the efforts made, in relation to the size and administrative resources of the employer's undertaking. This comparison cannot be made without this information.

22   With this information it will be necessary to consider all the vacancies and to list those which the worker could have been offered (within his/her capability). If none of these jobs was offered it will be necessary to ascertain at the hearing the reason why they had not been offered to the worker.

23   Needed to ascertain whether the selection of the worker was unfair. The most important criterion is the length of service (see p67 above).

24   Needed for the purpose of determining the question of alternative employment.

25   Needed to ascertain when the decision to dismiss was made, who made it and how it was proposed to deal with those workers being dismissed.

26 Standard request to prevent any damaging documents being presented on the day of the hearing.

27 Ibid.

28 This paragraph should be included so that the tribunal cannot say that it was not reasonable to expect the employer to comply with the request within the time limit given.

29 Always copy this letter to the tribunal.

30 In obtaining a witness order it is necessary to give the witnesses' full names and addresses (for the purpose of effecting service), a brief statement of their evidence, which must be material, and to state that they are not prepared to attend voluntarily.

31 Always put in a date for compliance, and always insist that claims for personal injury are excluded. ACAS will encourage this exception.

32 If a reference forms part of the agreement, which it should (see p161 above), this undertaking must be secured from the employer.

33 Set out in full the reference.

34 If the worker undertakes to withdraw the application on receipt of the sum, if there is non-payment the worker can return to the tribunal or sue for the agreed sum through the courts. If the worker returns to the tribunal s/he should apply for costs on the grounds of unreasonable conduct (Tribunal Rules of Procedure r11).

Index

Other LAG books

Practice and Procedure in Industrial Tribunals: A Guide to Unfair Dismissal and Redundancy
Clayton

This book comprises the series of articles by Richard Clayton first published in LAG's monthly journal, *Legal Action*. The full texts of the Industrial Tribunals and Employment Appeal Tribunal Rules of Procedure are included, with comprehensive tables and index.

Detailed guidance and practical advice on tactics are provided for the employment law adviser, from first application through to the substantive hearing, costs, reviews and enforcement, to appeals.

October 1986   142pp   £7.50

Claim in Time: time limits in social security law
second edition   Partington

Professor Martin Partington has updated his highly acclaimed book on the time limit rules in social security law.

Claim in Time considers all the relevant changes in the rules resulting from the new Claims and Payments Regulations and Adjudication Regulations. The book examines the time limits for payment of national insurance contributions, deals with housing benefit and provides detailed analysis of the commissioners' case-law on "good cause" for late claim.

The book is an indispensable aid to all who advise on social security. Of the first edition, it was said:

". . . thoroughly and clearly written . . . of most use to the welfare rights specialist" — *Journal of Social Welfare Law*

". . . a valuable reference work for those advising or representing claimants in appeals against adverse decisions, dealing with the issues often raised in relation to the various pensions and benefits and the different contexts in which difficulties arise" — *Paul Burgess, then of the Manchester Welfare Rights Service*

April 1989   120pp   £8.50

Action on Racial Harassment: Legal Remedies and Local Authorities
Forbes

Written by a solicitor who has specialised in the field, the book explores the wide-ranging powers of local authorities that can be utilised to combat racial harassment, not only on council housing estates, but also in the streets, in schools and social services accommodation.

Action on Racial Harassment is for councillors, local authority officers, solicitors, advisers and community organisations — and for victims of harassment themselves. It covers civil and criminal proceedings including court procedure, concentrating particularly on the rules of evidence and their implications for the interviewing of witnesses and the collection of evidence.

In conclusion, Duncan Forbes makes a series of recommendations for the improvement of local authority practices and for changes in the law, which, if implemented, could go a long way towards the eradication of this evil in our society.

The book is comprehensively tabled and indexed and the appendices include model tenancy agreements and precedents for court documents.

May 1988   355pp   £10.00

Police Powers: a practitioner's guide
second edition   Levenson and Fairweather

This book, written by two solicitors, is for the practitioner and gives practical, step-by-step guidance to the legislation and common law. It is the successor to the authors' highly acclaimed *Practitioner's Guide to the Police and Criminal Evidence Act 1984* and updates their earlier book.

Police Powers covers the considerable case-law that has grown up since the passing of the Police and Criminal Evidence Act and also covers police powers under the legislation relating to terrorism, drug trafficking, serious fraud, customs and excise, confiscation of proceeds of crime and interception of communications. A very useful chapter deals with the exclusion of confessions and other evidence, while the police complaints procedure and remedies for abuse of police powers are also considered.

"A thorough perusal of this book is mandatory" — *New Law Journal*

"Lucid and helpful" — *Criminal Law Review*

"A whole chapter on remedies . . . takes the work further than any other" — *Justice of the Peace* (on the first edition)

December 1990   580pp   £26.00

The Emergency Procedures Handbook
second edition   Dowell, Forbes, Hall, Olley and Wyld

In five main sections — relationship breakdown, children, housing, police station emergencies and debt crises — this *Handbook* provides time-saving precedents and checklists for taking instructions when situations demand immediate action.

Fully up-to-date, all the legislative changes that have been made since the 1986 edition was published have been taken into account.

It was said of the first edition:

". . . written with less experienced advisers in mind . . . [it] will concentrate your mind and organise your efforts . . . buy it" — *Roof*

"This is a book that can confidently be recommended to the busy practitioner" — *Solicitors Journal*

September 1989   456pp   £19.00

Defending Possession Proceedings
second edition   Luba, Madge and McConnell

Completely revised and updated to take into account the Housing Act 1988, this edition of LAG's best selling guide to procedure and tactics is for advisers of public and private sector tenants, *and* mortgagors.

The authors consider the position of diverse tenants, licensees, service occupiers, mortgagors, rental purchasers, squatters and short life occupiers, and explain housing benefit, problems arising on relationship breakdown, rights under homelessness legislation, bailiffs and legal aid.

Of the first edition it was said:

"A splendid manual . . . I can unreservedly recommend this book" — *Law Centres News*

". . . cannot be praised too highly . . . the authors are to be congratulated" — *Roof*

April 1989   347pp   £17.00

Homeless Persons: The Housing Act 1985 Part III
third edition   Arden

A third edition of LAG's popular guide to the homeless persons legislation, as consolidated by the Housing Act 1985 and amended by the Housing and Planning Act 1986.

Homeless Persons has been revised to cover the 1985 and 1986 legislation and the case-law. With an expanded index and comprehensive tables of statutes and cases, *Homeless Persons* reproduces the text of the Housing Act 1985 Part III, as amended, the Local Authority Agreement on local connection, the statutory instruments on the resolution of such disputes and the Code of Guidance.

Written by Andrew Arden, a practising barrister and well-known specialist in housing law, this LAG guide will be an indispensible addition to any housing practitioner's library.

July 1988   240pp   £12.00

Arden and Partington on Quiet Enjoyment
third edition   Carrott and Hunter

Tenants' remedies for illegal eviction and harassment by landlords are expertly and concisely explained in *Quiet Enjoyment*. The book covers all the law, both civil and criminal, relevant to this complex and technical area, and the full text of the Protection from Eviction Act 1977, as amended, is reproduced in an appendix.

Completely up-to-date, this third edition is a revision by two practising barristers who specialise in housing law. It takes into account the amendments made to the Protection from Eviction Act 1977, and the new tenancies and new tort of unlawful eviction created by the Housing Act 1988.

Essentially a practical guide, *Quiet Enjoyment* includes forms and precedents, and gives detailed descriptions of the steps for obtaining an injunction and how to complete the forms used in civil proceedings.

"This lucidly written book deserves a wide audience."
                                    — *Solicitors Journal* (on the 2nd edition)

March 1990   135pp   £11.00

Repairs: tenants' rights
second edition Luba

A guide to the diverse statutory and common law rights of tenants whose homes are in disrepair.

Successive chapters clearly explain the landlord's obligations and liabilities — and the tenant's remedies where these obligations are not met:

- the repairs problem
- contractual rights
- landlord's liability
- civil remedies
- using the Public Health Acts
- the Housing Act and bad housing
- displaced tenants
- related housing conditions

Repairs: Tenants' Rights takes account of the relevant legislative changes since the first edition in 1986. Written by Jan Luba, highly respected for his work in this field, this guide will prove indispensable to housing advisers and to solicitors.

> "gives a good, practical grounding for those helping tenants" — *Solicitors Journal* (on the first edition)

January 1991   225pp   £15.00

Using Civil Legal Aid: the 1989 scheme
second edition Hansen

Using Civil Legal Aid is LAG's guide to the legal aid scheme. It examines the green form scheme, assistance by way of representation, the legal aid certificate, emergency applications, family proceedings, costs and the statutory charge.

The 1988 Act and 1989 Regulations are reproduced in appendices, and the book is well indexed and cross-referenced.

In the *Law Society's Gazette*, it was said of the first edition.

> "It ought to be at the elbow of all legal aid practitioners . . . being admirably clear, concise and comprehensive . . . It ought also to be bought by every CAB and related advice agency."

April 1989   325pp   £15.00

All titles available from: LAG, 242 Pentonville Road, London N1 9UN, tel 071–833 2931.

Prices include postage and packing. Please send cash with orders, making cheques payable to: Legal Action Group.